Poetry Criticism & Practice: Developments since the Symbolists

A CASEBOOK

EDITED BY

A. E. DYSON

MACMILLAN

First published 1986

Published by
MACMILLAN EDUCATION LTD
Houndmills, Basingstoke, Hampshire RG21 2XS
and London
Companies and representatives
throughout the world

Typeset by Wessex Typesetters, Frome, Somerset

Printed in Hong Kong

British Library Cataloguing in Publication Data
Dyson, A. E.
Poetry criticism & practice : developments
since the symbolists : a casebook.—Casebook
series)
1. Poetry—History and criticism   2. Criticism
—History
I. Dyson, A. E.   II. Series
801'.951   PN1035
ISBN 0–333–23696–3
ISBN 0–333–23697–1 Pbk

CONTENTS

GENERAL EDITOR'S PREFACE

The Casebook series, launched in 1968, has become a well-regarded library of critical studies. The central concern of the series remains the 'single-author' volume, but suggestions from the academic community have led to an extension of the original plan, to include occasional volumes on such general themes as literary 'schools' and genres.

Each volume in the central category deals either with one well-known and influential work by an individual author, or with closely related works by one writer. The main section consists of critical readings, mostly modern, collected from books and journals. A selection of reviews and comments by the author's contemporaries is also included, and sometimes comment from the author himself. The Editor's Introduction charts the reputation of the work or works from the first appearance to the present time.

Volumes in the 'general themes' category are variable in structure but follow the basic purpose of the series in presenting an integrated selection of readings, with an Introduction which explores the theme and discusses the literary and critical issues involved.

A single volume can represent no more than a small selection of critical opinions. Some critics are excluded for reasons of space, and it is hoped that readers will pursue the suggestions for further reading in the Select Bibliography. Other contributions are severed from their original context, to which some readers may wish to turn. Indeed, if they take a hint from the critics represented here, they certainly will.

A. E. DYSON

INTRODUCTION

'All art aspires to the condition of music': this Symbolist insight of Walter Pater's,[1] which makes an implicit appearance in our earliest extract (Richard Wagner, in section 1 of Part Two), was seminal. In the first place, it announced a new school of French poets. Very soon, its influence permeated all of the other arts and spread over the whole of Europe. In England, Symbolist influences were diluted initially by 'Pre-Raphaelite', by 'fin-de-siècle' and later by Georgian trends. Nevertheless, they enriched Walter de la Mare (currently much underrated), Wilfred Owen, A. E. Housman, Edward Thomas, Robert Graves, Thomas Hardy – indeed, most poets of substance in the late-nineteenth/early-twentieth century period – even before they achieved a splendid flowering in T. S. Eliot and post-1914 Yeats.

At the same time, and on the international stage, dramatists and novelists learned from the tradition. Very soon, Ibsen, Chekhov and Strindberg among the former, James, Mann, Proust, Lawrence, Kafka and many more among the latter, were so influential, in the ranks of Symbolist writers, that the terms 'poetry' and 'poetic' became much extended in critical usage, to encompass them – as is the case to this day.

Indeed, as Wagner's role reminds us, Symbolism was only fleetingly French at its outset and was not restricted to 'poetry'. T. S. Eliot wrote poems called 'Preludes' in his early years, and *Four Quartets* is the title of his greatest work. Such titles indicate his belief in the essentially musical structure of all truly memorable poetry. Eliot's personal debts were as great, in *Four Quartets*, to late Beethoven and to Bartók as they were to his earlier mentors: Baudelaire, Mallarmé, Laforge.

Arguably, the aspiring of 'all art . . . to the condition of music' is both homage to music and also a salutary reminder that music has been the senior, and grandest, element in 'modernism' itself. Wagner's *Tristram and Isolde* is now widely recognised as formative, particularly when *Parsifal* and, of course, *The Ring* cycle are set beside it. The immense power of *Tristram and Isolde* derives, not from 'statement', but from resonance: from its intricate interweaving of themes, mottoes, images, archetypes and dramatic technique. When *Parsifal* is juxtaposed, there is the enrichment of counter-themes that both echo and balance tensions that are 'resolved' – on their own terms and in one of many possible ways – in the earlier work. Herein we encounter a further aspect of the Symbolist tradition – namely, a characteristic *accumulation* of individual works, each one interacting with all the others, to become so many landmarks in one whole lifetime's quest. Wagner's 'final' statement is neither in one opera nor in another, but in all his music taken together: and all held in mind, not only as 'sequence' (though it belongs in time, and naturally is sequential), but as autonomous artefacts – the earlier modified but in no sense superseded by the latter; and the whole *oeuvre*, 'Wagner'. The same perception holds true of all considerable artists, in any medium.

If we may remain with music for a little longer, we further recall Wagner's influence on 'Modern Music'. '*Tristram* is the link' – as William Mann put it in his programme notes for a series of concerts given by the Philharmonia Orchestra under Simon Rattle in London in April 1984. This remarkable enterprise was intended to show the 'link' from Wagner to the Second Viennese School (Schoenberg, Webern and Berg), by way of Richard Strauss and above all, of course, Mahler. In effect, it pointed beyond the Viennese to a great variety of more recent composers, a surprising number of whom find in Mahler's eleven major symphonies (I include among these *The Song of the Earth*) the living centre of Modernism. Mahler's symphonies, taken together, are a towering instance of a quest, by way of essentially Symbolist techniques, that spans a lifetime.[2] The link with poetry, through Symbolism, is of key significance.[3]

Symbolism is, then, a French poetic theory which appeared in the late nineteenth century. But, as very soon emerged, it is also an illumination turned upon all poetry and, indeed, upon all art. We may even consider that, through art, it reaches towards new explorations of the human psyche, including the unconscious: and so, towards the borderlands of religion itself. Just off-stage, Freud and Jung are always in waiting; and no enquirer, or compiling editor, can hope to keep them at bay.

Hence, the major problem confronting this volume's editor has been, not so much *how* to arrange the material, as *what* to exclude. The word 'art' will frequently appear, standing in for 'poetry'; at times we are threatened with confusion between the two. 'Poetry' is, of course, a particular art, a province of 'Literature', not of 'Music'; the 'art made with words' has rules and laws of its own.[4] Nevertheless, since it is an art, poetry shares common ground with all other arts, as well as differences. Symbolism belongs in, and near, this mysterious terrain.

At the same time, we are threatened with a possible confusion from the seemingly opposite direction. Poetry, though part of the 'art made with words', naturally differs from other purely literary genres. Yet once again, 'symbolism' blurs the distinctions – or, as I prefer to put it, offers insights in the shared, common ground. Thus: F. R. Leavis saw that novels are structurally close to poetry in some of their aspects, and that techniques of criticism deriving from 'symbolism' can, and do, shed light on novels as well. And it is not only post-Symbolist novelists (James, Conrad, Proust, Mann, Joyce, Kafka and many more) to whom this is relevant. It is relevant also to Dickens, the Brontës, Jane Austen, Sterne, Richardson . . . right back to early days. The post-Symbolist novelists had read the source-texts and been influenced directly; but clearly, the earlier writers can have done no such thing. In this wider viewpoint, then, it seems to me that the Symbolists did not just invent a 'school' or a passing theory. Rather, they perceived certain aspects which great novelists and dramatists and poets (in sum, great *artists*) have always known.

'Always known': by this I suggest that 'symbolism' is native to art and a true universal. 'The Symbolists' were a group who first clearly articulated deep general truths about the nature of art. How, without these insights, would we write now of Shakespeare? How, without them, could Greek tragedy be read?

As I have hinted already, these perceptions are central in Modernism – in music and literature especially; and they parallel the discoveries and speculations of Freud and Jung. As it happened, both these explorers of dreams, and of the 'unconscious', were also keen students of literature. Both wrote most illuminatingly on many aspects of literature – though with methods fascinatingly different from those of any 'critical' school that I know.[5] Their main concern was to probe dreams and the human unconscious, for the purpose of healing: though it is fair to say that each was obsessed, in his differing way, with exploring 'truth'. For both, 'dreams' were a natural symbolism, potent with meaning, but their sharp divergence (a famous episode) turned on their ultimate differences in religious stance. Freud, as an atheist, related dreams to the personal subconscious; for him, though symbols recur, particular dreams relate 'just' to a *self*. In contrast, Jung – a natural platonist and drawn, like Yeats, to the occult – came to find in dreams a 'collective unconscious' that transcended 'self'. His collective unconscious has much in common with Plotinus's *anima mundi* and similar mystical concepts. The doctrine of archetypes, which distinguishes Jung, cross-fertilised with literature. Indeed, many of the texts in this Casebook might have been selected with a demonstration of Jung's prophetic stature and relevance directly in mind.

Freud and Jung agreed in finding highly meaningful the 'natural' symbolism that occurs in dreams. Both asserted that the sensitive analysis of dreams is our essential entrée to individuality in its completeness and depth. For both, these truths were revelatory of the inner psyche. For Jung, they pointed towards religion also, and so towards 'realities' linking our 'unique self' with all human consciousness, and perhaps with 'the divine'.

But here we encounter the distinction crucial, also, to poetry; and crucial to the understanding of Symbolism peculiar to *art*. In dreams, 'natural symbols' are images thrown up by the unconscious. No creative act or rational intention is involved. Indeed, the absence of conscious 'intention' is the very nature of dream-symbols. Not only has the sleeper no control of them: he is even (with rare exceptions) unaware of his sleep and of the actual gulf between waking 'reality' and dream. Even so, the symbols, remembered when waking, are instinct with power and with the rich suggestion of meaning. For the psycho-analyst, they are clues to precisely those 'truths' which the 'conscious' may seek to repress or reject.

The symbols of art – crafted and selected and heightened by the mind at its most alert and creative – are in one sense, therefore, at a great remove from the 'natural symbols' of the dream-state. Yet these 'art symbols', too, are 'instinct with power'; they also work by suggestion. In their fullest resonance they can elude the creator – who also knows that his readers will respond, to a degree, in unguessable ways.[6] As the Symbolists show, they disturb and reverberate; they are the deep sources of art's power. Moreover, the religious differences between the Freudian and the Jungian approaches are equally relevant. For some critics, the 'revelation', through symbols, is of a 'self' (the particular poet or artist) and of nothing beyond this; for others, it borders on revelation in a mystical sense. It is fascinating to note that, whereas academic theorists and critics in English Literature have been 'Freudian', by and large, steering clear of religion, most of our great modern artists are 'Jungian' whether they like it or not. On the whole, most of them do 'like' it, whatever their own terms of reference – for most are indeed engaged, through art, on a life-long, super-personal quest.

This is no place to take *these* thoughts further (nor am I qualified to do so). Yet one earlier debate in this arena must be mentioned before we pass on. Coleridge's distinction between primary and secondary imagination has been dismissed by some as a distinction without a meaning. To my mind, it is of key importance, and very close to the matter in hand here. Coleridge's 'primary imagination', it will be recalled, is involuntary – our normal habit of perception. His 'secondary imagination' is a complex process of diffusing, dissecting, breaking-down, *in order to create*. Dreams, I would suggest, are a symbolism akin to Coleridge's 'primary imagination' – though they would exemplify this involuntary power at work in the dreaming, not the waking, world. The Symbolism of art demands some description akin to Coleridge's 'secondary imagination' – which accounts for the mingling of intention and non-intention in the symbols of art.

Interactions between literary criticism and psycho-analysis are naturally complex; but, from widely differing starting-points, they converge when imagination and image and creative insight become common ground. I would sugget that, in so far as the Symbolists discovered common properties of 'resonance' between art and dream-images, they guaranteed the constructive, not destructive, nature of analysis *when it is also a quest*.

In this Casebook I have neither opportunity, nor a brief, to pursue 'dream psychology'; I would merely note that the essays and extracts reproduced herein often point, by their nature, that way. I shall be content to use Alice's dream-musings on 'Jabberwocky' as one point of reference. Carroll's *Through the Looking-Glass* is dated 1872:

> 'It seems very pretty', she said, when she had finished it, 'but it's *rather* hard to understand!' (You see, she didn't want to confess, even to herself, that she couldn't make it out at all.) 'Somehow it seems to fill my head with ideas – only I don't exactly know what they *are*! However, *somebody* killed *something*: that's clear, at any rate. . . .'

Alice's first readings, and reactions, were surely right; she has the makings of a critic, if not yet the brazen gift-of-the-gab. Later, she is ready to learn from Humpty-Dumpty, whose high-handed, hard-line elucidations are interesting, if partial and arbitrary in the extreme. Humpty-Dumpty's 'way with words' is pure deconstruction (as we call it, these days). Alice's reservations about him commend, as ever, her unfailing good sense.

This Casebook charts a diversity of modern critical developments, leaving the contributors to speak for themselves. It remains for me to draw a sketch-map of the territory, with some comment on omissions, and to say a word on Movements, Manifestos and the present (very confused) state of play.

But before this is essayed, two persistent problems call for explicit comment, if only to put nagging doubts about them to rest.

1. The first problem is a pragmatic one and has already been touched on: namely, that in a great many of the extracts reproduced here emphasis falls not on the word 'poetry', but on the word 'art'.

This is true in Bradley's famous Inaugural Lecture at Oxford, which I have included with very special pleasure. Along with Henry James's Prefaces to his novels,[7] it has been seminal in my own teaching and criticism and actual enjoyment of life. I can imagine no better background, for any student of poetry and literature, than a reading and periodic re-reading of these two splendid statements.

Bradley, of course, has long been a centre for controversy in literary circles, as much for this particular essay as for *Shakespearean Tragedy* itself. As a schoolboy in the 1940s, I was told that Bradley had been refuted and relegated; but forty or so years later, his classic status is scarcely in doubt. Often, those who reacted against him most strongly took hints from one *part* of his work: and in this they surely read him as he would have wished. Whatever theory one adopts, and however different in detail, Bradley's quests, insights and methods may each play a part. Moral critics, Symbolist critics, critics focussing on structure or on imagery or on 'world pictures' – all have in his work their clear model for procedure. For it is 'art' that Bradley deals with, though his subject is 'poetry'; and all critical questioners must be aware, as he is, of the medium, since every possible aspect links inextricably with this.

Note, also, how instinctively Yeats talks of 'art' when he is writing of 'poetry' (in section 2 of Part Two, below), and how many of the other creative writers represented in Part Two do the same – whether overtly or by implication in their very diverse reflections. And note particularly how 'poetry for poetry's sake', in *this* aspect, presupposes experience and consciousness. In a word, let us perceive how it takes us from and back to the soil in which art is sown and then nurtured, rather than from and back to mere theories or mere games with words.

Most usually, it is those who try to by-pass 'art' and to start directly from 'life' who founder. How often does 'realism', as a slogan, end in ideology, dogma and mere moral cant? Bradley values poems as poems – which is to say, as artefacts. And the artefacts are, in the first place, words set out on a page. Then, they are words spoken, either aloud or inwardly, as the dance from writer to reader, through the artefact, starts to take place. All the art-ful resonances turn us back to 'experience', where they also started, and without which poetry would never have existed (though words, even words set out like poetry, might have done so, of course).

In great poetry, the resonances are at the peaks, or frontiers, of consciousness. At the very least, they are the artist's most remarkable trophies, won in his quest. And do not be fooled by 'subject'. Great 'subjects' may help great poetry, as Bradley acknowledges; yet Milton and Pope made unfortunate haircuts serve, for major art.

The Geneva critics – rescued from British and American neglect by J. Hillis Miller – speak of literature as the history of human consciousness.* If we turn (in Part One of our selection) to Cleanth Brooks or Frank Kermode – indeed, to all critics acutely aware of paradox and ambivalence – then they too extend paths charted, if not always followed, by Bradley himself. In yet other directions, Northrop Frye, C. S. Lewis, Helen Gardner and others ponder revelatory qualities inherent in human artefacts made, from human experience, in human words. For some, 'revelation' may point towards inward, psychic realities – the human consciousness stirred to that energy from which, and by which, it *makes*. For others, the focus of revelation will be on certain external experiences – biographical, historical, social, political or the like – that are the poetry's 'subject' abstracted, in so far as it can be, from particular form. For others again, revelation will imply 'logos' or incarnation – including perhaps religious implications – inherent in the process of creation itself. Be this as it may, all poems clearly point towards some kind of 'reality' now inseparable, whatever response we make, from the icons of art.

Once forget the art – the metre, rhythm, tone, movement and other ingredients of poetry – and any work can quickly be remade in the image of the reader himelf. Bradley remains, therefore, an essential bulwark against the most disabling kind of reductionism: notably, the abolition, through language, of human consciousness. (Writing thus in the mid-1980s, one understands only too readily the nightmare predictions of Orwell's *1984*.) My impression, indeed, is that it is precisely those who regard Bradley as an 'aesthete', in some disabling sense, who pose most danger to any supposedly less frivolous 'values' they purport to uphold.

2. My second general problem is one of definition and tradition. Where did 'Symbolism' originate, and where does it lead?

The Symbolists were working in the Romantic tradition and, to some degree, extending it. The Romantics, as critics like Stephen Spender have asserted, are the founding fathers of Modernism, as it is

---

* The scope and detail of J. Hillis Miller's discussion are of such a kind that, with great regret, I have had to exclude his survey of the Geneva School from this selection. But in signalising his important and innovatory study in the Select Reading List, I take the opportunity there of very briefly outlining its summation of the ideas and critical methods of Marcel Raymond, Albert Béguin, Georges Poulet, Jean Rousset, Jean-Pierre Richard and Jean Starobinski.

understood here. Theories of 'the imagination' deriving from German, British and French sources are central. So is the later development, through Imagism, to Eliot and Yeats, and thence to many more recent poets, including a few young poets of today.

This huge area assimilates literature, as I have argued, to 'modern consciousness', one major characteristic of which is the flexible, complex, non-dogmatic mind. Jung's *Modern Man in Search of a Soul* (1933) remains a brilliant classic statement for the larger perspectives. If a less religiously committed guide is wanted, from the ranks of the poets, then Stephen Spender's *The Struggle of the Modern* (1963) is lucid and searching.

The roots, then, are in Romanticism where, in the later years of the eighteenth and early years of the nineteenth centuries, a strong intellectual reaction – not unconnected with the French Revolution and the Industrial Revolution – set in. The Romantics reacted totally against purely empirical philosophy and against the deadly force they perceived this to be, in life and in art alike. The process has been charted by Basil Willey, Paul Hazard and others, and the merest outline is all that there is space for here. (Basic texts in this area of discussion are indicated in the Select Bibliography provided for this Casebook.)

The Romantics detested the reductive theory of human language which the eighteenth century had embraced almost universally: a usage attuned to scientific and rationalist-philosophic communication ('rational discourse'), and to little else. Precision was exalted as 'right judgement', but 'fancy' suffered. Any notion of 'imagination' as a source of truth had gone underground.[8] Poets were expected to discover 'truth' with their discursive intellect (like all other men) and then, at best, to adorn truths with 'just' wit, fancy, ornament and the like, as their own social role and contribution. Style was likewise caught in a trap, along with 'manners' and 'morals'. Style added elegance, wit, balance, epigram, charm and other such qualities – but it was kept to its due place. 'Enthusiasm' was a lost cause; so was 'originality'. The former term denoted fanaticism, notably among sectarian Christians; the latter signified eccentricity, which was not admired. This ethos was inimical to any delight in individuality or in the 'uniqueness' of self.

To read eighteenth-century poetry is occasionally to encounter genius: Pope; Blake; in his strange way, Smart. But who else? These are the striking exceptions in the field. More generally, there is well-crafted, immensely readable, highly pleasing verse by a great many writers – who seem almost, but never (alas!) wholly, to have believed in themselves.

Locke's *Essay Concerning Human Understanding*, though published as late as 1690, summed up a cultural outlook that had its roots in the Renaissance and seemed bespoke to fit the interests and claims of science. After the Stuart Restoration (1660 is a date of *European* significance), 'empiricism' attained a century or more of ascendance in Western intellectual society at large. In Britain a decisive influence was exerted by the Royal Society, which took an active part in 'reforming' our language and neutering our art. The strong reaction which set in, after 1660, against the 'metaphysical' poets was all-pervasive. Samuel Johnson's bizarre strictures against them, in his *Life of Cowley*, for long held the field. It is even the case that, within fifty years of its triumphant reception, the Authorised (or King James) Version of the Bible was an anachronism. For religious reasons, no doubt, it remained a fixed component of the Anglican liturgy, becoming the normative text for Dissenters, also. But its style was 'archaic' and few writers were influenced by it (outsiders like Bunyan were exceptions, proving the rule). The new rule, indeed, was that 'prose' should be shorn of 'poetry', in the cause of precision; and that 'poetry' should be receptive of the virtues of good prose and be guided by them. Poets could affirm and embellish truths, provided they did this decorously. Under no circumstances could they claim their own access to truth. The corresponding assumption was that certain truths could be known and demonstrated universally, and that these embraced science and philosophy, morals, religion and art.

Yet, though Locke was not easily displaced, this strong empirical position did come under pressure during the eighteenth century. For his determined followers unwelcome contradictions became apparent far inside the Lockean framework – notably with Butler's *Analogy of Religion* (1736). Then a coup-de-grâce was administered by Hume (*Treatise of Human Nature*, 1738). In the transition from Rationalism to Romanticism, Hume is a key figure, for all that (unlike Kant) he had no natural wish to play this part. Even Bertrand Russell, in his *History of Western Philosophy* (1946) found Hume unanswered and un-answerable (for all that consenting to this view went entirely against *his* grain too). Hume to some extent saved the doubtful day by 'good-humoured' antidotes. If philosophy disturbs us, 'why bother too much?' he virtually asks. 'Carelessness and inattention', he observes in the *Treatise*, 'alone can afford us a remedy. For this reason I rely entirely upon them; and take it for granted, whatever may be the reader's opinion at this present moment, that an hour hence he will be persuaded there is both an external and an internal world.' However, few other minds could treat Hume's insights with Hume's urbanity, and the *Treatise* proved to be the beginning of the end for classicism (a time-bomb fitted with a fifty-year fuse).

The Romantics were aware of some crumbling within the empirical castle; indeed, they assisted the process.[9] But their own chief impetus was a power in itself. They felt that the eighteenth century, far from liberating man, had imprisoned him. In confining art and religion to 'logic' and in banishing mystery, it had destroyed precisely those things (assured religion, assured morality, and the assured cluster of dogmas) that it had sought to make firm. In particular, emotion had been perceived by the empirical intellect as tainted, imagination as lying, impulse as folly. Repressing both imagination and emotional intensity, the empirical, rationalist outlook had undermined man's sense of wonder, of creativity, of divinity itself.

The early Romantics were all concerned to rediscover deep truths, based in feeling. For them, language was far more mysterious than Locke had assumed. Words could evoke, resonate, rouse memories (personal and super-personal); they could initiate men directly to truth far too high for discursive logic even to reach, far less grasp. The German Romantics put particular stress on intensity and complexity, being assured that, once freed from their fetters, these powers would unlock truth. Nearest to them among the English Romantics was Blake – not through direct influence but in the prophetic sweep of his vision and his blazing, personal style.

The Germans and Blake open a way towards Yeats, Jung and the very greatest 'moderns' – to explorations of ambivalence, multivalence and vision, as components in the true soil of art. That the way leads thereto via the Symbolists is our main theme in this Casebook's treatment of the Poet as Critic and Artist. We see also that notable academic critics followed, and added their insights. They followed methodically, cautiously and, as befits them, some decades late.

To my mind, the emergence of the Symbolists, and of the great art they helped to release in creative 'Modernism', is a continual unfolding of the original Romantic revolt. It was the Romantics who shaped 'modern consciousness' as I define it. The Symbolists are a new focus on a continuum, reaching from Blake to ourselves today.

As I have emphasised, 'modern' was the word chosen, by certain outstanding twentieth-century poets, to describe themselves. Michael Roberts's *Faber Book of Modern Verse* (1936) is a useful milestone, and in Part Two is reproduced the substance of his famous original Preface. Since Michael Roberts, the thesis of Modernism has often been challenged. In the 1950s, it was already seen by some as old-fashioned. In the 1980s, we are witnessing a resurgence of dogma, both political and religious. Those who approve of this development will almost certainly dislike Symbolism and, most possibly, art. If they study literature, they will be happier with structural 'theories' and pragmatic practice than with the main stream of poetry in Europe in the last hundred years. Any witness to complexity, to paradox, to frontiers beyond reach and problems beyond solution, will most likely affront them. Most likely they will resist 'literature', but it is not impossible that they may try to change it. Philistines take kindly to one myth, at least: that of the Trojan Horse.

Even so, the 'modern sensibility', for those I am calling Modernist, is a *fait accompli*. It is undeniably the direction of art and experience and humanity taken in this century, whether we like it or not. Academics may rebel, politicians oppose, Big Brother machinate, yet the ethos we live in cannot be undone or unmade. The insights of Freud and Jung, Yeats and Eliot, James and Kafka, and the many who follow them, are as irreversible as is the release into history, by scientists, of nuclear power. Unlike nuclear power, such insights are more constructive than explosive, in a balanced assessment: though undeniably they impose strain, as well as offering freedom, for those exposed to their force. Poetry is indeed dangerous as well as healing and life-giving, and it is up to academics to give warning. (Perhaps the texts herein do *that*.) In my experience, some university students discover this dangerous aspect of literature too late for their comfort. They did not really believe Auden's talk of poets 'exploding like bombs' ('Spain', 1937). Silas Wegg (in *Our Mutual Friend*) knew better when he haggled with Mr Boffin, in an exchange that could usefully be inscribed prominently in all Faculties of Art:

'As to the amount of strain upon the intellect, now. Was you thinking at all of poetry?' Mr Wegg inquired, musing.

'Would it come dearer?' Mr Boffin asked.

'It would come dearer', Mr Wegg returned. 'For when a person comes to grind off poetry night after night, it is but right he should expect to be paid for its weakening effect on his mind.'

In this Casebook extracts from poets (some in prose, some in verse) are challenging and diverse. All have something to show us of art in its wider potentials, as well as particular insights (of course) into particular writers. The counter-revolution is also represented and, though I think it abortive, readers can decide for themselves what, in the criticism to be found here, strengthens their own minds.

Here is a useful cue to lead me, in this brief preface to the anthology, to drawing a generalised map of the last hundred years of poetry.

★

As mentioned earlier, Symbolist influences came late to literature in Britain, and were at first diluted. Even so, Yeats and Eliot brought a notable flowering of the movement. Moreover, all major English poets and most presentable ones have something Symbolist in their bloodstream and bones.

In the early twentieth century our poetry was extremely diverse. Late Victorian Romanticism had often allowed stock rhymes, stock rhythms, stock responses generally to do its practitioner's work for him. When this was accompanied by somewhat jangling metres, used inflexibly, the results were seldom distinguished. The Pre-Raphaelites, Morris, Swinburne and other lesser figures had, however, developed recognisable, and sometimes powerful, personal styles. If they now seem to us faded, this must be due to an over-reliance on sound at the expense of sense; their music, instead of enforcing meaning, became an hypnotic distraction. Eliot in particular rebelled against such imprecise art. The excerpt printed from his essay on Swinburne (in section 2 of Part Two) is very acute.

The greatest poet of the period, though he was far better known as a novelist, was Hardy. Always apart from other poets, he achieved a remarkable personal 'flavour': one which was unmistakably his own (who is remotely like him?) and yet attuned to Modernism as it would shortly emerge. His rhythms, though 'difficult', are hand-made for each poem. The extreme precision of his imagery is inseparable from his sensibility and tone. Hardy's greatest poems are probably those written after the death of his first wife, Emma. They stand, on the very eve of the Modernist revolutions and the 1914 cataclysm, as a grand personal peak. Though Hardy did not often theorise, he is 'modern' in outlook. Only recently has his full poetic stature, and the extent of his influence, been recognised. Philip Larkin's *Oxford Book of Twentieth-Century Poetry* makes good amends for the earlier neglect, and the new regard for Hardy's poetic achievement is happily signalised in the Casebook edited by James Gibson and Trevor Johnson.

The first of the revolutions in this poetic development was initiated by the 'Georgians', as a group of poets anthologised by Sir Edward Marsh came to be called. (Marsh's first volume was published in 1912.) Their chief concern was with beauty, lyricism and celebration as antidotes to ugliness. Since the 'ugliness' was social, the link with the Pre-Raphaelites is clear. Yet for the Georgians 'beauty' was not an escape but a recall to 'reality'; they are sharper, more focussed than the tradition from which they emerge. Their technique is tighter, their imagery sparser, their best poems are individually memorable – as James Reeves's *Georgian Poetry* (the Penguin anthology) well shows. In this Casebook, D. H. Lawrence speaks for them – though as a group they were too individualistic to be seen as a 'school'. Their group-name relates to the accession of George v in 1910, when all were writing; but their achievements come best through a roll-call: Housman, Davies, de la Mare, Brooke, Owen, Lawrence, Graves, Sassoon. Some are better known now in other groupings ('War Poets', 'Moderns'). Clearly, they stimulated that fine late-emerging poet Edward Thomas. Their influence on even later poets – Day Lewis and Spender – can be readily traced.

Almost at once two events overtook the Georgians: one literary, the other all too grimly rooted in 'life'.

'The Imagists' speak for themselves here, through manifestos and pronouncements. The influence on them of the Symbolists is easy to discern. Even so, they add particular emphases (Pound is their most robust spokesman) in the direction of precision. Pound's 'make it new!' is a slogan which still resounds.

Eliot, who was deeply affected by Imagism, remained apart, as did Yeats also – though both added notes (and poems) in the Imagist vein. By an odd irony, the best Imagist poems were not written by the group who so named themselves but by later poets, achieving the effects they described. The quintessential idea was for poems short enough to be retained in the memory and for images precise enough to transfer a whole state of consciousness from writer to reader. If I were asked to name poems which succeed in this manner, I should go back to (say) 'Westron Wind', Rochester's 'Absent from these . . .', Blake's 'Sick Rose', or forward to Edward Thomas's 'Addlestrop', Eliot's 'Preludes', R. S. Thomas's 'Pietà' and similar poems. Even so, the Imagist poets themselves deserve study, as a salutary corrective to (then) recent excesses; and the Imagist theory remains an important transitional point in English poetic literature.

Imagism was a literary phenomenon, appealing for vividness. The 1914–18 war was a cataclysm, leaving nothing untouched. In its way, it defined 'the Modern', altered art, sealed off 'the Past'. As Philip Larkin was to put it, many years later, in his poem 'MCMXIV':

> . . .
> Never such innocence,
> Never before or since,
> As changed itself to past
> Without a word – the men
> Leaving the gardens tidy,
> The thousands of marriages
> Lasting a little while longer:
> Never such innocence again.

'The poetry is in the pity': Owen's famous dictum – which so offended

Yeats – seems to challenge 'mere' art, as if to counterbalance Symbolists and Bradley alike with a direct call from 'life'. No doubt it does. Yet Owen is a highly skilled craftsman; moreover, as a stylist he innovates more than any (except, perhaps, Lawrence) among his Georgian peers. If it is true that the Great War changed everything, then poetry is part of this. But Symbolist theory demands the fullest engagement, through art, with consciousness. There is no real contradiction to be found.

The destruction of Europe after 1914 is an unhealed trauma still. As Bertrand Russell put it, in an article on his ninetieth birthday, the war which was characterised as a war to end wars turned out to be a war to end peace. In 1945 Hiroshima and Nagasaki further distanced 'the past', as men had known it. In any social or political sense 'the future' has gone. Our own century, facing the abyss in crisis and loneliness, really is in the 'modern' predicament, come what may:

The man whom we can with justice call 'modern' is solitary. He is so of necessity and at all times, for every step towards a fuller consciousness of the present removes him further from his original *'participation mystique'* with the mass of men – from submersion in a common unconsciousness. Every step forward means an act of tearing himself loose from the all-embracing pristine unconsciousness which claims the bulk of mankind almost entirely. . . . Indeed, he is completely modern only when he has come to the very edge of the world, leaving behind him all that has been discarded and outgrown, and acknowledging that he stands before a void out of which all things may grow.

C. G. Jung, *Modern Man in Search of a Soul* (1933), pp. 227–8.

I think profane philosophy must come from terror. An abyss opens under our feet; inherited convictions, the presuppositions of our thoughts, those Fathers of the Church Lionel Johnson expounded, drop into the abyss. Whether we will or no we must ask the ancient questions: Is there a reality anywhere? Is there a God? Is there a Soul? We cry with the Indian Sacred Book: 'They have put a golden stopper into the neck of the bottle; pull it! Let out reality!'

W. B. Yeats, *Essays and Introductions* (1936), pp. 502–3.

In 1937, in his splendid poem 'Lapis Lazuli', Yeats extracts a triumphant, partial affirmation from this predicament:

> All things fall, and are built again:
> And those that build them again are gay!

But Yeats died too early to see the war he, like all men, expected. If he had lived on until the atomic age, would he still have been able to write those lines? Eliot's *Four Quartets* was published in its final complete form in 1944, just a year before Hiroshima. In itself it is a Symbolist masterpiece, not yet surpassed.

Since 1945, the history of poetry has taken two main directions, at least in Britain. (American developments have, throughout the period, criss-crossed with British and Continental experiences: some rather basic documents on this are included in our selection, as space permits.)

Dylan Thomas – who emerged in the 1930s but wrote his best poems in the following decade, shortly before his early death in 1953 – was a 'Celtic magician', a lone wizard: such unacademic phrases suggest themselves as we submit to his art. He was also a highly skilled craftsman and a slow perfectionist – qualities which academics have been less ready, or able, to perceive in him. There are poems like 'Refusal to Mourn', 'Poem in October', 'Fern Hill' which surpass analytical praise, yet which make an excellent touchstone for readers of this Casebook to keep well in mind. Again and again they interact (or so it strikes me) with the most diverse insights here. T. S. Eliot once suggested that Dryden is a test for a 'catholic appreciation of poetry'. Though I find this obscure, I sense Eliot's drift and would readily substitute the name of Dylan Thomas for such a test.

Unhappily, Thomas had self-appointed disciples to cope with (an already forgotten group called 'The Apocalyptics'); unaccountably, his own achievement was obscured by these. During the 1950s the wrath of Robert Conquest fell on the lot of them. 'The Movement' manifestos (which accompanied two sequential volumes of new poems) are included in section 3 of Part Two. Ostensibly, Conquest's call is for a return to discipline, to neo-classicism even; and to it academics like Donald Davie, and even Graham Hough, added their voice. Yet the two finest voices of 'The Movement' evade its precepts. Philip Larkin and Thom Gunn are unique talents and (of course) very much their own theorists and their own men.

Meanwhile, that extraordinary and transient phenomenon Sylvia Plath blazed her course, briefly, miles away from 'The Movement'. Indeed, the term 'confessional' was coined to describe her imitators (Anne Sexton and others) and her – mainly senior – American peers (Robert Lowell and one or two more). Arguably, Sylvia Plath is the first poet who attempted to engage the world in its nuclear turmoil; and arguably, 'The Movement' poets were prudent to seek disengagement in more 'domestic' themes. The strain of engagement killed Plath – and, God knows, it is hazardous to 'engage the world' at any time. 'Art' and 'life' at their most uncomfortable converge in her work.

In my view, though Larkin and Gunn run less risks than Plath, at the frontiers of sanity, even so they are closer to her than to the group with which they were linked. They are great poets to the very degree that they transcend 'The Movement' – each engaging in his own way with the metaphysical quest. Their poems are invariably subtle, disturbing, complex, however 'domestic' their subjects. Both are loners, treading harrowing paths (Gunn's often exhilarating, Larkin's seldom so); and paradoxically they touch *our* 'solitude' at hundreds of points. If I were compiling a Symbolist anthology, I should include them, of course. Among other things, they reconcile Hardy and Eliot (if that is still needed). But they are great poets in their own right and, not surprisingly, in the central stream.

Ted Hughes and R. S. Thomas steered clear of The Movement. They are, in my judgement, our outstanding poets today, along with Larkin and Gunn. Though they have little in common (or seemingly so) in their 'subjects', both are elemental; both engage, through resonance, with the great 'modern' themes. Each of their volumes is part of a quest, which still continues. Each is a marvellous observer in the manner captured by Blake in 'Auguries of Innocence':

> To see a world in a grain of sand
> And a heaven in a flower,
> Hold infinity in the palm of your hand
> And eternity in an hour.

Because they write of religious themes (in the broadest sense) they are universal. Their Collected Poems will stand in the end with Hardy, Yeats and Eliot.

Such is my sketch-map. I have skipped over the poets of the 1930s (notably Auden, Day Lewis, Spender, MacNeice), though Auden's critical viewpoint is epitomised in section 2 of Part Two. Though most often regarded as a 'group', the 'Thirties Poets' were never a *coterie*. Moreover, their 'political' themes were always Modern, in the larger sense. It could be argued that they brought politics back into English poetry for the first time, as a major 'subject', since (say) Wordsworth and Shelley. But is Wilfred Owen, in implication, not 'political' of necessity? Owen's view of 'war' is at once both post-Kipling and Aeschylean.

And so, I reach my main theme again. The Symbolists, while centrally modern, reach back to illuminate all earlier art.

Those who read this Casebook will keep up to date in their poetry reading. But the fortunes of 'Poetry Now' leave a critic behind. In the 1960s, Alvarez produced a Penguin anthology, *The New Poets*, in which he expounded the centrality of Plath and of the 'confessional' school. The most recent Penguin anthology turns to Craig Raine, Tony Harrison and others for a counterblast. How far these anthologies succeed is best left to the judgement of younger readers, particularly if they are trying to write poetry themselves.

More than most Casebooks, this volume *needs* no 'introduction'. Happily, it is full of major writers and critics who explain themselves. As the reader embarks, let me offer a parting exhortation. The poets I have discussed often have 'labels' affixed to them. This helps their 'image' but obscures whatever is best and truest in their work. Please remember also the poets who have no such labels yet who may prove very rewarding: the still under-rated names (though they belong with this general Symbolist grouping): – de la Mare; Robert Graves; Edwin Muir; Stevie Smith; Kathleen Raine . . . .

NOTES

1. The precise phrase, 'All art constantly aspires towards the condition of music', occurs in Walter Pater's essay, 'The School of Giorgione'.

2. Simon Rattle's 1984 initiative was followed by a larger festival in 1985 – organised by Claudio Abbado – called 'Mahler, Vienna and the Twentieth Century'. This major enterprise, ranging among several locations (the Barbican, the Royal Festival Hall, the Royal Albert Hall and elsewhere), spanned most of the year, with the London Symphony Orchestra at its centre, and included lectures specifically linking music with literature and philosophy. In his Introductory Note, Abbado commented:

> The plan is to trace the history of modern music, developing like a bridge between Mahler and the Viennese School, and then between the Viennese School and contemporary music, since many of today's composers are heirs to this development. Most of them, like Britten and Shostakovich, could be considered directly influenced by Mahler. All the other composers performed during the festival . . . are in turn influenced by the Viennese School. I do hope that this series of concerts, aided by a number of important exhibitions, lectures and theatre performances, will illustrate to the public that today's music is not an isolated occurrence, but the logical continuation of the great composers we all love.

During the extensive debates generated by Abbado's 1985 festival, links among music, poetry, art and 'the Modern' generally have been explored in ways germane to this Casebook's theme. I would, in particular, draw attention to two recurring insights that connect closely with my own perspective (already in press-preparation before this Note was added).

The first: many major modern composers, both inside the field chosen by Abbado and also belonging to apparently different traditions, have produced, in their *oeuvres*, a totality which is recognisable as coherent, probing and, in the broadest sense, 'Symbolist'. Names, in addition to Mahler, Schoenberg, Berg and Webern, would certainly include Brahms and Bruckner (from the late nineteenth century), Richard Strauss, Elgar, Sibelius, Bartók, Shostakovich, Britten, Messiaen, Tippet. . . .

The second: a characteristic convention of 'Modern' music includes major single works which, though not strictly 'symphonies', 'oratorios', 'requiems' (in the traditional sense) or 'chamber music', yet include aspects from all these *genres*, and seek to offer, in themselves, major resonant statements about human *meaning*. The roots of this phenomenon are to be found in (say) Beethoven's *Choral Symphony*, Berlioz's *La Damnation de Faust, Roméo et Juliette, L'enfance du Christ* and *Les Troyens*, Brahms's *German Requiem*, Verdi's *Requiem*, Wagner's major operas and similar nineteenth-century landmarks. Here also the reader will readily draw up his own list of 'Modern' works of this kind. My own list would certainly include four of Mahler's symphonies – No. 2 (1895), No. 3 (1902), No. 5 (1904), No. 8 (1910) – Elgar's *Dream of Gerontius* (1900) and, considered as one work, his *The Apostles* (1903) and *The Kingdom* (1906), Delius's *Mass of Life* (1909), Schoenberg's *Gurreleider* (1913), Janáček's *Glagolitic Mass* (1928), Messiaen's *Turangalîla Symphony* (1949), Britten's *War Requiem* (1962), Burgon's *Requiem* (1976), William Mathias's *Lux Aeterna* (1982), Michael Berkeley's *Or Shall We Die?* (1982) and Tippett's *A Mask of Time* (1984).

The link in each case with modern literature, and modern poetry in particular, is a main concern in this Introduction. Most of what I say about Symbolism applies, with a little adaptation, to this parallel musical tradition.

3. This Introduction is no place for attempted illustration, but if any reader wants to follow up my own application of this approach, it can be found in *Yeats, Eliot and R. S. Thomas: Riding the Echo* (London and Basingstoke, and New York, 1981).

4. This crucial matter also transcends the scope of the Introduction. My own reflections, if wanted, are given in *Between Two Worlds: Aspects of Literary Form* (London and Basingstoke, and New York, 1972).

5. Freud's use of Greek tragedy for his major categories of perception can be taken alongside his specific writings on (say) Shakespeare's *Merchant of Venice* and Ibsen's *Rosmersholme*. Jung's *Answer to Job* is a tour-de-force and among the wisest books known to me. How to categorise it is a terrible poser – it is not philosophy, not theology, not literary criticism, not psychology even, in the exclusive sense. Perhaps 'symbolist critique' will have to suffice.

· 6. For the first of these propositions, see (for instance) the extract from *The Use of Poetry and the Use of Criticism* (Eliot excerpt II in section 2 of Part Two, below). For the second, see the opening of his *Burnt Norton* (reproduced as Eliot excerpt IV in the same section).

7. James's Prefaces are conveniently collected in *The Art of the Novel: Critical Prefaces*, edited by R. P. Blackmur (New York, 1934).

8. I speak here of the main tradition of British and Continental philosophy. Neo-platonism carried on, of course – through the Third Earl of Shaftesbury, Bishop Berkeley and others, for those who read them; through mystics like Swedenborg and Thomas Taylor the platonist; through the strong mystical element in John and Charles Wesley and their followers; and in other places, more occult and, for the most part, well out of sight.

9. For example, Coleridge's *Biographia Literaria* (1817); this is the outstanding English contribution. However, many of the ideas it presents (no doubt passing verbally between Coleridge and Wordsworth) are developed very fully in the first version of Wordsworth's *Prelude* (finished 1805).

PART ONE

The Critic as Reader & Theorist

Walter Pater (1873)

'ART FOR ITS OWN SAKE'

. . . *Philosophiren*, says Novalis, *ist dephlegmatisiren, vivificiren.* The service of philosophy, of speculative culture, towards the human spirit, is to rouse, to startle it to a life of constant and eager observation. Every moment some form grows perfect in hand or face; some tone on the hills or the sea is choicer than the rest; some mood of passion or insight or intellectual excitement is irresistibly real and attractive to us – for that moment only. Not the fruit of experience, but experience itself, is the end. A counted number of pulses only is given to us of a variegated, dramatic life. How may we see in them all that is to be seen in them by the finest senses? How shall we pass most swiftly from point to point, and be present always at the focus where the greatest number of vital forces unite in their purest energy?

To burn always with this hard, gemlike flame, to maintain this ecstasy, is success in life. In a sense it might even be said that our failure is to form habits: for, after all, habit is relative to a stereotyped world, and meantime it is only the roughness of the eye that makes any two persons, things, situations, seem alike. While all melts under our feet, we may well grasp at any exquisite passion, or any contribution to knowledge that seems by a lifted horizon to set the spirit free for a moment, or any stirring of the senses, strange dyes, strange colours, and curious odours, or work of the artist's hands, or the face of one's friend. Not to discriminate every moment some passionate attitude in those about us, and in the very brilliancy of their gifts some tragic dividing of forces on their ways, is, on this short day of frost and sun, to sleep before evening. With this sense of the splendour of our experience and of its awful brevity, gathering all we are into one desperate effort to see and touch, we shall hardly have time to make theories about the things we see and touch. What we have to do is to be for ever curiously testing new opinions and courting new impressions, never acquiescing in a facile orthodoxy of Comte, or of Hegel, or of our own. Philosophical theories or ideas, as points of view, instruments of criticism, may help us to gather up what might otherwise pass unregarded by us. 'Philosophy is the microscope of thought.' The theory or idea or system which requires of us the sacrifice of any part of this experience, in consideration of some interest into which we cannot enter, or some abstract theory we have not identified with ourselves, or of what is only conventional, has no real claim upon us.

One of the most beautiful passages of Rousseau is that in the sixth book of the *Confessions*, where he describes the awakening in him of the literary sense. An undefinable taint of death had clung always about him, and now in early manhood he believed himself smitten by mortal disease. He asked himself how he might make as much as possible of the interval that remained; and he was not biassed by anything in his previous life when he decided that it must be by intellectual excitement, which he found just then in the clear, fresh writings of Voltaire. Well! we are all *condamnés* as Victor Hugo says: we are all under sentence of death but with a sort of indefinite reprieve – *les hommes sont tous condamnés à mort avec des sursis indéfinis*: we have an interval, and then our place knows us no more. Some spend this interval in listlessness, some in high passions, the wisest, at least among 'the children of this world', in art and song. For our one chance lies in expanding that interval, in getting as many pulsations as possible into the given time. Great passions may give us this quickened sense of life, ecstasy and sorrow of love, the various forms of enthusiastic activity, disinterested or otherwise, which come naturally to many of us. Only be sure it is passion – that it does yield you this fruit of a quickened, multipled consciousness. Of such wisdom, the poetic passion, the desire of beauty, the love of art for its own sake, has most. For art comes to you proposing frankly to give nothing but the highest quality to your moments as they pass, and simply for those moments' sake.

SOURCE: extract from 'Conclusion' in *Studies in the History of the Renaissance* (1873; new edition, New York, 1919), pp. 94–9.

Arthur Symons   (1899)

THE SYMBOLIST MOVEMENT

1. Dedication to W. B. Yeats

May I dedicate to you this book on the Symbolist movement in literature, both as an expression of a deep personal friendship and because you, more than any one else, will sympathise with what I say in it, being yourself the chief representative of that movement in our country? France is the country of movements, and it is naturally in France that I have studied the development of a principle which is spreading throughout other countries, perhaps not less effectually, if with less definite outlines. Your own Irish literary movement is one of its expressions; your own poetry and A. E.'s poetry belong to it in the most intimate sense. In Germany it seems to be permeating the whole of literature, its spirit is that which is deepest in Ibsen, it has absorbed the one new force in Italy, Gabriele d'Annunzio. I am told of a group of Symbolists in Russian literature, there is another in Dutch literature, in Portugal it has a little school of its own under Eugenio de Castro; I even saw some faint strivings that way in Spain, and the aged Spanish poet Campoamor has always fought on behalf of a 'transcendental' art in which we should recognise much of what is most essential in the doctrine of Symbolism. How often have you and I discussed all these questions, rarely arguing about them, for we rarely had an essential difference of opinion, but bringing them more and more clearly into light, turning our instincts into logic, digging until we reached the bases of our convictions. And all the while we were working as well as thinking out a philosophy of art; you, at all events, creating beautiful things, as beautiful, it seems to me, as anything that is being done in our time.

And we talked of other things besides art, and there are other sympathies, besides purely artistic ones, between us. I speak often in this book of Mysticism, and that I, of all people, should venture to speak, not quite as an outsider, of such things, will probably be a surprise to many. It will be no surprise to you, for you have seen me gradually finding my way, uncertainly but inevitably, in that direction which has always been to you your natural direction. Still, as I am, so meshed about with the variable and too clinging appearances of things, so weak before the delightfulness of earthly circumstance, I hesitate sometimes in saying what I have in my mind, lest I should seem to be saying more than I have any personal right to say. But what, after all, is one's personal right? How insignificant a matter to any one but oneself, a matter how deliberately to be disregarded in that surely impersonal utterance which comes to one in one's most intimate thinking about beauty and truth and the deeper issues of things!

It is almost worth writing a book to have one perfectly sympathetic reader, who will understand everything that one has said, and more than one has said, who will think one's own thought whenever one has said exactly the right thing, who will complete what is imperfect in reading it, and be too generous to think that it is imperfect. I feel that I shall have that reader in you; so here is my book in token of that assurance.

2. Introduction

> It is in and through Symbols that man, consciously or unconsciously, lives, works, and has his being: those ages, moreover, are accounted the noblest which can the best recognise symbolical worth, and prize it highest.
>
> CARLYLE

Without symbolism there can be no literature; indeed, not even language. What are words themselves but symbols, almost as arbitrary as the letters which compose them, mere sounds of the voice to which we have agreed to give certain significations, as we have agreed to translate these sounds by those combinations of letters? Symbolism began with the first words uttered by the first man, as he named every living thing; or before them, in heaven, when God named the world into being. And we see, in these beginnings, precisely what Symbolism in literature really is: a form of expression, at the best but approximate, essentially but arbitrary, until it has obtained the force of a convention, for an unseen reality apprehended by the consciousness. It is sometimes permitted to us to hope that our convention is indeed the reflection rather than merely the sign of that unseen reality. We have done much if we have found a recognisable sign.

'A symbol', says Comte Goblet d'Alviella, in his book on *The Migration of Symbols*, 'might be defined as a representation which does not aim at being a reproduction.' Originally, as he points out, used by the Greeks to denote 'the two halves of the tablet they divided between themselves as a pledge of hospitality', it came to be used of every sign, formula, or rite by which those initiated in any mystery made themselves secretly known to one another. Gradually the word extended its meaning, until it came to denote every conventional representation of idea by form, of the unseen by the visible. 'In a Symbol', says Carlyle, 'there is concealment and yet revelation: hence therefore, by Silence and by Speech acting together, comes a double significance.' And, in that fine chapter of *Sartor Resartus*, he goes further, vindicating for the word its full value: 'In the Symbol proper, what we can call a Symbol, there is ever, more or less distinctly and directly, some embodiment and revelation of the Infinite; the Infinite is made to blend itself with the Finite, to stand visible, and as it were, attainable there.'

It is in such a sense as this that the word Symbolism has been used to describe a movement which, during the last generation, has profoundly influenced the course of French literature. All such words, used of anything so living, variable, and irresponsible as literature, are, as symbols themselves must so often be, mere compromises, mere indications. Symbolism, as seen in the writers of our day, would have no value if it were not seen also, under one disguise or another, in every great imaginative writer. What distinguishes the Symbolism of our day from the Symbolism of the past is that it has now become conscious of itself, in a sense in which it was unconscious even in Gérard de Nerval, to whom I trace the particular origin of the literature which I call Symbolist. The forces which mould the thought of men change, or men's resistance to them slackens; with the change of men's thought comes a change of literature, alike in its inmost essence and in its outward form: after the world has starved its soul long enough in the contemplation and the re-arrangement of material things, comes the turn of the soul; and with it comes the literature of which I write in this volume, a literature in which the visible world is no longer a reality, and the unseen world no longer a dream.

The great epoch in French Literature which preceded this epoch was that of the offshoot of Romanticism which produced Baudelaire, Flaubert, the Goncourts, Taine, Zola, Leconte de Lisle. Taine was the philosopher both of what had gone before him and of what came immediately after; so that he seems to explain at once Flaubert and Zola. It was the age of Science, the age of material things; and words, with that facile elasticity which there is in them, did miracles in the exact representation of everything that visibly existed, exactly as it existed. Even Baudelaire, in whom the spirit is always an uneasy guest at the orgie of life, had a certain theory of Realism which tortures many of his poems into strange, metallic shapes, and fills them with imitative odours, and disturbs them with a too deliberate rhetoric of the flesh. Flaubert, the one impeccable novelist who has ever lived, was resolute to be the novelist of a world in which art, formal art, was the only escape from the burden of reality, and in which the soul was of use mainly as the agent of fine literature. The Goncourts caught at Impressionism to render the fugitive aspects of a world which existed only as a thing of flat spaces, and angles, and coloured movement, in which sun and shadow were the artists; as moods, no less flitting, were the artists of the merely receptive consciousness of men and women. Zola has tried to build in brick and mortar inside the covers of a book; he is quite sure that the soul is a nervous fluid, which he is quite sure some man of science is about to catch for us, as a man of science has bottled the air, a pretty, blue liquid. Leconte de Lisle turned the world to stone, but saw, beyond the world, only a pause from misery in a Nirvana never subtilised to the Eastern ecstasy. And, with all these writers, form aimed above all things at being precise, at saying rather than suggesting, at saying what they had to say so completely that nothing remained over, which it might be the business of the reader to divine. And so they have expressed, finally, a certain aspect of the world; and some of them have carried style to a point beyond which the style that says, rather than suggests, cannot go. The whole of that movement comes to a splendid funeral in Hérédia's sonnets, in which the literature of form says its last word, and dies.

Meanwhile, something which is vaguely called Decadence had come into being. That name, rarely used with any precise meaning, was usually either hurled as a reproach or hurled back as a defiance. It pleased some young men in various countries to call themselves Decadents, with all the thrill of unsatisfied virtue masquerading as uncomprehended vice. As a matter of fact, the term is in its place only when applied to style; to that ingenious deformation of the language, in Mallarmé, for instance, which can be compared with what we are accustomed to call the Greek and Latin of the Decadence. No doubt perversity of form and perversity of matter are often found together, and, among the lesser men especially, experiment was carried far, not only in the direction of style. But a movement which in this sense might be called Decadent could but have been a straying aside from the main road of literature. Nothing, not even conventional virtue, is so provincial as conventional vice; and the desire to 'bewilder the middle-classes' is itself middle-class. The interlude, half a mock-interlude, of Decadence, diverted the attention of the critics while something more serious was in preparation. That something more serious has crystallised, for the time, under the form of Symbolism, in which art returns to the one pathway, leading through beautiful things to the eternal beauty.

In most of the writers whom I have dealt with as summing up in themselves all that is best in Symbolism, it will be noticed that the form is very carefully elaborated, and seems to count for at least as much as in those writers of whose over-possession by form I have complained. Here, however, all this elaboration comes from a very different motive, and leads to other ends. There is such a thing as perfecting form that form may be annihilated. All the art of Verlaine is in bringing verse to a bird's song, the art of Mallarmé in bringing verse to the song of an orchestra. In Villiers de l'Isle-Adam drama becomes an embodiment of spiritual forces, in Maeterlinck not even their embodiment, but the remote sound of their voices. It is all an attempt to spiritualise literature, to evade the old bondage of rhetoric, the old bondage of exteriority. Description is banished that beautiful things may be evoked, magically; the regular beat of verse is broken in order that words may fly, upon subtler wings. Mystery is no longer feared, as the great mystery in whose midst we are islanded was feared by those to whom that unknown sea was only a great void. We are coming closer to nature, as we seem to shrink from it with something of horror, disdaining to catalogue the trees of the forest. And as we brush aside the accidents of daily life, in which men and women imagine that they are alone touching reality, we come closer to humanity, to everything in humanity that may have begun before the world and may outlast it.

Here, then, in this revolt against exteriority, against rhetoric, against a materialistic tradition; in this endeavour to disengage the ultimate essence, the soul, of whatever exists and can be realised by the consciousness; in this dutiful waiting upon every symbol by which the soul of things can be made visible; literature, bowed down by so many burdens, may at last attain liberty, and its authentic speech. In attaining this liberty, it accepts a heavier burden; for in speaking to us so intimately, so solemnly, as only religion had hitherto spoken to us, it becomes itself a kind of religion, with all the duties and responsibilities of the sacred ritual.

3. On Villiers de l'Isle-Adam

. . . For Villiers, to whom time, after all, was but a metaphysical abstraction, the age of the Crusaders had not passed. From a descendant of the Grand Master of the Knights of St John of Jerusalem, the nineteenth century demanded precisely the virtues which the sixteenth century had demanded of that ancestor. And these virtues were all summed up in one word, which, in its double significance, single to him, covered the whole attitude of life: the word 'nobility'. No word returns oftener to the lips in speaking of what is most characteristic in his work, and to Villiers moral and spiritual nobility seemed but the inevitable consequence of that other kind of nobility by which he seemed to himself still a Knight of the Order of St John of Jerusalem. It was his birthright.

To the aristocratic conception of things, nobility of soul is indeed a birthright, and the pride with which this gift of nature is accepted is a pride of exactly the opposite kind to that democratic pride to which nobility of soul is a conquest, valuable in proportion to its difficulty. This duality, always essentially aristocratic and democratic, typically Eastern and Western also, finds its place in every theory of religion, philosophy, and the ideal life. The pride of *being*, the pride of *becoming*: these are the two ultimate contradictions set before every idealist. Villiers' choice, inevitable indeed, was significant. In its measure, it must always be the choice of the artist, to whom, in his contemplation

of life, the means is often so much more important than the end. That
nobility of soul which comes without effort, which comes only with an
unrelaxed diligence over oneself, that I should be I: there can at least
be no comparison of its beauty with the stained and dusty onslaught
on a never quite conquered fort of the enemy, in a divided self. And, if
it be permitted to choose among degrees of sanctity, that, surely, is the
highest in which a natural genius for such things accepts its own
attainment with the simplicity of a birthright.

And the Catholicism of Villiers was also a part of his inheritance.
His ancestors had fought for the Church, and Catholicism was still a
pompous flag, under which it was possible to fight on behalf of the
spirit, against that materialism which is always, in one way or
another, atheist. Thus he dedicates one of his stories to the Pope,
chooses ecclesiastical splendours by preference among the many
splendours of the world which go to make up his stage-pictures, and is
learned in the subtleties of the Fathers. The Church is his favourite
symbol of austere intellectual beauty; one way, certainly, by which
the temptations of external matter may be vanquished, and a way,
also, by which the desire of worship may be satisfied.

But there was also, in his attitude towards the mysteries of the
spiritual world, that 'forbidden' curiosity which had troubled the
obedience of the Templars, and which came to him, too, as a kind of
knightly quality. Whether or not he was actually a Kabbalist,
questions of magic began, at an early age, to preoccupy him, and,
from the first wild experiment of *Isis* to the deliberate summing up of
Axël, the 'occult' world finds its way into most of his pages.

Fundamentally, the belief of Villiers is the belief common to all
Eastern mystics.[1] 'Know, once for all, that there is for thee no other
universe than that conception thereof which is reflected at the bottom
of thy thoughts.' 'What is knowledge but a recognition?' . . .

4. On Arthur Rimbaud

. . . What, then, is the actual value of Rimbaud's work, in verse and
prose, apart from its relative values of so many kinds? . . . He brought
into French verse something of that 'gipsy way of going with nature,
as with a woman'; a very young, very crude, very defiant and
sometimes very masterly sense of just those real things which are too
close to us to be seen by most people with any clearness. He could
render physical sensation, of the subtlest kind, without making any
compromise with language, forcing language to speak straight,
taming it as one would tame a dangerous animal. And he kneaded
prose as he kneaded verse, making it a disarticulated, abstract,

mathematically lyrical thing. In verse, he pointed the way to certain new splendours, as to certain new *naïvetés*; there is the *Bateau Ivre*, without which we might never have had Verlaine's *Crimen Amoris*. And, intertangled with what is ingenuous, and with what is splendid, there is a certain irony, which comes into that youthful work as if youth were already reminiscent of itself, so conscious is it that youth is youth, and that youth is passing.

In all these ways, Rimbaud had his influence upon Verlaine, and his influence upon Verlaine was above all the influence of the man of action upon the man of sensation; the influence of what is simple, narrow, emphatic, upon what is subtle, complex, growing. Verlaine's rich, sensitive nature was just then trying to realise itself. Just because it had such delicate possibilities, because there were so many directions in which it could grow, it was not at first quite sure of its way. Rimbaud came into the life and art of Verlaine, troubling both, with that trouble which reveals a man to himself. Having helped to make Verlaine a great poet, he could go. . . .

5. On Paul Verlaine

. . . Verlaine may be said to have learnt nothing from experience, in the sense that he learnt everything direct from life, and without comparing day with day. That the exquisite artist of the *Fêtes Galantes* should become the great poet of *Sagesse*, it was needful that things should have happened as disastrously as they did: the marriage with the girl-wife, that brief idyl, the passion for drink, those other forbidden passions, vagabondage, an attempted crime, the eighteen months of prison, conversion; followed, as it had to be, by relapse, bodily sickness, poverty, beggary almost, a lower and lower descent into mean distresses. It was needful that all this should happen, in order that the spiritual vision should eclipse the material vision; but it was needful that all this should happen in vain, so far as the conduct of life was concerned. Reflection, in Verlaine, is pure waste; it is the speech of the soul and the speech of the eyes, that we must listen to in his verse, never the speech of the reason. And I call him fortunate because, going through life with a great unconsciousness of what most men spend their lives in considering, he was able to abandon himself entirely to himself, to his unimpeded vision, to his unchecked emotion, to the passionate sincerity which in him was genius.

French poetry, before Verlaine, was an admirable vehicle for a really fine, a really poetical, kind of rhetoric. With Victor Hugo, for the first time since Ronsard (the two or three masterpieces of Ronsard and his companions) it had learnt to sing; with Baudelaire it had invented a new vocabulary for the expression of subtle, often perverse, essentially modern emotion and sensation. But with Victor Hugo, with Baudelaire, we are still under the dominion of rhetoric. 'Take eloquence, and wring its neck!' said Verlaine in his *Art Poétique*; and he showed, by writing it, that French verse could be written without rhetoric. It was partly from his study of English models that he learnt the secret of liberty in verse, but it was much more a secret found by the way, in the mere endeavour to be absolutely sincere, to express exactly what he saw, to give voice to his own temperament, in which intensity of feeling seemed to find its own expression, as if by accident. *L'art, mes enfants, c'est d'être absolument soi-même*, he tells us in one of his later poems; and, with such a pesonality as Verlaine's to express, what more has art to do, if it would truly, and in any interesting manner, hold the mirror up to nature?

For, consider the natural qualities which this man had for the task of creating a new poetry. 'Sincerity, and the impression of the moment followed to the letter': that is how he defined his theory of style, in an article written about himself.

> Car nous voulons la nuance encor,
> Pas la couleur, rien que la nuance!

as he cries, in his famous *Art Poétique*. Take, then, his susceptibility of the senses, an emotional susceptibility not less delicate; a life sufficiently troubled to draw out every emotion of which he was capable, and, with it, that absorption in the moment, that inability to look before or after; the need to love and the need to confess, each a passion; an art of painting the fine shades of landscape, of evoking atmosphere, which can be compared only with the art of Whistler; a simplicity of language which is the direct outcome of a simplicity of temperament, with just enough consciousness of itself for a final elegance, and, at the very depth of his being, an almost fierce humility, by which the passion of love, after searching furiously through all his creatures, finds God by the way, and kneels in the dust before him. Verlaine was never a theorist: he left theories to Mallarmé. He had only his divination; and he divined that poetry, always desiring that miracles should happen, had never waited patiently enough upon the miracle. It was by that proud and humble mysticism of his temperament that he came to realise how much could be done by, in a sense, trying to do nothing.

And then: *De la musique avant toute chose; De la musique encore et toujours!* There are poems of Verlaine which go as far as verse can go to become pure music, the voice of a bird with a human soul. It is part of his simplicity, his divine childishness, that he abandons himself, at times, to the song which words begin to sing in the air, with the same wise confidence with which he abandons himself to the other miracles about him. He knows that words are living things, which we have not created, and which go their way without demanding of us the right to live. He knows that words are suspicious, not without their malice, and that they resist mere force with the impalpable resistance of fire or water. They are to be caught only with guile or with trust. Verlaine has both, and words become Ariel to him. They bring him not only that submission of the slave which they bring to others, but all the soul, and in a happy bondage. They transform themselves for him into music, colour, and shadow; a disembodied music, diaphanous colours, luminous shadow. They serve him with so absolute a self-negation that he can write *romances sans paroles*, songs almost without words, in which scarcely a sense of the interference of human speech remains. The ideal of lyric poetry, certainly, is to be this passive, flawless medium for the deeper consciousness of things, the mysterious voice of that mystery which lies about us, out of which we have come, and into which we shall return. It is not without reason that we cannot analyse a perfect lyric.

With Verlaine the sense of hearing and the sense of sight are almost interchangeable: he paints with sound, and his line and atmosphere become music. It was with the most precise accuracy that Whistler applied the terms of music to his painting, for painting, when it aims at being the vision of reality, *pas la couleur, rien que la nuance*, passes almost into the condition of music. Verlaine's landscape painting is always an evocation, in which outline is lost in atmosphere.

> C'est des beaux yeux derrière des voiles,
>   C'est le grand jour tremblant de midi,
>   C'est, par un ciel d'automne attiédi,
> Le bleu fouillis des claires étoiles!

He was a man, certainly, 'for whom the visible world existed', but for whom it existed always as a vision. He absorbed it through all his senses, as the true mystic absorbs the divine beauty. And so he created in verse a new voice for nature, full of the humble ecstasy with which he saw, listened, accepted.

> Cette âme qui se lamente
> En cette plaine dormante
>   C'est la nôtre, n'est-ce pas?
> La mienne, dis, et la tienne,
> Dont s'exhale l'humble antienne
>   Par ce tiède soir, tout bas?

And with the same attentive simplicity with which he found words for the sensations of hearing and the sensations of sight, he found words for the sensations of the soul, for the fine shades of feeling. From the moment when his inner life may be said to have begun, he was occupied with the task of an unceasing confession, in which one seems to overhear him talking to himself, in that vague, preoccupied way which he often had. Here again are words which startle one by their delicate resemblance to thoughts, by their winged flight from so far, by their alighting so close. The verse murmurs, with such an ingenuous confidence, such intimate secrets. That 'setting free' of verse, which is one of the achievements of Verlaine, was itself mainly an attempt to be more and more sincere, a way of turning poetic artifice to new account, by getting back to nature itself, hidden away under the eloquent rhetoric of Hugo, Baudelaire, and the Parnassians. In the devotion of rhetoric to either beauty or truth, there is a certain consciousness of an audience, of an external judgment: rhetoric would convince, be admired. It is the very essence of poetry to be unconscious of anything between its own moment of flight and the supreme beauty which it will never attain. Verlaine taught French poetry that wise and subtle unconsciousness. It was in so doing that he 'fused his personality', in the words of Verhaeren, 'so profoundly with beauty, that he left upon it the imprint of a new and henceforth eternal attitude.'

J'ai la fureur d'aimer, says Verlaine, in a passage of very personal significance.

> J'ai la fureur d'aimer. Mon cœur si faible est fou.
> N'importe quand, n'importe quel et n'importe où,
> Qu'un éclair de beauté, de vertu, de vaillance,
> Luise, il s'y précipite, il y vole, il y lance,
> Et, le temps d'une étreinte, il embrasse cent fois
> L'être ou l'objet qu'il a poursuivi de son choix;
> Puis, quand l'illusion a replié son aile,
> Il revient triste et seul bien souvent, mais fidèle,
> Et laissant aux ingrats quelque chose de lui,
> Sang ou chair . . . .
> J'ai la fureur d'aimer. Qu'y faire? Ah, laissez faire!

And certainly this admirable, and supremely dangerous, quality was at the root of Verlaine's nature. Instinctive, unreasoning as he was, entirely at the mercy of the emotion or impression which, for the moment, had seized upon him, it was inevitable that he should be completely at the mercy of the most imperious of instincts, of passions, and of intoxications. And he had the simple and ardent nature, in this again consistently childlike, to which love, some kind of affection, given or returned, is not the luxury, the exception, which it is to many natures, but a daily necessity. To such a temperament there may or may not be the one great passion; there will certainly be many passions. And in Verlaine I find that single, child-like necessity of loving and being loved, all through his life and on every page of his works; I find it, unchanged in essence, but constantly changing form, in his chaste and unchaste devotions to women, in his passionate friendships with men, in his supreme mystical adoration of God. . . .

6. On Jules Laforgue

. . . It is an art of the nerves, this art of Laforgue, and it is what all art would tend towards if we followed our nerves on all their journeys. There is in it all the restlessness of modern life, the haste to escape from whatever weighs too heavily on the liberty of the moment, that capricious liberty which demands only room enough to hurry itself weary. It is distressingly conscious of the unhappiness of mortality, but it plays, somewhat uneasily, at a disdainful indifference. And it is out of these elements of caprice, fear, contempt, linked together by an embracing laughter, that it makes its existence.

Il n'y a pas de type, il y a la vie, Laforgue replies to those who come to him with classical ideals. *Votre idéal est bien vite magnifiquement submergé,* in life itself, which should form its own art, an art deliberately ephemeral, with the attaching pathos of passing things. There is a great pity at the root of this art of Laforgue: self-pity, which extends, with the artistic sympathy, through mere clearness of vision, across the world. His laughter, which Maeterlinck has defined so admirably as 'the laughter of the soul', is the laughter of Pierrot, more than half a sob, and shaken out of him with a deplorable gesture of the thin arms, thrown wide. He is a metaphysical Pierrot, *Pierrot lunaire,* and it is of abstract notions, the whole science of the unconscious, that he makes his showman's patter. As it is part of his manner not to distinguish between irony and pity, or even belief, we need not attempt to do so. Heine should teach us to understand at least so much of a poet who could not otherwise resemble him less. In Laforgue, sentiment is squeezed out of the world before one begins to play at ball with it.

And so, of the two, he is the more hopeless. He has invented a new manner of being René or Werther: an inflexible politeness towards man, woman, and destiny. He composes love-poems hat in hand, and smiles with an exasperating tolerance before all the transformations of the eternal feminine. He is very conscious of death, but his *blague* of death is, above all things, gentlemanly. He will not permit himself, at any moment, the luxury of dropping the mask: not at any moment. . . .

And yet one realises, if one but reads him attentively enough, how much suffering and despair, and resignation to what is, after all, the inevitable, are hidden away under this disguise, and also why this disguise is possible. Laforgue died at twenty-seven: he had been a dying man all his life, and his work has the fatal evasiveness of those who shrink from remembering the one thing which they are unable to forget. Coming as he does after Rimbaud, turning the divination of the other into theories, into achieved results, he is the eternally grown up, mature to the point of self-negation, as the other is the eternal *enfant terrible*. He thinks intensely about life, seeing what is automatic, pathetically ludicrous in it, almost as one might who has no part in the comedy. He has the double advantage, for his art, of being condemned to death, and of being, in the admirable phrase of Villiers, 'one of those who come into the world with a ray of moonlight in their brains'.

7. On Stéphane Mallarmé

. . . 'Poetry', said Mallarmé, 'is the language of a state of crisis'; and all his poems are the evocation of a passing ecstasy, arrested in mid-flight. This ecstasy is never the mere instinctive cry of the heart, the simple human joy or sorrow, which, like the Parnassians, but for not quite the same reason, he did not admit in poetry. It is a mental transposition of emotion or sensation, veiled with atmosphere, and becoming, as it becomes a poem, pure beauty. . . .

It is the distinction of Mallarmé to have aspired after an impossible liberation of the soul of literature from what is fretting and constraining in 'the body of that death', which is the mere literature of words. Words, he has realised, are of value only as a notation of the free breath of the spirit; words, therefore, must be employed with an extreme care, in their choice and adjustment, in setting them to reflect and chime upon one another; yet least of all for their own sake, for what they can never, except by suggestion, express. 'Every soul is a melody', he has said, 'which needs to be readjusted; and for that are the flute or viol of each.' The word, treated indeed with a kind of 'adoration', as he says, is so regarded in a magnificent sense, in which it is apprehended as a living thing, itself the vision rather than the reality; at least the philtre of the evocation. The word, chosen as he chooses it, is for him a liberating principle, by which the spirit is extracted from matter; takes form, perhaps assumes immortality. Thus an artificiality, even, in the use of words, that seeming artificiality which comes from using words as if they had never been used before, that chimerical search after the virginity of language, is but the paradoxical outward sign of an extreme discontent with even the best of their service. Writers who use words fluently, seeming to disregard their importance, do so from an unconscious confidence in their expressiveness, which the scrupulous thinker, the precise dreamer, can never place in the most carefully chosen among them. To evoke, by some elaborate, instantaneous magic of language, without the formality of an after all impossible description; to be, rather than to express: that is what Mallarmé has consistently, and from the first, sought in verse and prose. And he has sought this wandering, illusive, beckoning butterfly, the soul of dreams, over more and more entangled ground; and it has led him into the depths of many forests, far from the sunlight. To say that he has found what he sought is impossible; but (is it possible to avoid saying?) how heroic a search, and what marvellous discoveries by the way!

I think I understand, though I cannot claim his own authority for my supposition, the way in which Mallarmé wrote verse, and the reason why it became more and more abstruse, more and more unintelligible. Remember his principle: that to name is to destroy, to suggest is to create. Note, further, that he condemns the inclusion in verse of anything but, 'for example, the horror of the forest, or the silent thunder afloat in the leaves; not the intrinsic, dense wood of the trees'. He has received, then, a mental sensation: let it be the horror of the forest. This sensation begins to form in his brain, at first probably no more than a rhythm, absolutely without words. Gradually thought begins to concentrate itself (but with an extreme care, lest it should break the tension on which all depends) upon the sensation, already struggling to find its own consciousness. Delicately, stealthily, with infinitely timid precaution, words present themselves, at first in silence. Every word seems like a desecration, seems, the clearer it is, to throw back the original sensation farther and farther into the darkness. But, guided always by the rhythm, which is the executive soul (as, in Aristotle's definition, the soul is the form of the body), words come slowly, one by one, shaping the message. Imagine the poem already written down, at least composed. In its very imperfection, it is clear, it shows the links by which it has been riveted together; the whole process of its construction can be studied. Now most writers would be content; but with Mallarmé the work has only begun. In the final result there must be no sign of the making, there must be only the thing made. He works over it, word by word, changing a word here, for its colour, which is not precisely the colour required, a word there, for the break it makes in the music. A new image occurs to him, rarer, subtler, than the one he has used; the image is transferred. By the time the poem has reached, as it seems to him, a flawless unity, the steps of the progress have been only too effectually effaced; and while the poet, who has seen the thing from the beginning, still sees the relation of point to point, the reader, who comes to it only in its final stage, finds himself in a not unnatural bewilderment. Pursue this manner of writing to its ultimate development; start with an enigma, and then withdraw the key of the enigma; and you arrive, easily, at the frozen impenetrability of those latest sonnets, in which the absence of all punctuation is scarcely a recognisable hindrance.

That, I fancy to myself, was his actual way of writing; here, in what I prefer to give as a corollary, is the theory. 'Symbolist, Decadent, or Mystic, the schools thus called by themselves, or thus hastily labelled by our information-press, adopt, for meeting-place the point of an Idealism which (similarly as in fugues, in sonatas) rejects the "natural" materials, and, as brutal, a direct thought ordering them; to retain no more than suggestion. To be instituted, a relation between images, exact; and that therefrom should detach itself a third aspect, fusible and clear, offered to the divination. Abolished, the pretension, aesthetically an error, despite its dominion over almost all the masterpieces, to enclose within the subtle paper other than, for example, the horror of the forest, or the silent thunder afloat in the leaves; not the intrinsic, dense wood of the trees. Some few bursts of personal pride, veridically trumpeted, awaken the architecture of the palace, alone habitable; not of stone, on which the pages would close but ill.' For example (it is his own): 'I say: a flower! and out of the oblivion to which my voice consigns every contour, so far as anything save the known calyx, musically arises, idea, and exquisite, the one flower absent from all bouquets'. 'The pure work', then, 'implies the elocutionary disappearance of the poet, who yields place to the words, immobilised by the shock of their inequality; they take light from mutual reflection, like an actual trail of fire over precious stones, replacing the old lyric afflatus or the enthusiastic personal direction of the phrase.' 'The verse which out of many vocables remakes an entire word, unknown to the language, and as if magical, attains this isolation of speech.' Whence, it being 'music which rejoins verse, to form, since Wagner, Poetry', the final conclusion: 'That we are now precisely at the moment of seeking, before that breaking up of the large rhythms of literature, and their scattering in articulate, almost instrumental, nervous waves, an art which shall complete the transposition, into the Book, of the symphony, or simply recapture our own: for, it is not in elementary sonorities of brass, strings, wood, unquestionably, but in the intellectual word at its utmost, that, fully and evidently, we should find, drawing to itself all the correspondences of the universe, the supreme Music.'

Here, literally translated, in exactly the arrangement of the original, are some passages out of the theoretic writings, which I have brought together, to indicate what seem to me the main lines of Mallarmé's doctrine. It is the doctrine which . . . had been divined by Gérard de Nerval; but what, in Gérard, was pure vision, becomes in Mallarmé a logical sequence of meditation. Mallarmé was not a mystic, to whom anything came unconsciously; he was a thinker, in whom an extraordinary subtlety of mind was exercised on always explicit, though by no means the common, problems. 'A seeker after something in the world, that is there is no satisfying measure, or not at all', he pursued his search with unwearying persistence, with a sharp mental division of dream and idea, certainly very lucid to himself, however he may have failed to render his expression clear to others. And I, for one, cannot doubt that he was, for the most part, entirely right in his statement and analysis of the new conditions under which we are now privileged or condemned to write. His obscurity was partly his failure to carry out the spirit of his own directions; but, apart from obscurity, which we may all be fortunate enough to escape, is it possible for a writer, at the present day, to be quite simple, with the old, objective simplicity, in either thought or expression? To be *naïf*, to be archaic, is not to be either natural or simple; I affirm that it is not natural to be what is called 'natural' any longer. We have no longer the mental attitude of those to whom a story was but a story, and all stories good; we have realised, since it was proved to us by Poe, not merely that the age of epics is past, but that no long poem was ever written; the finest long poem in the world being but a series of short poems linked together by prose. And, naturally, we can no longer write what we can no longer accept. Symbolism, implicit in all literature from the beginning, as it is implicit in the very words we use, comes to us now, at last quite conscious of itself, offering us the only escape from our many imprisonments. We find a new, an older, sense in the so worn out forms of things; the world, which we can no longer believe in as the satisfying material object it was to our grandparents, becomes transfigured with a new light; words, which long usage had darkened almost out of recognition, take fresh lustre. And it is on the lines of that spiritualising of the word, that perfecting of form in its capacity for allusion and suggestion, that confidence in the eternal correspondences between the visible and the invisible universe, which Mallarmé taught, and too intermittently practised, that literature must now move, if it is in any sense to move forward.

8. Conclusion

Our only chance, in this world, of a complete happiness, lies in the measure of our success in shutting the eyes of the mind, and deadening its sense of hearing, and dulling the keenness of its apprehension of the unknown. Knowing so much less than nothing, for we are entrapped in smiling and many-coloured appearances, our life may seem to be but a little space of leisure, in which it will be the necessary business of each of us to speculate on what is so rapidly becoming the past and so rapidly becoming the future, that scarcely existing present which is after all our only possession. Yet, as the present passes from us, hardly to be enjoyed except as memory or as hope, and only with an at best partial recognition of the uncertainty or inutility of both, it is with a kind of terror that we wake up, every now and then, to the whole knowledge of our ignorance, and to some perception of where it is leading us. To live through a single day with that overpowering consciousness of our real position, which, in the moments in which alone it mercifully comes, is like blinding light or the thrust of a flaming sword, would drive any man out of his senses. It is our hesitations, the excuses of our hearts, the compromises of our intelligence, which save us. We can forget so much, we can bear suspense with so fortunate an evasion of its real issues; we are so admirably finite.

And so there is a great, silent conspiracy between us to forget death; all our lives are spent in busily forgetting death. That is why we are active about so many things which we know to be unimportant; why we are so afraid of solitude, and so thankful for the company of our fellow-creatures. Allowing ourselves, for the most part, to be but vaguely conscious of that great suspense in which we live, we find our escape from its sterile, annihilating reality in many dreams, in religion, passion, art; each a forgetfulness, each a symbol of creation; religion being the creation of a new heaven, passion the creation of a new earth, and art, in its mingling of heaven and earth, the creation of heaven out of earth. Each is a kind of sublime selfishness, the saint, the lover, and the artist having each an incommunicable ecstasy which he esteems as his ultimate attainment, however, in his lower moments, he may serve God in action, or do the will of his mistress, or minister to men by showing them a little beauty. But it is, before all things, an escape; and the prophets who have redeemed the world, and the artists who have made the world beautiful, and the lovers who have quickened the pulses of the world, have really, whether they knew it or not, been fleeing from the certainty of one thought: that we have, all of us, only our one day; and from the dread of that other thought: that the day, however used, must after all be wasted.

The fear of death is not cowardice; it is, rather, an intellectual dissatisfaction with an enigma which has been presented to us, and which can be solved only when its solution is of no further use. All we have to ask of death is the meaning of life, and we are waiting all through life to ask that question. That life should be happy or unhappy, as those words are used, means so very little; and the heightening or lessening of the general felicity of the world means so little to any individual. There is something almost vulgar in happiness which does not become joy, and joy is an ecstasy which can rarely be maintained in the soul for more than the moment during which we recognise that it is not sorrow. Only very young people want to be happy. What we all want is to be quite sure that there is something which makes it worth while to go on living, in what seems to us our best way, at our finest intensity; something beyond the mere fact that we are satisfying a sort of inner logic (which may be quite faulty) and that we get our best makeshift for happiness on that so hazardous assumption.

Well, the doctrine of Mysticism, with which all this symbolical literature has so much to do, of which it is all so much the expression, presents us, not with a guide for conduct, not with a plan for our happiness, not with an explanation of any mystery, but with a theory of life which makes us familiar with mystery, and which seems to harmonise those instincts which make for religion, passion, and art, freeing us at once of a great bondage. The final uncertainty remains, but we seem to knock less helplessly at closed doors, coming so much closer to the once terrifying eternity of things about us, as we come to look upon these things as shadows, through which we have our shadowy passage. 'For in the particular acts of human life', Plotinus tells us, 'it is not the interior soul and the true man, but the exterior shadow of the man alone, which laments and weeps, performing his part on the earth as in a more ample and extended scene, in which many shadows of souls and phantom scenes appear.' And as we realise the identity of a poem, a prayer, or a kiss, in that spiritual universe which we are weaving for ourselves, each out of a thread of the great fabric; as we realise the infinite insignificance of action, its immense distance from the current of life; as we realise the delight of feeling ourselves carried onward by forces which it is our wisdom to obey; it is at least with a certain relief that we turn to an ancient doctrine, so much the more likely to be true because it has so much the air of a dream. On this theory alone does all life become worth living, all art worth making, all worship worth offering. And because it might slay as well as save, because the freedom of its sweet captivity might so easily become deadly to the fool, because it is the hardest path to walk in where you are told only, walk well: it is perhaps the only counsel of perfection which can ever really mean much to the artist.

SOURCE: extracts from *The Symbolist Movement* (London, 1899; 2nd edn revised, 1908), pp. *v–vii*, 1–9, 38–41, 72–3, 82–91, 108–10, 111, 120, 126–34, 170–5.

NOTE

1. 'I am far from sure', wrote Verlaine, 'that the philosophy of Villiers will not one day become the formula of our century.' [Symons's note in the original.]

A. C. Bradley   (1901)

POETRY FOR POETRY'S SAKE

The words 'Poetry for poetry's sake' recall the famous phrase, 'Art for Art'. It is far from my purpose to examine the possible meanings of that phrase, or all the questions it involves. I propose to state briefly what I understand by 'Poetry for poetry's sake', and then, after guarding against one or two misapprehensions of the formula, to consider more fully a single problem connected with it. And I must premise, without attempting to justify them, certain explanations. We are to consider poetry in its essence, and apart from the flaws which in most poems accompany their poetry. We are to include in the idea of poetry the metrical form, and not to regard this as a mere accident or a mere vehicle. And, finally, poetry being poems, we are to think of a poem as it actually exists; and, without aiming here at accuracy, we may say that an actual poem is the succession of experiences – sounds, images, thoughts, emotions – through which we pass when we are reading as poetically as we can. Of course this imaginative experience – if I may use the phrase for brevity – differs with every reader and every time of reading: a poem exists in innumerable degrees. But that insurmountable fact lies in the nature of things and does not concern us now.

What then does the formula 'Poetry for poetry's sake' tell us about this experience? It says, as I understand it, these things. First, this experience is an end in itself, is worth having on its own account, has an intrinsic value. Next, its *poetic* value is this intrinsic worth alone. Poetry may have also an ulterior value as a means to culture or religion; because it conveys instruction, or softens the passions, or furthers a good cause; because it brings the poet fame or money or a quiet conscience. So much the better: let it be valued for these reasons too. But its ulterior worth neither is nor can directly determine its poetic worth as a satisfying imaginative experience; and this is to be judged entirely from within. And to these two positions the formula would add, though not of necessity, a third. The consideration of ulterior ends, whether by the poet in the act of composing or by the reader in the act of experiencing, tends to lower poetic value. It does so because it tends to change the nature of poetry by taking it out of its own atmosphere. For its nature is to be not a part, nor yet a copy, of the real world (as we commonly understand that phrase), but to be a world by itself, independent, complete, autonomous; and to possess it fully you must enter that world, conform to its laws, and ignore for the time the beliefs, aims, and particular conditions which belong to you in the other world of reality.

Of the more serious misapprehensions to which these statements may give rise I will glance only at one or two. The offensive consequences often drawn from the formula 'Art for Art' will be found to attach not to the doctrine that Art is an end in itself, but to the doctrine that Art is the whole or supreme end of human life. And as this latter doctrine, which seems to me absurd, is in any case quite different from the former, its consequences fall outside my subject. The formula 'Poetry is an end in itself' has nothing to say on the various questions of moral judgment which arise from the fact that poetry has its place in a many-sided life. For anything it says, the intrinsic value of poetry might be so small, and its ulterior effects so mischievous, that it had better not exist. The formula only tells us that we must not place in antithesis poetry and human good, for poetry is one kind of human good; and that we must not determine the intrinsic value of this kind of good by direct reference to another. If we do, we shall find ourselves maintaining what we did not expect. If poetic value lies in the stimulation of religious feelings, *Lead, kindly Light* is no better a poem than many a tasteless version of a Psalm: if in the excitement of patriotism, why is *Scots, wha hae* superior to *We don't want to fight*? if in the mitigation of the passions, the Odes of Sappho will win but little praise: if in instruction, Armstrong's *Art of preserving Health* should win much.

Again, our formula may be accused of cutting poetry away from its connection with life. And this accusation raises so huge a problem that I must ask leave to be dogmatic as well as brief. There is plenty of connection between life and poetry, but it is, so to say, a connection underground. The two may be called different forms of the same thing: one of them having (in the usual sense) reality, but seldom fully satisfying imagination; while the other offers something which satisfies imagination but has not full 'reality'. They are parallel developments which nowhere meet, or, if I may use loosely a word which will be serviceable later, they are analogues. Hence we understand one by help of the other, and even, in a sense, care for one because of the other; but hence also, poetry neither is life, nor, strictly speaking, a copy of it. They differ not only because one has more mass and the other a more perfect shape, but because they have different *kinds* of existence. The one touches us as beings occupying a given position in space and time, and having feelings, desires, and purposes due to that position: it appeals to imagination, but appeals to much besides. What meets us in poetry has not a position in the same series of time and space, or, if it has or had such a position, it is taken apart from much that belonged to it there; and therefore it makes no direct appeal to those feelings, desires, and purposes, but speaks only to contemplative imagination – imagination the reverse of empty or emotionless, imagination saturated with the results of 'real' experience, but still contemplative. Thus, no doubt, one main reason why poetry has poetic value for us is that it presents to us in its own way something which we meet in another form in nature or life; and yet the test of its poetic value for us lies simply in the question whether it satisfies our imagination; the rest of us, our knowledge or conscience, for example, judging it only so far as they appear transmuted in our imagination. So also Shakespeare's knowledge or his moral insight, Milton's greatness of soul, Shelley's 'hate of hate' and 'love of love', and that desire to help men or make them happier which may have influenced a poet in hours of meditation – all these have, as such, no poetical worth: they have that worth only when, passing through the unity of the poet's being, they reappear as qualities of imagination, and then are indeed mighty powers in the world of poetry.

I come to a third misapprehension, and so to my main subject. This formula, it is said, empties poetry of its meaning: it is really a doctrine of form for form's sake. 'It is of no consequence what a poet says, so long as he says the thing well. The *what* is poetically indifferent: it is the *how* that counts. Matter, subject, content, substance, determines nothing; there is no subject with which poetry may not deal: the form, the treatment, is everything. Nay, more: not only is the matter indifferent, but it is the secret of Art to "eradicate the matter by means of the form",' – phrases and statements like these meet us everywhere in current criticism of literature and the other arts. They are the stock-in-trade of writers who understand of them little more than the fact that somehow or other they are not 'bourgeois'. But we find them also seriously used by writers whom we must respect, whether they are anonymous or not; something like one or another of them might be quoted, for example, from Professor Saintsbury, the late R. A. M. Stevenson, Schiller, Goethe himself; and they are the watchwords of a school in the one country where Aesthetics has flourished. They come, as a rule, from men who either practise one of the arts, or, from study of it, are interested in its methods. The general reader – a being so general that I may say what I will of him – is outraged by them. He feels that he is being robbed of almost all that he cares for in a work of art. 'You are asking me', he says, 'to look at the Dresden Madonna as if it were a Persian rug. You are telling me that the poetic value of *Hamlet* lies solely in its style and versification, and that my interest in the man and his fate is only an intellectual or moral interest. You allege that, if I want to enjoy the poetry of *Crossing the Bar*, I must not mind what Tennyson says there, but must consider solely his way of saying it. But in that case I can care no more for a poem than I do for a set of nonsense verses; and I do not believe that the authors of *Hamlet* and *Crossing the Bar* regarded their poems thus.'

These antitheses of subject, matter, substance on the one side, form, treatment, handling on the other, are the field through which I especially want, in this lecture, to indicate a way. It is a field of battle; and the battle is waged for no trivial cause; but the cries of the combatants are terribly ambiguous. Those phrases of the so-called formalist may each mean five or six different things. Taken in one sense they seem to me chiefly true; taken as the general reader not unnaturally takes them, they seem to me false and mischievous. It would be absurd to pretend that I can end in a few minutes a controversy which concerns the ultimate nature of Art, and leads perhaps to problems not yet soluble; but we can at least draw some plain distinctions which, in this controversy, are too often confused.

In the first place, then, let us take 'subject' in one particular sense; let us understand by it that which we have in view when, looking at the title of an un-read poem, we say that the poet has chosen this or that for his subject. The subject, in this sense, so far as I can discover, is generally something, real or imaginary, as it exists in the minds of fairly cultivated people. The subject of *Paradise Lost* would be the story of the Fall as that story exists in the general imagination of a Bible-reading people. The subject of Shelley's stanzas *To a Skylark* would be the ideas which arise in the mind of an educated person when, without knowing the poem, he hears the word 'skylark'. If the title of a poem conveys little or nothing to us, the 'subject' appears to be either what we should gather by investigating the title in a dictionary or other book of the kind, or else such a brief suggestion as might be offered by a person who had read the poem, and who said, for example, that the subject of *The Ancient Mariner* was a sailor who killed an albatross and suffered for his deed.

Now the subject, in this sense (and I intend to use the word in no other), is not, as such, inside the poem, but outside it. The contents of the stanzas *To a Skylark* are not the ideas suggested by the word 'skylark' to the average man; they belong to Shelley just as much as the language does. The subject, therefore, is not the matter *of* the poem at all; and its opposite is not the *form* of the poem, but the whole poem. The subject is one thing; the poem, matter and form alike, another thing. This being so, it is surely obvious that the poetic value cannot lie in the subject, but lies entirely in its opposite, the poem. How can the subject determine the value when on one and the same subject poems may be written of all degrees of merit and demerit; or when a perfect poem may be composed on a subject so slight as a pet sparrow, and, if Macaulay may be trusted, a nearly worthless poem on a subject so stupendous as the omnipresence of the Deity? The 'formalist' is here perfectly right. Nor is he insisting on something unimportant. He is fighting against our tendency to take the work of art as a mere copy or reminder of something already in our heads, or at the best as a suggestion of some idea as little removed as possible from the familiar. The sightseer who promenades a picture-gallery, remarking that this portrait is so like his cousin, or that landscape the very image of his birthplace, or who, after satisfying himself that one picture is about Elijah, passes on rejoicing to discover the subject, and nothing but the subject, of the next – what is he but an extreme example of this tendency? Well, but the very same tendency vitiates much of our criticism, much criticism of Shakespeare, for example, which, with all its cleverness and partial truth, still shows that the critic never passed from his own mind into Shakespeare's; and it may be traced even in so fine a critic as Coleridge, as when he dwarfs the sublime struggle of Hamlet into the image of his own unhappy weakness. Hazlitt by no means escaped its influence. Only the third of that great trio, Lamb, appears almost always to have rendered the conception of the composer.

Again, it is surely true that we cannot determine beforehand what subjects are fit for Art, or name any subject on which a good poem might not possibly be written. To divide subjects into two groups, the beautiful or elevating, and the ugly or vicious, and to judge poems according as their subjects belong to one of these groups or the other, is to fall into the same pit, to confuse with our pre-conceptions the meaning of the poet. What the thing is in the poem he is to be judged by, not by the thing as it was before he touched it; and how can we venture to say beforehand that he cannot make a true poem out of something which to us was merely alluring or dull or revolting? The question whether, having done so, he ought to publish his poem; whether the thing in the poet's work will not be still confused by the incompetent Puritan or the incompetent sensualist with the thing in *his* mind, does not touch this point: it is a further question, one of ethics, not of art. No doubt the upholders of 'Art for art's sake' will generally be in favour of the courageous course, of refusing to sacrifice the better or stronger part of the public to the weaker or worse; but their maxim in no way binds them to this view. Rossetti suppressed one of the best of his sonnets, a sonnet chosen for admiration by Tennyson, himself extremely sensitive about the moral effect of poetry; suppressed it, I believe, because it was called fleshly. One may regret Rossetti's judgment and at the same time respect his scrupulousness; but in any case he judged in his capacity of citizen, not in his capacity of artist.

So far then the 'formalist' appears to be right. But he goes too far, I think, if he maintains that the subject is indifferent and that all subjects are the same to poetry. And he does not prove his point by observing that a good poem might be written on a pin's head, and a bad one on the Fall of Man. That truth shows that the subject *settles* nothing, but not that it counts for nothing. The Fall of Man is really a more favourable subject than a pin's head. The Fall of Man, that is to say, offers opportunities of poetic effects wider in range and more penetrating in appeal. And the fact is that such a subject, as it exists in the general imagination, has some aesthetic value before the poet touches it. It is, as you may choose to call it, an inchoate poem or the débris of a poem. It is not an abstract idea or a bare isolated fact, but an assemblage of figures, scenes, actions, and events, which already appeal to emotional imagination; and it is already in some degree organized and formed. In spite of this a bad poet would make a bad poem on it; but then we should say he was unworthy of the subject. And we should not say this if he wrote a bad poem on a pin's head. Conversely, a good poem on a pin's head would almost certainly transform its subject far more than a good poem on the Fall of Man. It might revolutionize its subject so completely that we should say, 'The subject may be a pin's head, but the substance of the poem has very little to do with it.'

This brings us to another and a different antithesis. Those figures, scenes, events, that form part of the subject called the Fall of Man, are not the substance of *Paradise Lost*; but in *Paradise Lost* there are figures, scenes, and events resembling them in some degree. These, with much more of the same kind, may be described as its substance, and may then be contrasted with the measured language of the poem, which will be called its form. Subject is the opposite not of form but of the whole poem. Substance is within the poem, and its opposite, form, is also within the poem. I am not criticizing this antithesis at present, but evidently it is quite different from the other. It is practically the distinction used in the old-fashioned criticism of epic and drama, and it flows down, not unsullied, from Aristotle. Addison, for example, in examining *Paradise Lost* considers in order the fable, the characters, and the sentiments; these will be the substance: then he considers the language, that is, the style and numbers; this will be the form. In like manner, the substance or meaning of a lyric may be distinguished from the form.

Now I believe it will be found that a large part of the controversy we are dealing with arises from a confusion between these two distinctions of substance and form, and of subject and poem. The extreme formalist lays his whole weight on the form because he thinks its opposite is the mere subject. The general reader is angry, but makes the same mistake, and gives to the subject praises that rightly belong to the substance.[1] I will read an example of what I mean. I can only explain the following words of a good critic by supposing that for the moment he has fallen into this confusion: 'The mere matter of all poetry – to wit, the appearances of nature and the thoughts and feelings of men – being unalterable, it follows that the difference between poet and poet will depend upon the manner of each in applying language, metre, rhyme, cadence, and what not, to this invariable material.' What has become here of the substance of *Paradise Lost* – the story, scenery, characters, sentiments, as they are in the poem? They have vanished clean away. Nothing is left but the form on one side, and on the other not even the subject, but a supposed invariable material, the appearances of nature and the thoughts and feelings of men. Is it surprising that the whole value should then be found in the form?

So far we have assumed that this antithesis of substance and form is valid, and that it always has one meaning. In reality it has several, but we will leave it in its present shape, and pass to the question of its validity. And this question we are compelled to raise, because we have to deal with the two contentions that the poetic value lies wholly or mainly in the substance, and that it lies wholly or mainly in the form. Now these contentions, whether false or true, may seem at least to be clear; but we shall find, I think, that they are both of them false, or both of them nonsense: false if they concern anything outside the poem, nonsense if they apply to something in it. For what do they evidently imply? They imply that there are in a poem two parts, factors, or components, a substance and a form; and that you can conceive them distinctly and separately, so that when you are speaking of the one you are not speaking of the other. Otherwise how can you ask the question, In which of them does the value lie? But really in a poem, apart from defects, there are no such factors or components; and therefore it is strictly nonsense to ask in which of them the value lies. And on the other hand, if the substance and the form referred to are not in the poem, then both the contentions are false, for its poetic value lies in itself.

What I mean is neither new nor mysterious; and it will be clear, I believe, to any one who reads poetry poetically and who closely examines his experience. When you are reading a poem, I would ask – not analysing it, and much less criticizing it, but allowing it, as it proceeds, to make its full impression on you through the exertion of your recreating imagination – do you then apprehend and enjoy as one thing a certain meaning or substance, and as another thing certain articulate sounds, and do you somehow compound these two? Surely you do not, any more than you apprehend apart, when you see some one smile, those lines in the face which express a feeling, and the feeling that the lines express. Just as there the lines and their meaning are to you one thing, not two, so in poetry the meaning and the sounds are one: there is, if I may put it so, a resonant meaning, or a meaning resonance. If you read the line, 'The sun is warm, the sky is clear', you do not experience separately the image of a warm sun and clear sky, on the one side, and certain unintelligible rhythmical sounds on the other; nor yet do you experience them together, side by side; but you experience the one *in* the other. And in like manner, when you are really reading *Hamlet*, the action and the characters are not something which you conceive apart from the words; you apprehend them from point to point *in* the words, and the words as expressions of them. Afterwards, no doubt, when you are out of the poetic experience but remember it, you may by analysis decompose this unity, and attend to a substance more or less isolated, and a form more or less isolated. But these are things in your analytic head, not in the poem, which is *poetic* experience. And if you want to have the poem again, you cannot find it by adding together these two products of decomposition; you can only find it by passing back into poetic experience. And then what you recover is no aggregate of factors, it is a unity in which you can no more separate a substance and a form than you can separate living blood and the life in the blood. This unity has, if you like, various 'aspects' or 'sides', but they are not factors or parts; if you try to examine one, you find it is also the other. Call them substance and form if you please, but these are not the reciprocally exclusive substance and form to which the two contentions *must* refer. They do not 'agree', for they are not apart: they are one thing from different points of view, and in that sense identical. And this identity of content and form, you will say, is no accident; it is of the essence of poetry in so far as it is poetry, and of all art in so far as it is art. Just as there is in music not sound on one side and a meaning on the other, but expressive sound, and if you ask what is the meaning you can only answer by pointing to the sounds; just as in painting there is not a meaning *plus* paint, but a meaning *in* paint, or significant paint, and no man can really express the meaning in any other way than in paint and in *this* paint; so in a poem the true content and the true form neither exist nor can be imagined apart. When then you are asked whether the value of a poem lies in a substance got by decomposing the poem, and present, as such, only in reflective analysis, or whether the value lies in a form arrived at and existing in the same way, you will answer, 'It lies neither in one, nor in the other, nor in any addition of them, but in the poem, where they are not.'

We have then, first, an antithesis of subject and poem. This is clear and valid; and the question in which of them does the value lie is intelligible; and its answer is, In the poem. We have next a distinction of substance and form. If the substance means ideas, images, and the like taken alone, and the form means the measured language taken by itself, this is a possible distinction, but it is a distinction of things not in the poem, and the value lies in neither of them. If substance and form mean anything *in* the poem, then each is involved in the other, and the question in which of them the value lies has no sense. No doubt you may say, speaking loosely, that in this poet or poem the aspect of substance is the more noticeable, and in that the aspect of form; and you may pursue interesting discussions on this basis, though no principle or ultimate question of value is touched by them. And apart from that question, of course, I am not denying the usefulness and necessity of the distinction. We cannot dispense with it. To consider separately the action or the characters of a play, and separately its style or versification, is both legitimate and valuable, so long as we remember what we are doing. But the true critic in speaking of these apart does not really think of them apart; the whole, the poetic experience, of which they are but aspects, is always in his mind; and he is always aiming at a richer, truer, more intense repetition of that experience. On the other hand, when the question of principle, of poetic value, is raised, these aspects *must* fall apart into components, separately conceivable; and then there arise two heresies, equally false, that the value lies in one of two things, both of which are outside the poem, and therefore where its value cannot lie.

On the heresy of the separable substance a few additional words will suffice. This heresy is seldom formulated, but perhaps some unconscious holder of it may object: 'Surely the action and the characters of *Hamlet* are in the play; and surely I can retain these, though I have forgotten all the words. I admit that I do not possess the whole poem, but I possess a part, and the most important part.' And I would answer: 'If we are not concerned with any question of principle, I accept all that you say except the last words, which do raise such a question. Speaking loosely, I agree that the action and characters, as you perhaps conceive them, together with a great deal more, are in the poem. Even then, however, you must not claim to possess all of this kind that is in the poem; for in forgetting the words you must have lost innumerable details of the action and the characters. And, when the question of value is raised, I must insist that the action and characters, as you conceive them, are not in *Hamlet* at all. If they are, point them out. You cannot do it. What you find at any moment of that succession of experiences called *Hamlet* is words. In these words, to speak loosely again, the action and characters (more of them than you can conceive apart) are focussed; but your experience is not a combination of them, as ideas, on the one side, with certain sounds on the other; it is an experience of something in which the two are indissolubly fused. If you deny this, to be sure I can make no answer, or can only answer that I have reason to believe that you cannot read poetically, or else are misinterpreting your experience. But if you do not deny this, then you will admit that the action and characters of the poem, as you separately imagine them, are no part of it, but a product of it in your reflective imagination, a faint analogue of one aspect of it taken in detachment from the whole. Well, I do not dispute, I would even insist, that, in the case of so long a poem as *Hamlet*, it may be necessary from time to time to interrupt the poetic experience, in order to enrich it by forming such a product and dwelling on it. Nor, in a wide sense of "poetic", do I question the poetic value of this product, as you think of it apart from the poem. It resembles our recollections of the heroes of history or legend, who move about in our imaginations, "forms more real than living man", and are worth much to us though we do not remember anything they said. Our ideas and images of the "substance" of a poem have this poetic value, and more, if they are at all adequate. But they cannot determine the poetic value of the poem, for (not to speak of the competing claims of the "form") nothing that is outside the poem can do that, and they, as such, are outside it.'[2]

Let us turn to the so-called form – style and versification. There is no such thing as mere form in poetry. All form is expression. Style may have indeed a certain aesthetic worth in partial abstraction from the particular matter it conveys, as in a well-built sentence you may take pleasure in the build almost apart from the meaning. Even so, style is expressive – presents to sense, for example, the order, ease, and rapidity with which ideas move in the writer's mind – but it is not expressive of the meaning of that particular sentence. And it is possible, interrupting poetic experience, to decompose it and abstract for comparatively separate consideration this nearly formal element of style. But the aesthetic value of style so taken is not considerable;[3] you could not read with pleasure for an hour a composition which had no other merit. And in poetic experience you never apprehend this value by itself; the style is here expressive also of a particular meaning, or rather is one aspect of that unity whose other aspect is meaning. So that what you apprehend may be called indifferently an expressed meaning or a significant form. Perhaps on this point I may in Oxford appeal to authority, that of Matthew Arnold and Walter Pater, the latter at any rate an authority whom the formalist will not despise. What is the gist of Pater's teaching about style, if it is not that in the end the one virtue of style is truth or adequacy; that the word, phrase, sentence, should express perfectly the writer's perception, feeling, image, or thought; so that, as we read a descriptive phrase of Keats's, we exclaim, 'That is the thing itself'; so that, to quote Arnold, the words are 'symbols equivalent with the thing symbolized', or, in our technical language, a form identical with its content? Hence in true poetry it is, in strictness, impossible to express the meaning in any but its own words, or to change the words without changing the meaning. A translation of such poetry is not really the old meaning in a fresh dress; it is a new product, something like the poem, though, if one chooses to say so, more like it in the aspect of meaning than in the aspect of form.

No one who understands poetry, it seems to me, would dispute this, were it not that, falling away from his experience, or misled by theory, he takes the word 'meaning' in a sense almost ludicrously inapplicable to poetry. People say, for instance, 'steed' and 'horse' have the same meaning; and in bad poetry they have, but not in poetry that *is* poetry.

> 'Bring forth the horse!' The horse was brought:
> In truth he was a noble steed!

says Byron in *Mazeppa*. If the two words mean the same here, transpose them:

> 'Bring forth the steed!' The steed was brought:
> In truth he was a noble horse!

and ask again if they mean the same. Or let me take a line certainly very free from 'poetic diction':

To be or not to be, that is the question.

You may say that this means the same as 'What is just now occupying my attention is the comparative disadvantages of continuing to live or putting an end to myself.' And for practical purposes – the purpose, for example, of a coroner – it does. But as the second version altogether misrepresents the speaker at that moment of his existence, while the first does represent him, how can they for any but a practical or logical purpose be said to have the same sense? Hamlet was well able to 'unpack his heart with words', but he will not unpack it with our paraphrases.

These considerations apply equally to versification. If I take the famous line [in Virgil's *Aeneid*] which describes how the souls of the dead stood waiting by the river, imploring a passage from Charon:

Tendebantque manus ripae ulterioris amore;

and if I translate it, 'and were stretching forth their hands in longing for the further bank', the charm of the original has fled. Why has it fled? partly (but we have dealt with that) because I have substituted for five words, and those the words of Virgil, twelve words, and those my own. In some measure because I have turned into rhythmless prose a line of verse which, as mere sound, has unusual beauty. But much more because in doing so I have also changed the *meaning* of Virgil's line. What that meaning is *I* cannot say: Virgil has said it. But I can see this much, that the translation conveys a far less vivid picture of the outstretched hands and of their remaining outstretched, and a far less poignant sense of the distance of the shore and the longing of the souls. And it does so partly because this picture and this sense are conveyed not only by the obvious meaning of the words, but through the long-drawn sound of 'tendebantque,' through the time occupied by the five syllables and therefore by the idea of 'ulterioris', and through the identity of the long sound 'or' in the penultimate syllables of 'ulterioris amore' – all this, and much more, apprehended not in this analytical fashion, nor as *added* to the beauty of mere sound and to the obvious meaning, but in unity with them and so as expressive of the poetic meaning of the whole.

It is always so in fine poetry. The value of versification, when it is indissolubly fused with meaning, can hardly be exaggerated. The gift for feeling it, even more perhaps than the gift for feeling the value of style, is the *specific* gift for poetry, as distinguished from other arts. But versification, taken, as far as possible, all by itself, has a very different worth. Some aesthetic worth it has; how much, you may experience by reading poetry in a language of which you do not understand a syllable. The pleasure is quite appreciable, but it is not great; nor in actual poetic experience do you meet with it, as such, at all. For, I repeat, it is not *added* to the pleasure of the meaning when you read poetry that you do understand: by some mystery the music is then the music *of* the meaning, and the two are one. However fond of versification you might be, you would tire very soon of reading verses in Chinese; and before long of reading Virgil and Dante if you were ignorant of their languages. But take the music as it is *in* the poem, and there is a marvellous change. Now

> It gives a very echo to the seat
> Where love is throned;

or 'carries far into your heart', almost like music itself, the sound

> Of old, unhappy, far-off things
> And battles long ago.

What then is to be said of the following sentence of the critic quoted before: 'But when any one who knows what poetry is reads –

> Our noisy years seem moments in the being
> Of the eternal silence,

he sees that, quite independently of the meaning, . . . there is one note added to the articulate music of the world – a note that never will leave off resounding till the eternal silence itself gulfs it'? I must think that the writer is deceiving himself. For I could quite understand his enthusiasm, if it were an enthusiasm for the music of the meaning; but as for the music, 'quite independently of the meaning', so far as I can hear it thus (and I doubt if any one who knows English can quite do so), I find it gives some pleasure, but only a trifling pleasure. And indeed I venture to doubt whether, considered as mere sound, the words are at all exceptionally beautiful, as Virgil's line certainly is.

When poetry answers to its idea and is purely or almost purely poetic, we find the identity of form and content; and the degree of purity attained may be tested by the degree in which we feel it hopeless to convey the effect of a poem or passage in any form but its own. Where the notion of doing so is simply ludicrous, you have quintessential poetry. But a great part even of good poetry, especially in long works, is of a mixed nature; and so we find in it no more than a partial agreement of a form and substance which remain to some extent distinct. This is so in many passages of Shakespeare (the greatest of poets when he chose, but not always a conscientious poet); passages where something was wanted for the sake of the plot, but he did not care about it or was hurried. The conception of the passage is then distinct from the execution, and neither is inspired. This is so also, I think, wherever we can truly speak of merely decorative effect. We seem to perceive that the poet had a truth or fact – philosophical, agricultural, social – distinctly before him, and then, as we say, clothed it in metrical and coloured language. Most argumentative, didactic, or satiric poems are partly of this kind; and in imaginative poems anything which is really a mere 'conceit' is mere decoration. We often deceive ourselves in this matter, for what we call decoration has often a new and genuinely poetic content of its own; but wherever there is mere decoration, we judge the poetry to be not wholly poetic. And so when Wordsworth inveighed against poetic diction, though he hurled his darts rather wildly, what he was rightly aiming at was a phraseology, not the living body of a new content, but the mere worn-out body of an old one.

In pure poetry it is otherwise. Pure poetry is not the decoration of a preconceived and clearly defined matter: it springs from the creative impulse of a vague imaginative mass pressing for development and definition. If the poet already knew exactly what he meant to say, why should he write the poem? The poem would in fact already be written. For only its completion can reveal, even to him, exactly what he wanted. When he began and while he was at work, he did not possess his meaning; it possessed him. It was not a fully formed soul asking for a body: it was an inchoate soul in the inchoate body of perhaps two or three vague ideas and a few scattered phrases. The growing of this body into its full stature and perfect shape was the same thing as the gradual self-definition of the meaning. And this is the reason why such poems strike us as creations, not manufactures, and have the magical effect which mere decoration cannot produce. This is also the reason why, if we insist on asking for the meaning of such a poem, we can only be answered 'It means itself.'

And so at last I may explain why I have troubled myself and you with what may seem an arid controversy about mere words. It is not so. These heresies which would make poetry a compound of two factors – a matter common to it with the merest prose, *plus* a poetic form, as the one heresy says: a poetical substance *plus* a negligible form, as the other says – are not only untrue, they are injurious to the dignity of poetry. In an age already inclined to shrink from those higher realms where poetry touches religion and philosophy, the formalist heresy encourages men to taste poetry as they would a fine wine, which has indeed an aesthetic value, but a small one. And then the natural man, finding an empty form, hurls into it the matter of cheap pathos, rancid sentiment, vulgar humour, bare lust, ravenous vanity – everything which, in Schiller's phrase,[4] the form should extirpate, but which no mere form can extirpate. And the other heresy – which is indeed rather a practice than a creed – encourages us in the habit so dear to us of putting our own thoughts or fancies into the place of the poet's creation. What he meant by *Hamlet*, or the *Ode to a Nightingale*, or *Abt Vogler*, we say, is this or that which we knew already; and so we lose what he had to tell us. But he meant what he said, and said what he meant.

Poetry in this matter is not, as good critics of painting and music often affirm, different from the other arts; in all of them the content is one thing with the form. What Beethoven meant by his symphony, or Turner by his picture, was not something which you can name, but the picture and the symphony. Meaning they have, but *what* meaning can be said in no language but their own: and we know this, though some strange delusion makes us think the meaning has less worth because we cannot put it into words. Well, it is just the same with poetry. But because poetry is words, we vainly fancy that some other words than its own will express its meaning. And they will do so no more – or, if you like to speak loosely, only a trifle more – than words will express the meaning of the Dresden Madonna. Something a little like it they may indeed express. And we may find analogues of the meaning of poetry outside it, which may help us to appropriate it. The other arts, the best ideas of philosophy or religion, much that nature and life offer us or force upon us, are akin to it. But they are only akin. Nor is it the expression of them. Poetry does not present to imagination our highest knowledge or belief, and much less our dreams and opinions; but it, content and form in unity, embodies in its own irreplaceable way something which embodies itself also in other irreplaceable ways, such as philosophy or religion. And just as each of these gives a satisfaction which the other cannot possibly give, so we find in poetry, which cannot satisfy the needs they meet, that which by their natures they cannot afford us. But we shall not find it fully if we look for something else.

And now, when all is said, the question will still recur, though now in quite another sense, What does poetry mean? This unique expression, which cannot be replaced by any other, still seems to be trying to express something beyond itself. And this, we feel, is also what the other arts, and religion, and philosophy are trying to express: and that is what impels us to seek in vain to translate the one into the other. About the best poetry, and not only the best, there floats an atmosphere of infinite suggestion. The poet speaks to us of one thing, but in this one thing there seems to lurk the secret of all. He said what he meant, but his meaning seems to beckon away beyond itself, or rather to expand into something boundless which is only focussed in it; something also which, we feel, would satisfy not only the imagination, but the whole of us; that something within us, and without, which everywhere

> makes us seem
> To patch up fragments of a dream,
> Part of which comes true, and part
> Beats and trembles in the heart.

Those who are susceptible to this effect of poetry find it not only, perhaps not most, in the ideals which she has sometimes described, but in a child's song by Christina Rossetti about a mere crown of wind-flowers, and in tragedies like *Lear*, where the sun seems to have set for ever. They hear this spirit murmuring its undertone through the *Aeneid*, and catch its voice in the song of Keats's nightingale, and its light upon the figures on the Urn, and it pierces them no less in Shelley's hopeless lament, *O world, O life, O time*, than in the rapturous ecstasy of his *Life of Life*. This all-embracing perfection cannot be expressed in poetic words or words of any kind, nor yet in music or in colour, but the suggestion of it is in much poetry, if not all, and poetry has in this suggestion, this 'meaning', a great part of its value. We do it wrong, and we defeat our own purposes, when we try to bend it to them:

> We do it wrong, being so majestical,
> To offer it the show of violence;
> For it is as the air invulnerable,
> And our vain blows malicious mockery.

It is a spirit. It comes we know not whence. It will not speak at our bidding, nor answer in our language. It is not our servant; it is our master.

SOURCE: from Bradley's Inaugural Lecture as Professor of Poetry at Oxford, 1901; reprinted with revisions and annotations in *Oxford Lectures on Poetry* (London, 1909; several times reprinted), pp. 4–27.

NOTES

[Reorganised and renumbered from the 1909 edition – Ed.]

1. What is here called 'substance' is what people generally mean when they use the word 'subject' and insist on the value of the subject. I am not arguing against this usage, or in favour of the usage which I have adopted for

the sake of clearness. It does not matter which we employ, so long as we and others know what we mean. (I use 'substance' and 'content' indifferently.)

2. These remarks hold good, *mutatis mutandis*, if by 'substance' is understood the 'moral' or the 'idea' of a poem, although perhaps in one instance out of five thousand this may be found in so many words in the poem.

3. On the other hand, the absence, or worse than absence, of style, in this sense, is a serious matter.

4. Not that to Schiller 'form' meant mere style and versification.

J. Middleton Murry   (1919)

'THE SUPREME POETIC ACT'

... The poetic process is, we believe, two-fold. The one part, the discovery of symbol, the establishment of an equivalence, is what we may call poetic method. It is concerned with the transposition and communication of emotion, no matter what the emotion may be, for to poetic method the emotional material is, strictly, indifferent. The other part is an aesthetic apprehension of significance, the recognition of the all in the one. This is a specifically poetic act, or rather the supreme poetic act. Yet it may be absent from poetry. For there is no necessary connection between poetic apprehension and poetic method. Poetic method frequently exists without poetic apprehension; and there is no reason to suppose that the reverse is not also true, for the recognition of greatness in poetry is probably not the peculiar privilege of great poets. We have here, at least a principle of division between major and minor poetry.

... we are impelled to seek further and ask what it is that enables [a major] poet to perform this sovereign act of apprehension and to recognise the quality of the all in the quality of the one. We believe that the answer is simple. The great poet knows what he is looking for ... We speak too precisely, and so falsely, being compelled to use the language of the kingdom of logic to describe what is being done in the kingdom of art. The poet, we say, knows the quality for which he seeks; but this knowledge is rather a condition than a possession of soul. It is a state of responsiveness rather than a knowledge of that to which he will respond. But it is knowledge inasmuch as the choice of that to which he will respond is determined by the condition of his soul. On the purity of that condition depends his greatness as a poet, and that purity in turn depends upon his denying no element of his profound experience. If he denies or forgets, the synthesis – again the word is a metaphor – which must establish itself within him is fragmentary and false. The new event can wake but partial echoes in his soul or none at all; it can neither be received into, nor can it create, a complete relation, and so it passes incommensurable from limbo into forgetfulness.

. . . Life . . . scatters her roses chiefly on the paths of those who forget her thorns. But the great poet remembers both rose and thorn; and it is beyond his power to remember them otherwise than together. . . .

SOURCE: extract from essay on Hardy in *Athenaeum* (Nov. 1919); reprinted in Murry's *Aspects of Literature* (London, 1920), pp. 149–50.

Edmund Wilson (1931)

'THE FIRST SYMBOLISTS'

[Wilson has been discussing leading figures in the literary movements of the eighteenth and nineteenth centuries, 'purposely selecting writers who seemed to represent some tendency or school in its purest or most highly developed form'.] We must . . . now consider some Romantics who, in certain ways, carried Romanticism further than even Chateaubriand or Musset, or than Wordsworth or Byron, and who became the first precursors of Symbolism and were afterwards placed among its saints.

One of these was the French writer who called himself Gérard de Nerval.[1] Gérard de Nerval suffered from spells of insanity; and, partly no doubt as a result of this, habitually confused his own fancies with external reality. He believed, even in his lucid periods – and no doubt Whitehead[2] would approve his metaphysics – that the world we see about us is involved in some more intimate fashion than is ordinarily supposed with the things that go on in our minds, that even our deepest dreams and hallucinations are somehow bound up with reality. And in one of his sonnets he outdoes Wordsworth, with his 'Presences of Nature in the sky' and 'Souls of lonely places', by imagining shuttered eyes coming to life in the very walls and 'a pure spirit under the bark of stones'.

But a more important prophet of Symbolism was Edgar Allan Poe. It was in general true that, by the middle of the century, the Romantic writers in the United States – Poe, Hawthorne, Melville, Whitman and even Emerson – were, for reasons which it would be interesting to determine, developing in the direction of Symbolism; and one of the events of prime importance was the discovery of Poe by Baudelaire. When Baudelaire, a late Romantic, first read Poe in 1847, he 'experienced a strange commotion'. When he began to look up Poe's writings in the files of American magazines, he found among them stories and poems which he said that he himself had already 'thought vaguely and confusedly' of writing, and his interest became a veritable passion. In 1852, Baudelaire published a volume of translations of Poe's tales; and from then on the influence of Poe played an important part in French literature. Poe's critical writings provided the first scriptures of the Symbolist Movement, for he had formulated what amounted to a new literary programme which corrected the Romantic looseness and lopped away the Romantic extravagance, at the same time that it aimed, not at Naturalistic, but at ultra-Romantic effects. There was, of course, a good deal in common between Poe's poetry and such Romantic poetry as Coleridge's 'Kubla Khan', as there was between his poems in prose and such Romantic prose as that of De Quincey. But Poe, by insisting on and specially cultivating certain aspects of Romanticism, helped to transform it into something different. 'I know', we find Poe writing, for example, 'that indefiniteness is an element of the true music [of poetry] – I mean of the true musical expression . . . a suggestive indefiniteness of vague and therefore of spiritual *effect*.' And to approximate the indefiniteness of music was to become one of the principal aims of Symbolism.

This effect of indefiniteness was produced not merely by the confusion I have mentioned [in previous discussion – Ed.] between the imaginary world and the real; but also by means of a further confusion between the perceptions of the different senses.

> Comme de longs échos qui de loin se confondent
> . . .
> Les parfums, les couleurs et les sons se répondent

wrote Baudelaire. And we find Poe, in one of his poems, *hearing* the approach of the darkness, or writing such a description as the following of the sensations which follow death: 'Night arrived; and with its shadows a heavy discomfort. It oppressed my limbs with the oppression of some dull weight, and was palpable. There was also a moaning sound, not unlike the distant reverberation of surf, but more continuous, which beginning with the first twilight, had grown in strength with the darkness. Suddenly lights were brought into the room . . . and issuing from the flame of each lamp, there flowed unbrokenly into my ears a strain of melodious monotone.'

This notation of super-rational sensations was a novelty in the forties of the last century – as was the dreamlike irrational musical poetry of 'Annabel Lee' and 'Ullalume'; and they helped to effect a revolution in France. For an English-speaking reader of today [c. 1930 – Ed.], Poe's influence may be hard to understand; and even when such a reader comes to examine the productions of French Symbolism, it may surprise him that they should have caused amazement. The medley of images; the deliberately mixed metaphors; the combination of passion and wit – of the grand and the prosaic manners; the bold amalgamation of material with spiritual: all these may seem to him quite proper and familiar. He has always known them in the English poetry of the sixteenth and seventeenth centuries – Shakespeare and the other Elizabethans did all these things without theorising about them. Is this not the natural language of poetry? Is it not the norm against which, in English literature, the eighteenth century was a heresy and to which the Romantics did their best to return?

But we must remember that the development of French poetry has been quite different from that of English. Michelet says that in the sixteenth century the future of French literature hung in the balance between Rabelais and Ronsard, and he regrets that it was Ronsard who triumphed. For Rabelais in France was a sort of equivalent to our own Elizabethans, whereas Ronsard, who represented to Michelet all that was poorest, dryest and most conventional in the French genius, was one of the fathers of that classical tradition of lucidity, sobriety and purity which culminated in Molière and Racine. In comparison with the Classicism of the French, which has dominated their literature since the Renaissance, the English Classicism of the eighteenth century, the age of Dr Johnson and Pope, was a brief ineffective deviation. And from the point of view of English readers, the most daring innovations of the Romantic revolution in France, in spite of all the excitement which accompanied them, must appear of an astonishingly moderate character. But the age and the rigour of the tradition were the measure of the difficulty of breaking out of it. After all, Coleridge, Shelley and Keats – in spite of Pope and Dr Johnson – had only to look back to Milton and Shakespeare, whose dense forests had all along been in view beyond the formal eighteenth-century gardens. But to an eighteenth-century Frenchman like Voltaire, Shakespeare was incomprehensible; and to the Frenchman of the classical tradition of the beginning of the nineteenth century, the rhetoric of Hugo was a scandal: the French were not used to such rich colours or to so free a vocabulary; moreover, the Romantics broke metrical rules far stricter than any we have had in English. Yet Victor Hugo was still very far from the variety and freedom of Shakespeare. It is enlightening to compare Shelley's lyric which begins, 'O World! O Life! O Time!' with the poem of Alfred de Musset's which begins, 'J'ai perdu ma force et ma vie'. These two lyrics are in some ways curiously similar: each is the breath of a Romantic sigh over the passing of the pride of youth. Yet the French poet, even in his wistfulness, makes epigrammatic points: his language is always logical and precise; whereas the English poet is vague and gives us images unrelated by logic. And it will not be till the advent of the Symbolists that French poetry will really become capable of the fantasy and fluidity of English.

The Symbolist Movement broke those rules of French metrics which the Romantics had left intact, and it finally succeeded in throwing overboard completely the clarity and logic of the French classical tradition, which the Romantics had still to a great extent respected. It was nourished from many alien sources – German, Flemish, modern Greek – and especially, precisely, from English. Verlaine had lived in England, and knew English well; Mallarmé was a professor of English; and Baudelaire, as I have said, had provided the movement with its first programmes by translating the essays of Poe. Two of the Symbolist poets, Stuart Merrill and Francis Vielé-Griffin, were Americans who lived in Paris and wrote French; and an American, reading today the latter's 'Chevauchée d'Yeldis', for example, may wonder how, when Symbolism was new, such a poem could ever have been regarded as one of the movement's acknowledged masterpieces: to us, it seems merely agreeable, not in the least revolutionary or novel, but like something which might not impossibly have been written by Thomas Bailey Aldrich[3] if he had been influenced by Browning. We are surprised to learn that Vielé-Griffin is still considered an important poet. But the point was that he had performed a feat which astonished and impressed the French and of which it is probable that no Frenchman was capable: he had succeeded in wrecking once for all the classical Alexandrine, hitherto the basis of French poetry – or rather, as an English reader at once recognises, he had dispensed with it altogether and begun writing English metres in French. The French called this *vers libre*, but it is free only in the sense of being irregular, like many poems of Matthew Arnold and Browning.

What made Poe particularly acceptable to the French, however, was what had distinguished him from most of the other Romantics of the English-speaking countries: his interest in aesthetic theory. The

French have always reasoned about literature far more than the English have; they always want to know what they are doing and why they are doing it: their literary criticism has acted as a constant interpreter and guide to the rest of their literature. And it was in France that Poe's literary theory, to which no one seems to have paid much attention elsewhere, was first studied and elucidated. So that – though the effects and devices of Symbolism were of a kind that was familiar in English, and though the Symbolists were sometimes indebted to English literature directly – the Symbolist Movement itself, by reason of its origin in France, had a deliberate self-conscious aesthetic which made it different from anything in English. One must go back to Coleridge to find in English a figure comparable to the Symbolist leader, Stéphane Mallarmé. Paul Valéry says of Mallarmé that, as he was the greatest French poet of his time, he could also have been one of the most popular. But Mallarmé was an unpopular poet: he taught English for a living, and wrote little and published less. Yet, ridiculed and denounced by the public, who reiterated that his poetry was nonsense and yet were irritated by his seriousness and obstinacy, he exercised, from his little Paris apartment, where he held Tuesday receptions, an influence curiously far-reaching over the young writers – English and French alike – of the end of the century. There in the sitting-room which was also the dining-room on the fourth floor in the Rue de Rome, where the whistle of the locomotives came in through the windows to mingle with the literary conversation, Mallarmé, with his shining pensive gaze from under his long lashes and always smoking a cigarette 'to put some smoke', as he used to say, 'between the world and himself', would talk about the theory of poetry in a 'mild, musical and unforgettable voice'. There was an atmosphere 'calm and almost religious'. Mallarmé had 'the pride of the inner life', said one of his friends; his nature was 'patient, disdainful and imperiously gentle'. He always reflected before he spoke and always put what he said in the form of a question. His wife sat beside him embroidering; his daughter answered the door. Here came Huysmans, Whistler, Degas, Moréas, Laforgue, Vielé-Griffin, Paul Valéry, Henri de Régnier, Pierre Louys, Paul Claudel, Remy de Gourmont, André Gide, Oscar Wilde, Arthur Symons, George Moore and W. B. Yeats. For Mallarmé was a true saint of literature: he had proposed to himself an almost impossible object, and he pursued it without compromise or distraction. His whole life was dedicated to the effort to do something with the language of poetry which had never been done before. 'Donner un sens plus pur', he had written in a sonnet on Poe, 'aux mots de la tribu.' He was, as Albert Thibaudet has said, engaged in 'a disinterested experiment on the confines of poetry, at a limit where other lungs would find the air unbreathable'.

What, then, was this purer sense which Mallarmé believed he was following Poe in wishing to give to the words of tribe? What, precisely, was the nature of this experiment on the confines of poetry which Mallarmé found so absorbing and which so many other writers tried to repeat? What, precisely, did the Symbolists propose? I have called attention, in speaking of Poe, to the confusion between the perceptions of the different senses, and to the attempt to make the effects of poetry approximate to those of music. And I should add, in this latter connection, that the influence on Symbolist poetry of Wagner was as important as that of any poet: at a time when Romantic music had come closest to literature, literature was attracted toward music. I have also spoken, in connection with Gérard de Nerval, of the confusion between the imaginary and the real, between our sensations and fancies, on the one hand, and what we actually do and see, on the other. It was the tendency of Symbolism – that second swing of the pendulum away from a mechanistic view of nature and from a social conception of man – to make poetry even more a matter of the sensations and emotions of the individual than had been the case with Romanticism: Symbolism, indeed, sometimes had the result of making poetry so much a private concern of the poet's that it turned out to be incommunicable to the reader. The peculiar subtlety and difficulty of Symbolism is indicated by the name itself. This name has often been complained of as being inadequate for the movement to which it was given and inappropriate to certain of its aspects; and it may prove misleading to English readers. For the symbols of Symbolism have to be defined a little differently from symbols in the ordinary sense – the sense in which the Cross is the symbol of Christianity or the Stars and Stripes the symbol of the United States. This symbolism differs even from such symbolism as Dante's. For the familiar kind of symbolism is conventional and fixed; the symbolism of the Divine Comedy is conventional, logical and definite. But the symbols of the Symbolist school are usually chosen arbitrarily by the poet to stand for special ideas of his own – they are a sort of disguise for these ideas. 'The Parnassians, for their part', wrote Mallarmé, 'take the thing just as it is and put it before us – and consequently they are deficient in mystery: they deprive the mind of the delicious joy of believing that it is creating. To name an object is to do away with the three-quarters of the enjoyment of the poem which is derived from the satisfaction of guessing little by little: to suggest it, to evoke it – that is what charms the imagination.'

To intimate things rather than state them plainly was thus one of the primary aims of the Symbolists. But there was more involved in their point of view than Mallarmé here explains. The assumptions which underlay Symbolism lead us to formulate some such doctrine as the following: Every feeling or sensation we have, every moment of consciousness, is different from every other; and it is, in consequence, impossible to render our sensations as we actually experience them through the conventional and universal language of ordinary literature. Each poet has his unique personality; each of his moments has its special tone, its special combination of elements. And it is the poet's task to find, to invent, the special language which will alone be capable of expressing his personality and feelings. Such a language must make use of symbols: what is so special, so fleeting and so vague cannot be conveyed by direct statement or description, but only by a succession of words, of images, which will serve to suggest it to the reader. The Symbolists themselves, full of the idea of producing with poetry effects like those of music, tended to think of these images as possessing an abstract value like musical notes and chords. But the words of our speech are not musical notation, and what the symbols of Symbolism really were, were metaphors detached from their subjects – for one cannot, beyond a certain point, in poetry, merely enjoy colour and sound for their own sake: one has to guess what the images are being applied to. And Symbolism may be defined as an attempt by carefully studied means – a complicated association of ideas represented by a medley of metaphors – to communicate unique personal feelings.

The Symbolist Movement proper was first largely confined to France and principally limited to poetry of rather an esoteric kind; but it was destined, as time went on, to spread to the whole western world and its principles to be applied on a scale which the most enthusiastic of its founders could scarcely have foreseen. Remy de Gourmont, who was eventually to become the most distinguished critical champion of the movement, tells of his excitement, one afternoon in the eighties, at discovering the new poetry in a little magazine he had picked up at a bookstall in the Odéon: 'As I looked through it, I experienced the little aesthetic thrill and that exquisite impression of novelty which has so much charm for youth. I seem to myself to have been dreaming rather than reading. The Luxembourg was pink with early April: I crossed it toward the Rue d'Assas, thinking a great deal more about the new literature which was coinciding for me that day with the renewal of the world than about the business which had brought me to that part of Paris. All that I had written up to that time inspired me with profound disgust. In less than an hour my literary orientation was radically modified.' And Yeats wrote in 1897: 'The reaction against the rationalism of the eighteenth century has mingled with a reaction against the materialism of the nineteenth century, and the symbolical movement, which has come to perfection in Germany in Wagner, in England in the Pre-Raphaelites, and in France in Villiers de L'Isle-Adam and Mallarmé and Maeterlinck, and has stirred the imagination of Ibsen and D'Anunzio, is certainly the only movement that is saying new things.'

We do not talk about Symbolism today in dealing with English literature; we do not even, as Yeats did at the end of the last century, think of the writers whom he mentions as all belonging to a 'symbolical movement'; yet the influence of Mallarmé and his fellow poets was felt widely and deeply outside of France, and it is difficult to understand certain of the things which have been happening lately in English literature without some knowledge of the Symbolist school. I believe, in fact, that if English and American criticism have sometimes shown themselves at a loss when confronted with the work of certain recent writers, it is partly because the work of these writers is the result of a literary revolution which occurred outside English literature. The case of the Romantic Movement was different: Wordsworth's prefaces were English manifestoes; Lockhart's attack on Keats and Byron's attack on Jeffrey were blows struck in an English civil war. But in spite of the Pre-Raphaelites, who were launched by an impulse somewhat similar to that of the Symbolists, and in spite of the English 'aesthetics' and 'decadents', who for the most part imitated the French without very much originality, the battle of Symbolism has never properly been fought out in English. So that whereas French writers like Valéry and Proust who have grown out of the Symbolist Movement, are well understood and appreciated by French literary criticism, the critics of the English-speaking countries have often seemed not to know how to deal with such writers as Eliot and Joyce. Even when these writers have brought back into English qualities which are natural to it and resources which it originally possessed, these elements have returned by way of France and have taken on the complexion of the French mind – critical, philosophical, much occupied with aesthetic theory and tending always to aim self-consciously at particular effects and to study scrupulously appropriate means.

It has perhaps been peculiarly easy for certain of the leaders of contemporary English literature – that is, of the literature since the War – to profit by the example of Paris, because they have themselves not been English. Of the writers in English I shall discuss . . . Yeats is an Irishman who turns almost as easily toward Paris as toward London; Joyce an Irishman who has done most of his work on the Continent and who has scarcely lived in England at all; and T. S. Eliot and Gertrude Stein are Americans living abroad. The work of these writers has been largely a continuance or extension of Symbolism. Yeats, the ablest of the *fin de siècle* group who tried in London to emulate the French, managed to make Symbolism flourish triumphantly by transplanting it to the more favourable soil of Ireland. T. S. Eliot in his earliest poems seems to have been as susceptible to the influence of the Symbolists as to that of the English Elizabethans. Joyce, a master of Naturalism as great as Flaubert, has at the same time succeeded in dramatising Symbolism by making use of its methods for differentiating between his various characters and their varying states of mind. And Gertrude Stein has carried Mallarmé's principles so far in the direction of that limit where other lungs find the air unbreathable as perhaps finally to reduce them to absurdity. It is true, however, that under proper conditions, these principles remain valid; and both the strength and the weaknesses characteristic of much of the literature since the War derive mainly from the Symbolist poets and may already be studied in their work. The literary history of our time is to a great extent that of the development of Symbolism and of its fusion or conflict with Naturalism.

Sources: extract from *Axel's Castle: A Study in the Imaginative Literature of 1870–1930* (New York, and London, 1931; Fontana paperback edition, 1961, cited here), pp. 16–27.

NOTES

1. [Ed.] Gérard de Nerval: pen-name of G. Labrunie (1808–55); his verse includes *Les Chimères* (sonnets, 1854), and his prose writings *Sylvie* (1853), *Les Filles du Feu* (1854) and *Aurélia* (1855).

2. [Ed.] Alfred North Whitehead (1861–1947): English philosopher and mathematician, teaching at Cambridge, in London University, and at Harvard; co-author with Bertrand Russell of *Principia Mathematica* (1910–12), his wide-ranging interests produced such studies in general philosophy and metaphysics as *Science and the Modern World* (1926), *Symbolism, Its Meaning and Effect* (1927), *Process and Reality* (1929), *Adventures of Ideas* (1933) and *Nature and Life* (1934).

3. [Ed.] Thomas Bailey Aldrich (1836–1907): popular American writer, editor in the 1880s of the *Atlantic Monthly*.

Maud Bodkin (1934)

... [Earlier in this study] an hypothesis was proposed for investigation, formulated in terms suggested by Dr Jung, that archetypal patterns, or images, are present within the experience communicated through poetry, and may be discovered there by reflective analysis. These patterns were likened ... to the culture-patterns studied by anthropologists. As corresponding to certain ancient and recurring themes of poetry – such as that of a usurping monarch overthrown by an heir of the king he has displaced – the patterns, viewed psychologically, may be described as organisations of emotional tendencies, determined partly through the distinctive experience of the race or community within whose history the theme has arisen. When [later] the patterns studied were analysed to their most universal elements, the relation to particular culture-patterns, on the one side, was shown as balanced by a relation to the most general conceptions of philosophy. Thus, the patterns we have called the Rebirth and Paradise-Hades archetypes, while finding expression in myths and legends of particular communities, could also be felt as characterising the flow, or texture, of universal experience. Similarly, the images studied of man, woman, god, devil, in any particular instance of their occurrence in poetry can be considered either as related to the sensibility of a certain poet, and a certain age and country, or as a mode of expressing something potentially realisable in human experience of any time or place.

In reviewing the argument thus developed ..., I wish to deal with certain objections to which it perhaps lies open. Corresponding to the more distinctive and more general aspects of the patterns studied, I see two possible forms of criticism. A reader might object: 'these patterns that you say are discoverable in the experience of poetry are not distinctive of it; they merely happen to form part of the content of the poems you have chosen to study. The *Divine Comedy* and *Paradise Lost* contain images of God and Devil, Heaven and Hell, taken over from the religious beliefs of the time; not all poetry contains such conceptions.' On the other hand, one might urge: 'it is true that all experience shows certain general characters, such as the contrast studied by philosophers, of "eternal objects" and "temporal flux", or the alternation, within the flux, of storage and release of energy, rest and renewal of life. If we examine the objectification of experience in imaginative literature, we are bound to find these contrasts illustrated. Is this all you set out to prove?'

To the first criticism I would reply that I have indeed chosen, for illustration of the patterns, poems that exhibit them with special power and fullness; but I have studied these poems – the *Comedy* for instance – as experience communicable to minds of our own day, not bound by the beliefs current in the poet's time. Also I have compared classical poems setting forth the established traditions of a period with romantic poems wherein similar imagery appears, arising in dream-like fashion within an individual mind. Other images and themes than those I have chosen might have been selected; but those studied perhaps serve to confirm the view that such ancient patterns are present in poetry not casually, but as an essential element in the power it has over us as an expression of the forces of our nature.

We may turn to the second criticism: 'if the patterns are taken in sufficient generality, it is nothing very startling to say that they may be discovered in any vivid experience of poetry; do they not characterise any experience whatever, provided it be realised in some scope and fullness?' To this, I reply that I am not indeed seeking to prove anything very new as to the nature of poetry; rather I am trying to show that its recognised nature may be felt and utilised in ways that are perhaps partly new. Just because universal characters of experience, and images of almost universal range, are communicated and realised in unique scope and fullness through the medium of poetry, poetic experience has special relations both to religion and to philosophy that are worth investigation.

The approach through poetry, it seems to me, can bring new light to bear upon the great images that appear in religious experience: the divine man, the divine mother, Heaven and Hell, rebirth from death to life. Also, the realisation in varied forms, through the writings of different poets, of the universal characters of experience, in its inward texture and flow, may provide data supplementing or correcting the generalisations concerning experience which psychologists working in other fields contribute towards the final synthesis of the philosopher.

It is particularly these issues of my argument, concerning the relations of poetry, religion, and philosophy, that I wish to develop more fully in this concluding section. But there is an objection that may be brought against my whole procedure, which I desire to meet before going farther. It is that felt by many minds against the application of any kind of reflective analysis to poetic experience.

This objection has been expressed forcibly, if only incidentally, in the interesting lecture by A. E. Housman, *The Name and Nature of Poetry* (1933). The essence of poetry, Professor Housman urges, is not realised in its intellectual content, or meaning: the attempt to draw out, or analyse, the meaning, in his experience often destroys the poetry. He gives, from the lyrics of Blake, examples which he regards as 'poetry neat, or adulterated with so little meaning that nothing except poetic emotion is perceived and matters' (p. 41). The first of these examples I will quote here, since I should like to make it, for the moment, our text in considering under what conditions intellectual analysis of meaning will destroy, or may enhance, the realisation and enjoyment of poetry.

Amongst the many passages of Blake's poetry that seem to me full of meaning that will repay examination by psychologist or philosopher, I should place perhaps first this lyric that Housman quotes as illustrating a 'celestial tune', with meaning 'unimportant or virtually non-existent':

> Hear the voice of the Bard,
>   Who present, past, and future sees;
> Whose ears have heard
> The Holy Word
>   That walk'd among the ancient trees,
>
> Calling the lapsèd soul
>   And weeping in the evening dew;
> That might control
> The starry pole,
>   And fallen, fallen light renew.
>
> 'O Earth, O Earth, return!
>   Arise from out the dewy grass;
> Night is worn,
> And the morn
>   Rises from the slumberous mass.
>
> 'Turn away no more;
>   Why wilt thou turn away?
> The starry floor,
> The watery shore
>   Is giv'n thee till the break of day.'

'That mysterious grandeur would be less grand', Housman observes, 'if it were less mysterious; if the embryo ideas which are all that it contains should endue form and outline, and suggestion condense itself into thought.' Has he in mind something like a paraphrase of the poem, in intellectually definite terms? The analysis I should wish to offer here, as in the case of other poems, is not an attempt to translate into logical form any supposed argument in the poem. I would not, any more than Housman, subordinate to logical thought the poem's music and magic. It is the emotional and intuitive experience communicated by these very words, that I suggest the reader should analyse for himself.

If he should feel with Professor Housman about poetry, he will refuse the suggestion; but the reader who has accompanied me so far in these essays is conscious, probably, of somewhat less repugnance to the attempt to apply thought to feeling. 'Somewhat less' – one can venture no stronger assertion; since perhaps every sensitive critic can sympathize with a certain reluctance in undertaking analysis of poetry, and mistrust of it as offered by others.

The author of a work of penetrating literary criticism has submitted a Rabelaisian metaphor to express his reader's possible repugnance to critics, as 'barking dogs', 'of two sorts, those who merely relieve themselves against the flower of beauty, and those, less continent, who afterwards scratch it up.'[1] In his own case, he confesses, 'unexplained beauty arouses an irritation in me, a sense that this would be a good place to scratch;' though he disclaims the arrogance of fancying that his investigations could ever violate the deep roots of beauty.

The type of analysis to which Mr Empson finds himself provoked by the beauty, and the 'ambiguities', of poetic speech is the same to which I find incitement in the magic of Blake's language in this poem. It was not till, knowing the poem by heart, I was able to feel, as it were simultaneously, the contribution of each word and its fused associations to the total suggested meaning, that I realised how much, for me, the meaning here depends upon that kind of sharp collision between different groups, or orders, of imagery that Empson terms an ambiguity.

Such collision occurs first, in my experience of the poem, in passing from the second to the third clause characterising the voice of the Bard. The imagery that the second clause revives from the Old Testament story, of God calling through the evening dews of the Garden, qualifies the Bard's voice only indirectly: the poet is one who sees and hears the Divine communication. But the third clause, and the words that follow, as one realises their cosmic and tremendous imagery, make the poet's voice itself divine. It is the poet's voice that, like the voice of God, can be imaged calling the lapsed soul – that might answer the call, rising, as repentant Eve might rise, from out the dewy grass – and is felt also as having power over vast spiritual revolutions, symbolised by the turning of the earth on its axis.

Before I had applied thought keenly to my feeling of the poem's harmony, I had a dim sense of unresolved discord within it – a clash of imagery. How could the earth, seen revolving on its axis-pole amid the stars, rise from the grass borne on its surface? The cosmic order of imagery clashed with the personal – Eve hiding, crouched in the grass, from the voice of the Holy One.

With the recognition of the imagery and its interrelations, came enhanced feeling of the beauty and wonder of the poem. Of God as the religious soul conceives Him, of poetry as experienced by its lovers, may be affirmed just this duality in unity, and harmonised clash, of cosmic and personal that Blake has woven into the texture of his verses. Each body of imagery: the Bard in his trance of vision, the God calling the fallen figure among the trees, the turning spheres and revolving earth, and those other memories through which one knows how morning clearness rises 'from the slumbrous mass' of landscapes seen at dawn – each of these yields up and fuses its distinct value within that shaping force of Idea animating the poem, at once thought and feeling, that I have termed the Rebirth archetype.

Having made, in relation to the poem, the positive effort of reflective analysis and construction, I pass, in alternation, to the negative phase of feeling – the nemesis of analysis and reflection. Carefully as I may choose my words to convey that which I have seen and felt in the poem with joy, yet, as I look back over those words, I am aware of the reaction of a possible reader: 'Here you are producing again your archetypes, your old labels. What can be more tedious?'

Any thought that is, from within, the divination of a force of meaning active within a unique living whole, may, from without, appear but the dull mechanical attaching of a name, a label. Always it is possible for living thought in its reception to be diminished to that kind of thinking that Jung has described as the 'nothing but' mode – this poem (or whatever the subject of thought may be) – is 'nothing but' an example of some class, some stereotype: you label it and pass on.

It is this kind of thinking that, applied to poetry, must be hateful to any poet; most of all if he should be himself – as A. E. Housman perhaps may be – a poet of divided, almost dissociated, mind, creating subconsciously, and with another part of his mind thinking in hard intellectual terms. Then his own habit of conscious thought, if he turns it upon poetry, will tend to belittle and destroy the living whole which he so intensely and delicately feels.

Yet thought need not be of the hard destructive type. Thought may be subtle, pliant, yielding itself to serve and follow the living imaginative activity. It is only so far as reflective analysis is part of thought of this nature, penetrated by feeling, docile and reverent toward its object, though loyal to its own standards, that analysis can be helpful in the appreciation of poetry.

There is another aspect of the nature of poetry emphasised in Housman's argument – an aspect which even sympathetic analysis of poetic content is apt to ignore. Professor Housman speaks of poetry as recognisable in his own experience by the symptoms it provokes – such bodily reactions as the shiver down the spine, constriction of the throat. The consideration of the factor of participation by the body in the experience of poetry suggests certain further lines of thought.

Bodily participation need not be mainly of that convulsive involuntary type of which shivering and tears are examples. Speaking of one of those passages whose fused variant shades of meaning he has been analysing, Empson says, 'The grace, the pathos, the "sheer song" of the couplet is given by the break in the voice, an enforced subtlety of intonation, from the difficulty of saying all these at once'.[2] So with the verses quoted from Blake, their grace of 'sheer song' is barely realised till they repeat themselves in inner speech and hearing, like an incantation, charged with those conflicting, yet ultimately harmonised, meanings and feelings of which they make possible the utterance 'all at once'. The 'enforced subtlety of intonation' of which Empson speaks is itself a dramatic achievement of the body, the inherited outcome of ages of discipline and refining of the art of passionate speech, whereby the felt significance of a wealth of overt action and gesture is condensed within slight changes in the governing of the breath, the inflecting of the voice.

The body's enactment, through changes of speech-rhythm and intonation, of changes in the dramatic content of poetry, is the factor that links the reading of verse – even though silent, reduced to sub-articulation – with the ritual dance, conceived as the prototype of the arts. As the wild rhythms of the ancient dance tended to annul the participant's consciousness of separate personality, exalting him to union with his group and with his God, so, in fainter degree, the rhythms of poetry still serve to hold the reader apart from his everyday self and cares, caught up into the thought and feeling communicated. As the regulated mimesis of the dance served to relieve tensions of fear and desire, so the participation of the body, through delicate adaptations of inner speech, in harmonies revealed to the spirit, helps to relieve emotional tensions developed by the strain of the personal life.

It would seem to be the relation to the dance, the experienced presence of motor schemata, wraiths of gesture and action, that constitutes, even more than sound, the link between the arts of poetry and music.[3] When, for instance, Eliot's *Waste Land* is compared to a symphony, 'a music of ideas,' it would seem that the analogy is felt in the whole movement of the poem, as we realise it schematically. In our experience of the poem, as of the symphony, there is present at any point an attitude, or set of mind and body, which involves felt reverberations from what has preceded, adjustments for what is to come – the fullness and exactness of such realisation of context depending, of course, upon the aptitude of the individual, and the attention he may have given to the grasp of this particular whole.

A whole of music – music of certain types, and to some hearers – communicates experience showing the same emotional patterns which we have traced in poetry. A symphony may, like a poem, be felt to carry us through Hell and Heaven, to plunge us in underworlds of despair, and raise us again from the dead. A critic, commenting on Beethoven's Eroica symphony, has observed: 'as one listens to the gay Scherzo and triumphant Finale, which follows [the Funeral March], instinctively one's inner voice repeats, "And the third day he rose again".'[4] Even for those who do not interpret music thus dramatically, there may be something in the texture of musical experience, with its recurring factors of pain or tension of discord, followed by relief in its resolution, and delight in harmony, that corresponds to the continual interplay of opposites, glimpses of heaven's joy amidst earthly frustration and pain, by which poetry renders the sense of our mortal state.

Our comparison of poetic speech with the dance, and with music, may lead us to the relation between poetry and religion.

Unless we grant poetic speech a reference to reality we cannot regard it as closely akin to religion. The contention throughout these essays has been that poetry – the attitude of poetic faith – does include such reference, though not in the same manner that reference is claimed by scientific statement. The emotive speech of poetry, it was urged, communicates attitudes interrelated in ways valid for many minds – for all who fulfil certain conditions of apprehension. The conditions are different from those to be fulfilled before the truth of reference of a scientific statement can be appreciated. Where science uses abstraction, narrowing and hardening the meaning of its terms to make communication exact, poetry uses suggestion, multiplying the evocative stimuli brought to bear in each particular instance, that communication may become complete. That a reader may participate in the truth of a scientific statement, he must be intellectually competent in the technique through which the terms mediate between sensuous experience and a system of abstract relations; that he may participate in the truth of poetic speech he must be emotionally responsive to the technique through which attitudes and imagery of sensuous experience are evoked to constitute a new imaginative whole. In both cases communication aims at transcending the limitations of the private perspective of reality, rendering those who participate free of a vision which, as shared, communicable, is, to that degree, objective.

It is the nature of the ritual dance, as communication of a complete experience, that makes it an illuminating prototype of the various differentiated modes of art. In the dance, communication is achieved through a sequence of bodily attitudes so related that each, within the total rhythm, enhances the experience of the rest; this vivid sensuous experience becoming the vehicle of a shared imaginative vision of reality. Similarly essential for communication, in drama, in music, in visual art, and in poetry, is the sensible object created by the artist – the spatial form seen, the sequence of sound, or of action sensuously imagined – that serves as vehicle of a vision, intuition, or emotional understanding, of certain aspects of our common reality.

Religion also, in its present varied institutional forms, may be considered genetically as having differentiated from the ritual dance. Religions have elaborated their ordered systems of worship and of dogma as vehicles for the communication, to those who are conditioned to respond, of a certain intuition of reality, involving a new relation towards it of emotional understanding.

Poetry, Santayana has observed,[5] 'is religion without points of application in conduct, and without an expression in worship and dogma'. In asking the reader to consider with me the Gospel story as poetry rather than from a religious standpoint, I implied some such distinction as Santayana makes in this statement. I wished to suggest a study divested of bonds of loyalty to any church that, for purposes of common worship and action, has elaborated a dogmatic interpretation of the sacred text.

An individual's religion, understood, in Santayana's phrase, as the poetry in which he believes,[6] may, by peculiarity of personal bent, remain aloof from expression in public worship and dogma. To such a one – and here I express my own position – there may be no distinction between religious and poetic faith. For me, the passage '*Except a grain of wheat . . .*' is a focus not of the teaching of a church, but of the total spiritual heritage communicated by poetry – all the poetry that has become alive for me through personal response.

So to identify religious and poetic faith is not to ignore that other element by which, in Santayana's dictum, religion and poetry are distinguished. Religion must have 'points of application in conduct'. Poetic assent is of the imagination, not of will and character. Yet

Santayana withdraws his negative description of poetry where the poet has 'dug his well deep enough to tap the subterranean springs of his own life'.[7] Imaginative insight may fail of practical efficacy for lack of the subordinate systems needed to carry over vision into conduct. Yet for the poet, or for the lover of poetry, who has realised by its means something of the deepest forces and demands of his own nature, poetry cannot be without influence on life. Rather, we may make for it the claim that Shelley urges in his *Defence*: that only through the attraction of that poetic, or aesthetic, order which men at different times imaginatively apprehended, have been achieved the imperfect embodiments of such order that we recognise in the actual world.[8]

What relation, or what distinction, shall we assert between poetry, so understood, and philosophy?

Again, I would say that for an individual mind there may be no difference. Of Shelley one would say that his poetic faith was his philosophy, as it was also his religion. Of Shelley's early theories and arguments a critic writes: these 'were merely the intellectual foam of his mind. His real philosophy lay deep down in his imagination; and though it developed as he learnt wisdom, its main tendency was never changed.'[9] A man's philosophy, in this sense, is is *Weltanschauung* – the individual vision, or perspective of reality, determined by his own nature and the main events and conditions of his life. According as this essential vision is communicated in imaginative or in reflective speech, we call an author poet or philosopher. Yet in every great writer thought and imagination interpenetrate; so that, according to our bent, we may enjoy the poetry of Plato or Spinoza, or seek the philosophy within the poetry of Shelley or of Shakespeare.[10]

If we refuse to apply the term 'philosophy' in his extended sense, and define the word's meaning more exactly – as a system of thought, reflective and critical, concerned with the most general characters of experience – we shall not attribute philosophy to Shakespeare or to Shelley, and we shall agree with T. S. Eliot, that a poem such as Dante's *Comedy*, making extensive use (as Shakespeare's drama does not) of a contemporary system of philosophy, is not greater poetry on that account.

The relation between poetry and systematic philosophy which is of concern from the standpoint of these essays is that indicated by Dr Whitehead, when he urges that the philosopher, as a critic of abstractions, should study the great poets, that he may compare their more concrete intuitions of the universe with the abstract formulations of the various sciences.[11] At the outset of these studies in regard to psychology in particular, the need was urged of an enrichment of the results of the science by reference to experience communicated through poetry. Psychologists, whether of the school of Freud, or engaged in various lines of academic research, are liable – in the terms of Whitehead's criticism – to attend only to those aspects of concrete experience which lie within some limited scheme. There would seem a place, within the general field of psychology, for students, both sensitive to literary values and familiar with psychological and philosophic method, who will play a part intermediary between the poet and the philosopher.

The poet – especially the epic and tragic poet, and, in another manner, in our own day, the more imaginative writer of fiction – performs for the community, as we have tried to show, the function of objectifying in imaginative form experience potentially common to all, but exceptionally deep and vivid, and revealing a certain tension and ideal reconcilment of opposite forces present in actual life. It is the insight of the poet into the nature of these forces, that we feel might do much, if it could be made available, toward the criticism and enrichment of the often arid-seeming generalisations which the scientific psychologist offers to the philosopher seeking to systematise the most general truths of existence.

But along the path from communicated imaginative experience to reflective statement of truth there are many pitfalls. Freudian researches into dream and fantasy have given us some indication both of a path to be followed, and of obstructions and dangers in the way. We owe a great debt in this respect to Freud and to his disciples. Yet it seems that both the master and many of his school have failed to fulfil the necessary conditions of apprehension in regard to the truths of philosophy and of poetry. To the kind of experience communicated by poetry they have not been sensitive, and they have despised philosophy.

For this reason it seems to me especially important that the highly interesting generalisations in regard to social experience, elaborated by Freud on the basis of clinical work, should be brought into relation with the results of psychological study of experience communicated through poetry.

Concerning my own work, set in relation to Freud's results, the criticism will naturally be made that it is highly subjective – a single individual's interpretation. My only defence against the charge must be that some escape from subjectivity is possible through its recognition. The results of an individual may have value, if presented, as individual results, with sincerity, after persistent application of the mind to the material, and comparison with the available recorded results of others.

From these studies of imaginative experience, I find one result, perhaps the most important, to be awareness of the individual as having his reality in relation to a larger life, communicated to him under different conditions, in varying degree. The patterns here illustrated in detail from different kinds of poetic material seem to converge upon this relation of the individual to a life within and beyond him. This life I have considered – in relation to Durkheim's hypothesis – as a power present within the community. It is for the philosopher, comparing the results of workers in all fields, to determine how far we may pass beyond this formula. In the psychological study of poetry it seems to me to have value, partly because it helps us to relate to the facts of poetic experience, in a manner more true to their nature, those facts which Freud has formulated under the hypothesis of the parent-imago, or super-ego.

The powerful and continuing influence upon an individual's sensibility of the early relation to his parents is a factor we have found objectified again and again within poetic imagery. We have studied it as communicated in the relation of Dante to the accusing Beatrice, compared with the relation of Orestes to the Erinys (p. 185), and again in Dante's imagery of approach to the supreme vision (p. 266); in Shelley's Jupiter (p. 256), and in the God of *Paradise Lost* (p. 261); and have commented on it in regard to such contrasting, diverse material as the Gospel story (p. 287) and Virginia Woolf's *Orlando* (p. 301). Always we found in the experience, together with the binding influence of the parent-imago, a movement toward freedom and fulfilment. This freedom did not appear as – in Freudian terms – an elevation of the ego to the role of supreme regulator (cf. p. 181). On the contrary, in the most intense and complete forms of poetic experience there persists the distinction between the limited individual self and a higher power; though this distinction is felt no longer as painful tension and conflict, but as harmony, difference within unity, the surrender and fulfilment of love.

From the standpoint of the psychologist – requiring for his working hypothesis not ultimate truth, but rather, in Durkheim's works, 'the highest reality in the intellectual and moral order that we can know by observation' [12] – it seemed possible in each case to interpret the transformation which the poem's action presents as corresponding to a re-ordering of the powers of the individual mind under a stimulus communicated from the social heritage. A form of control outgrown and become oppressive is replaced by a control objectified under a different symbol, transcending still the individual, but deeply akin to him, sustaining and renewing within him the values which he most intimately accepts.

There seems to me a need to translate – so far as this may be possible – from the terms of mystic and poetic faith into terms which a psychologist can use, the reality of this interaction, so central in poetic and religious experience. Freud's terminology cannot do justice to it, because the postulates within which he works require that later and higher products of the life process be explained in terms of elements present at the beginning. Also, the concentration of Freudian writers upon the physical relation of parent and child cuts off that other equally valid viewpoint, from which the parent's magic for the child, and overpowering influence, appear due to his acting as the first channel of the wider influence of the community and its stored achievement.

It is the environing larger life of the community, past and present, stored within the heritage of literary art, springing to creative activity within the minds of individual readers, that I have attempted, in these essays, to study and illustrate. The work will have achieved its purpose if, for some readers, it ministers to a keener sense of the values of poetry; still more, if to some it prove a stimulus to further study of the patterns of that inner imaginative life that poetry makes communicable.

SOURCE: extract from *Archetypal Patterns in Poetry: Psychological Studies of Imagination* (Oxford, 1934; paperback edn 1963), pp. 314–30.

NB The page references on p. 84 are to *this* text.

NOTES

[Reorganised and renumbered from the original – Ed.]

1. William Empson, *Seven Types of Ambiguity* (London, 1930), p. 12.

2. Ibid., p. 36.

3. Cf. the discussion, in Vernon Lee's *Music and its Lovers* (London, 1932), of movement schemata in the experience of music.

4. H. N. Brailsford, writing in the *Radio Times* (21 Feb. 1930).

5. George Santayana, *Interpretations of Poetry and Religion* (London, 1900), p. 289.

6. Ibid., p. 26; 'Our religion is the poetry in which we believe.'

7. Ibid., p. 289.

8. One should perhaps note, in qualification of this statement, that truth once imaginatively realised may be shorn of its poetic glory when it has become a familiar object of practical assent and endeavour. A. E. Housman quotes the saying, 'Whosoever will lose his life shall find it', describing it as the most important truth ever uttered and greatest discovery ever made in the moral world, yet for him not poetry – not arousing the bodily thrill of the response to poetic speech (*The Name and Nature of Poetry*, p. 36). I would agree that one may hear or read this saying of Christ, even in the thrilling form in which it occurs in St John, and give assent as a matter of intellectual

recognition and practical loyalty, with no emotional awareness of the glory of the speech communicating so great and dramatic a vision of life. Yet one may know the poetry is there for realisation, when imagination, awakening, escapes the inhibitions of familiarity and the practical life.

9. O. W. Campbell, *Shelley and the Unromantics*, p. 279.

10. From this standpoint one must disagree with T. S. Eliot when he asserts that the depth of the philosophy behind a man's poetry makes no difference to its value. . . . If we seek the philosophy behind Shakespeare's poetry, we attempt to render, in reflective speech for the intellect, that which is implicit in the vision of life which Shakespeare presents in dramatic terms to the imagination.

11. A. N. Whitehead, *Science and the Modern World*, ch. V.

12. E. Durkheim, *Elementary Forms of the Religious Life*, p. 16.

Cleanth Brooks   (1947)

THE LANGUAGE OF PARADOX

Few of us are prepared to accept the statement that the language of poetry is the language of paradox. Paradox is the language of sophistry, hard, bright, witty; it is hardly the language of the soul. We are willing to allow that paradox is a permissible weapon which a Chesterton may on occasion exploit. We may permit it in epigram, a special subvariety of poetry; and in satire, which though useful, we are hardly willing to allow to be poetry at all. Our prejudices force us to regard paradox as intellectual rather than emotional, clever rather than profound, rational rather than divinely irrational.

Yet there is a sense in which paradox is the language appropriate and inevitable to poetry. It is the scientist whose truth requires a language purged of every trace of paradox; apparently the truth which the poet utters can be approached only in terms of paradox. I overstate the case, to be sure; it is possible that the title of this chapter is itself to be treated as merely a paradox. But there are reasons for thinking that the overstatement which I propose may light up some elements in the nature of poetry which tend to be overlooked.

The case of William Wordsworth, for instance, is instructive on this point. His poetry would not appear to promise many examples of the language of paradox. He usually prefers the direct attack. He insists on simplicity; he distrusts whatever seems sophistical. And yet the typical Wordsworth poem is based upon a paradoxical situation. Consider his celebrated

> It is a beauteous evening, calm and free,
> The holy time is quiet as a Nun
> Breathless with adoration. . . .

The poet is filled with worship, but the girl who walks beside him is not worshiping. The implication is that she should respond to the holy time, and become like the evening itself, nunlike; but she seems less worshipful than inanimate nature itself. Yet

> If thou appear untouched by solemn thought,
> Thy nature is not therefore less divine:
> Thou liest in Abraham's bosom all the year;
> And worship'st at the Temple's inner shrine,
> God being with thee when we know it not.

The underlying paradox (of which the enthusiastic reader may well be unconscious) is nevertheless thoroughly necessary, even for that reader. Why does the innocent girl worship more deeply than the self-conscious poet who walks beside her? Because she is filled with an unconscious sympathy for *all* of nature, not merely the grandiose and solemn. One remembers the lines from Wordsworth's friend, Coleridge:

> He prayeth best, who loveth best
> All things both great and small.

Her unconscious sympathy is the unconscious worship. She is in communion with nature 'all the year', and her devotion is continual whereas that of the poet is sporadic and momentary. But we have not done with the paradox yet. It not only underlies the poem, but something of the paradox informs the poem, though, since this is Wordsworth, rather timidly. The comparison of the evening to the nun actually has more than one dimension. The calm of the evening obviously means 'worship', even to the dull-witted and insensitive. It corresponds to the trappings of the nun, visible to everyone. Thus, it suggests not merely holiness, but, in the total poem, even a hint of Pharisaical holiness, with which the girl's careless innocence, itself a symbol of her continual secret worship, stands in contrast.

Or consider Wordsworth's sonnet, 'Composed upon Westminster Bridge'. I believe that most readers will agree that it is one of Wordsworth's most successful poems; yet most students have the greatest difficulty in accounting for its goodness. The attempt to account for it on the grounds of nobility of sentiment soon breaks down. On this level, the poem merely says: that the city in the morning light presents a picture which is majestic and touching to all but the most dull of soul; but the poem says very little more about the

sight: the city is beautiful in the morning light and it is awfully still.
The attempt to make a case for the poem in terms of the brilliance of
its images also quickly breaks down: the student searches for graphic
details in vain; there are next to no realistic touches. In fact, the poet
simply huddles the details together:

> silent, bare,
> Ships, towers, domes, theatres, and temples lie
> Open unto the fields. . . .

We get a blurred impression – points of roofs and pinnacles along the
skyline, all twinkling in the morning light. More than that, the sonnet
as a whole contains some very flat writing and some well-worn
comparisons.

The reader may ask: Where, then, does the poem get its power? It
gets it, it seems to me, from the paradoxical situation out of which the
poem arises. The speaker is honestly surprised, and he manages to get
some sense of awed surprise into the poem. It is odd to the poet that
the city should be able to 'wear the beauty of the morning' at all.
Mount Snowden, Skiddaw, Mont Blanc – these wear it by natural
right, but surely not grimy, feverish London. This is the point of the
almost shocked exclamation:

> Never did sun more beautifully steep
> In his first splendour, *valley, rock*, or *hill* . . .

The 'smokeless air' reveals a city which the poet did not know existed:
man-made London is a part of nature too, is lighted by the sun of
nature, and lighted to as beautiful effect.

> The river glideth at his own sweet will . . .

A river is the most 'natural' thing that one can imagine; it has the
elasticity, the curved line of nature itself. The poet had never been
able to regard this one as a real river – now, uncluttered by barges, the
river reveals itself as a natural thing, not at all disciplined into a rigid
and mechanical pattern: it is like the daffodils, or the mountain
brooks, artless, and whimsical, and 'natural' as they. The poem
closes, you will remember, as follows:

> Dear God! the very houses seem asleep;
> And all that mighty heart is lying still!

The city, in the poet's insight of the morning, has earned its right to be
considered organic, not merely mechanical. That is why the stale
metaphor of the sleeping houses is strangely renewed. The most
exciting thing that the poet can say about the houses is that they are
asleep. He has been in the habit of counting them dead – as just

mechanical and inanimate; to say they are 'asleep' is to say that they are alive, that they participate in the life of nature. In the same way, the tired old metaphor which sees a great city as a pulsating heart of empire becomes revivified. It is only when the poet sees the city under the semblance of death that he can see it as actually alive – quick with the only life which he can accept, the organic life of 'nature'.

It is not my intention to exaggerate Wordsworth's own consciousness of the paradox involved. In this poem, he prefers, as is usual with him, the frontal attack. But the situation is paradoxical here as in so many of his poems. In his preface to the second edition of the *Lyrical Ballads* Wordsworth stated that his general purpose was 'to choose incidents and situations from common life' but so to treat them that 'ordinary things should be presented to the mind in an unusual aspect'. Coleridge was to state the purpose for him later, in terms which make even more evident Wordsworth's exploitation of the paradoxical: 'Mr. Wordsworth . . . was to propose to himself as his object, to give the charm of novelty to things of every day, and to excite a feeling analogous to the supernatural, by awakening the mind's attention from the lethargy of custom, and directing it to the loveliness and the wonders of the world before us . . .' Wordsworth, in short, was consciously attempting to show his audience that the common was really uncommon, the prosaic was really poetic.

Coleridge's terms, 'the charm of novelty to things of every day', 'awakening the mind', suggest the Romantic preoccupation with wonder – the surprise, the revelation which puts the tarnished familiar world in a new light. This may well be the *raison d'être* of most Romantic paradoxes; and yet the neo-classic poets use paradox for much the same reason. Consider Pope's lines from 'The Essay on Man':

> In doubt his Mind or Body to prefer;
> Born but to die, and reas'ning but to err;
> Alike in ignorance, his Reason such,
> Whether he thinks too little, or too much
> . . .
> Created half to rise, and half to fall;
> Great Lord of all things, yet a Prey to all;
> Sole Judge of Truth, in endless Error hurl'd;
> The Glory, Jest, and Riddle of the world!

Here, it is true, the paradoxes insist on the irony, rather than the wonder. But Pope too might have claimed that he was treating the things of everyday, man himself, and awakening his mind so that he would view himself in a new and blinding light. Thus, there is a certain awed wonder in Pope just as there is a certain trace of irony implicit in the Wordsworth sonnets. There is, of course, no reason why they should not occur together, and they do. Wonder and irony merge in many of the lyrics of Blake; they merge in Coleridge's *Ancient Mariner*. The variations in emphasis are numerous. Gray's 'Elegy' uses a typical Wordsworth 'situation' with the rural scene and with peasants contemplated in the light of their 'betters'. But in the 'Elegy' the balance is heavily tilted in the direction of irony, the revelation an ironic rather than a startling one:

> Can storied urn or animated bust
> Back to its mansion call the fleeting breath?
> Can Honour's voice provoke the silent dust?
> Or Flatt'ry sooth the dull cold ear of Death?

But I am not here interested in enumerating the possible variations; I am interested rather in our seeing that the paradoxes spring from the very nature of the poet's language: it is a language in which the connotations play as great a part as the denotations. And I do not mean that the connotations are important as supplying some sort of frill or trimming, something external to the real matter in hand. I mean that the poet does not use a notation at all – as the scientist may properly be said to do so. The poet, within limits, has to make up his language as he goes.

T. S. Eliot has commented upon 'that perpetual slight alteration of language, words perpetually juxtaposed in new and sudden combinations', which occurs in poetry. It *is* perpetual; it cannot be kept out of the poem; it can only be directed and controlled. The tendency of science is necessarily to stabilise terms, to freeze them into strict denotations; the poet's tendency is by contrast disruptive. The terms are continually modifying each other, and thus violating their dictionary meanings. To take a very simple example, consider the adjectives in the first lines of Wordsworth's evening sonnet: *beauteous, calm, free, holy, quiet, breathless*. The juxtapositions are hardly startling; and yet notice this: the evening is like a nun breathless with adoration. The adjective 'breathless' suggests tremendous excitement; and yet the evening is not only quiet but *calm*. There is no final contradiction, to be sure: it is *that* kind of calm and *that* kind of excitement, and the two states may well occur together. But the poet has no one term. Even if he had a polysyllabic technical term, the term would not provide the solution for his problem. He must work by contradiction and qualification.

We may approach the problem in this way: the poet has to work by analogies. All of the subtler states of emotion, as I. A. Richards has pointed out, necessarily demand metaphor for their expression. The poet must work by analogies, but the metaphors do not lie in the same plane or fit neatly edge to edge. There is a continual tilting of the planes; necessary overlappings, discrepancies, contradictions. Even the most direct and simple poet is forced into paradoxes far more often than we think, if we are sufficiently alive to what he is doing.

But in dilating on the difficulties of the poet's task, I do not want to leave the impression that it is a task which necessarily defeats him, or even that with his method he may not win to a fine precision. To use Shakespeare's figure, he can

<blockquote>
with assays of bias
By indirections find directions out.
</blockquote>

Shakespeare had in mind the game of lawnbowls in which the bowl is distorted, a distortion which allows the skillful player to bowl a curve. To elaborate the figure, science makes use of the perfect sphere and its attack can be direct. The method of art can, I believe, never be direct – is always indirect. But that does not mean that the matter of the game cannot place the bowl where he wants it. The serious difficulties will only occur when he confuses his game with that of science and mistakes the nature of his appropriate instrument. Mr Stuart Chase a few years ago, with a touching naïveté, urged us to take the distortion out of the bowl – to treat language like notation.

I have said that even the apparently simple and straightforward poet is forced into paradoxes by the nature of his instrument. Seeing this, we should not be surprised to find poets who consciously employ it to gain a compression and precision otherwise unobtainable. Such a method, like any other, carries with it its own perils. But the dangers are not overpowering; the poem is not predetermined to a shallow and glittering sophistry. The method is an extension of the normal language of poetry, not a perversion of it.

I should like to refer the reader to a concrete case. Donne's 'Canonisation' ought to provide a sufficiently extreme instance. The basic metaphor which underlies the poem (and which is reflected in the title) involves a sort of paradox. For the poet daringly treats profane love as if it were divine love. The canonisation is not that of a pair of holy anchorites who have renounced the world and the flesh. The hermitage of each is the other's body; but they do renounce the world, and so their title to sainthood is cunningly argued. The poem then is a parody of Christian sainthood; but it is an intensely serious parody of a sort that modern man, habituated as he is to an easy yes or no, can hardly understand. He refuses to accept the paradox as a serious rhetorical device; and since he is able to accept it only as a cheap trick, he is forced into this dilemma. Either: Donne does not take love seriously; here he is merely sharpening his wit as a sort of mechanical exercise. Or: Donne does not take sainthood seriously; here he is merely indulging in a cynical and bawdy parody.

Neither account is true; a reading of the poem will show that Donne takes both love and religion seriously; it will show, further, that the paradox is here his inevitable instrument. But to see this plainly will require a closer reading than most of us give to poetry.

The poem opens dramatically on a note of exasperation. The 'you' whom the speaker addresses is not identified. We can imagine that it is a person, perhaps a friend, who is objecting to the speaker's love affair. At any rate, the person represents the practical world which regards love as a silly affectation. To use the metaphor on which the poem is built, the friend represents the secular world which the lovers have renounced.

Donne begins to suggest this metaphor in the first stanza by the contemptuous alternatives which he suggests to the friend:

> . . . chide my palsie, or my gout,
> My five gray haires, or ruin'd fortune flout. . . .

The implications are: (1) All right, consider my love as an infirmity, as a disease, if you will, but confine yourself to my other infirmities, my palsy, my approaching old age, my ruined fortune. You stand a better chance of curing those; in chiding me for this one, you are simply wasting your time as well as mine. (2) Why don't you pay attention to your own welfare – go on and get wealth and honor for yourself. What should you care if I do give these up in pursuing my love.

The two main categories of secular success are neatly, and contemptuously epitomised in the line

> Or the Kings reall, or his stamped face . . .

Cultivate the court and gaze at the king's face there, or, if you prefer, get into business and look at his face stamped on coins. But let me alone.

This conflict between the 'real' world and the love absorbed in the world of love runs through the poem; it dominates the second stanza in which the torments of love, so vivid to the lover, affect the real world not at all –

> What merchants ships have my sighs drown'd?

It is touched on in the fourth stanza in the contrast between the word 'Chronicle' which suggests secular history with its pomp and magnificence, the history of kings and princes, and the word 'sonnets' with its suggestions of trivial and precious intricacy. The conflict appears again in the last stanza, only to be resolved when the unworldly lovers, love's saints who have given up the world, paradoxically achieve a more intense world. But here the paradox is still contained in, and supported by, the dominant metaphor: so does the holy anchorite win a better world by giving up this one.

But before going on to discuss this development of the theme, it is important to see what else the second stanza does. For it is in this second stanza and the third, that the poet shifts the tone of the poem, modulating from the note of irritation with which the poem opens into the quite different tone with which it closes.

Donne accomplishes the modulation of tone by what may be called an analysis of love-metaphor. Here, as in many of his poems, he shows that he is thoroughly self-conscious about what he is doing. This second stanza, he fills with the conventionalised figures of the Petrarchan tradition: the wind of lovers' sighs, the floods of lovers' tears, etc. – extravagant figures with which the contemptuous secular friend might be expected to tease the lover. The implication is that the poet himself recognises the absurdity of the Petrarchan love metaphors. But what of it? The very absurdity of the jargon which lovers are expected to talk makes for his argument: their love, however absurd it may appear to the world, does no harm to the world. The practical friend need have no fears: there will still be wars to fight and lawsuits to argue.

The opening of the third stanza suggests that this vein of irony is to be maintained. The poet points out to his friend the infinite fund of such absurdities which can be applied to lovers:

> Call her one, mee another flye,
> We'are Tapers too, and at our owne cost die. . . .

For that matter, the lovers can conjure up for themselves plenty of such fantastic comparisons: *they* know what the world thinks of them. But these figures of the third stanza are no longer the threadbare Petrarchan conventionalities; they have sharpness and bite. The last one, the likening of the lovers to the phoenix, is fully serious, and with it, the tone has shifted from ironic banter into a defiant but controlled tenderness.

The effect of the poet's implied awareness of the lovers' apparent madness is to cleanse and revivify metaphor; to indicate the sense in which the poet accepts it, and thus to prepare us for accepting seriously the fine and seriously intended metaphors which dominate the last two stanzas of the poem.

The opening line of the fourth stanza,

> Wee can dye by it, if not live by love,

achieves an effect of tenderness and deliberate resolution. The lovers
are ready to die to the world; they are committed; they are not callow
but confident. (The basic metaphor of the saint, one notices, is being
carried on; the lovers in their renunciation of the world, have
something of the confident resolution of the saint. By the bye, the
word 'legend' –

> . . . if unfit for tombes and hearse
> Our legend bee –

in Donne's time meant 'the life of a saint'.) The lovers are willing to
forego the ponderous and stately chronicle and to accept the trifling
and insubstantial 'sonnet' instead; but then if the urn be well
wrought, it provides a finer memorial for one's ashes than does the
pompous and grotesque monument. With the finely contemptuous,
yet quiet phrase, 'half-acre tombes', the world which the lovers reject
expands into something gross and vulgar. But the figure works
further; the pretty sonnets will not merely hold their ashes as a decent
earthly memorial. Their legend, their story, will gain them
canonisation; and approved as love's saints, other lovers will invoke
them.

In this last stanza, the theme receives a final complication. The
lovers in rejecting life actually win to the most intense life. This
paradox has been hinted at earlier in the phoenix metaphor. Here it
receives a powerful dramatisation. The lovers in becoming hermits,
find that they have not lost the world, but have gained the world in
each other, now a more intense, more meaningful world. Donne is
not content to treat the lovers' discovery as something which comes to
them passively, but rather as something which they actively achieve.
They are like the saint, God's athlete:

> Who did the whole worlds soule *contract*, and *drove*
> Into the glasses of your eyes. . . .

The image is that of a violent squeezing as of a powerful hand. And
what do the lovers 'drive' into each other's eyes? The 'Countries,
Townes', and 'Courtes', which they renounced in the first stanza of
the poem. The unworldly lovers thus become the most 'worldly' of all.

The tone with which the poem closes is one of triumphant
achievement, but the tone is a development contributed to by various
earlier elements. One of the more important elements which works
toward our acceptance of the final paradox is the figure of the
phoenix, which will bear a little further analysis.

The comparison of the lovers to the phoenix is very skilfully related to the two earlier comparisons, that in which the lovers are like burning tapers, and that in which they are like the eagle and the dove. The phoenix comparison gathers up both: the phoenix is a bird, and like the tapers, it burns. We have a selected series of items: the phoenix figure seems to come in a natural stream of association. 'Call us what you will', the lover says, and rattles off in his desperation the first comparisons that occur to him. The comparison to the phoenix seems thus merely another outlandish one, the most outrageous of all. But it is this most fantastic one, stumbled over apparently in his haste, that the poet goes on to develop. It really describes the lovers best and justifies their renunciation. For the phoenix is not two but one, 'we two being one, are it'; and it burns, not like the taper at its own cost, but to live again. Its death is life: 'Wee dye and rise the same . . .' The poet literally justifies the fantastic assertion. In the sixteenth and seventeenth centuries to 'die' means to experience the consummation of the act of love. The lovers after the act are the same. Their love is not exhausted in mere lust. This is their title to canonisation. Their love is like the phoenix.

I hope that I do not seem to juggle the meaning of *die*. The meaning that I have cited can be abundantly justified in the literature of the period; Shakespeare uses 'die' in this sense; so does Dryden. Moreover, I do not think that I give it undue emphasis. The word is in a crucial position. On it is pivoted the transition to the next stanza,

> Wee can dye by it, if not live by love,
> And if unfit for tombes . . .

Most important of all, the sexual submeaning of 'die' does not contradict the other meanings; the poet is saying: 'Our death is really a more intense life'; 'We can afford to trade life (the world) for death (love), for that death is the consummation of life'; 'After all, one does not expect to live *by* love, one expects, and wants, to die *by* it.' But in the total passage he is also saying: 'Because our love is not mundane, we can give up the world'; 'Because our love is not merely lust, we can give up the other lusts, the lust for wealth and power'; 'because', and this is said with an inflection of irony as by one who knows the world too well, 'because our love can outlast its consummation, we are a minor miracle, we are love's saints'. This passage with its ironical tenderness and its realism feeds and supports the brilliant paradox with which the poem closes.

There is one more factor in developing and sustaining the final effect. The poem is an instance of the doctrine which it asserts; it is both the assertion and the realisation of the assertion. The poet has actually before our eyes built within the song the 'pretty room' with which he says the lovers can be content. The poem itself is the well-wrought urn which can hold the lovers' ashes and which will not suffer in comparison with the prince's 'halfe-acre tomb'.

And how necessary are the paradoxes? Donne might have said directly, 'Love in a cottage is enough'. 'The Canonisation' contains this admirable thesis, but it contains a great deal more. He might have been as forthright as a later lyricist who wrote, 'We'll build a sweet little nest,/ Somewhere out in the West,/ And let the rest of the world go by'. He might even have imitated that more metaphysical lyric, which maintains, 'You're the cream in my coffee'. 'The Canonisation' touches on all these observations, but it goes beyond them, not merely in dignity, but in precision.

I submit that the only way by which the poet could say what 'The Canonisation' says is by paradox. More direct methods may be tempting, but all of them enfeeble and distort what is to be said. This statement may seem the less surprising when we reflect on how many of the important things which the poet has to say have to be said by means of paradox: most of the language of lovers is such – 'The Canonisation' is a good example; so is most of the language of religion – 'He who would save his life, must lose it'; 'The last shall be first'. Indeed, almost any insight important enough to warrant a great poem apparently has to be stated in such terms. Deprived of the character of paradox with its twin concomitants of irony and wonder, the matter of Donne's poem unravels into 'facts', biological, sociological, and economic. What happens to Donne's lovers if we consider them 'scientifically', without benefit of the supernaturalism which the poet confers upon them? Well, what happens to Shakespeare's lovers, for Shakespeare uses the basic metaphor of 'The Canonisation' in his *Romeo and Juliet*? In their first conversation, the lovers play with the analogy between the lover and the pilgrim to the Holy Land. Juliet says:

> For saints have hands that pilgrims' hands do touch
> And palm to palm is holy palmers' kiss.

Considered scientifically, the lovers become Mr Aldous Huxley's animals, 'quietly sweating, palm to palm'.

For us today, Donne's imagination seems obsessed with the problem of unity; the sense in which the lovers become one – the sense in which the soul is united with God. Frequently, as we have seen, one type of union becomes a metaphor for the other. It may not be too far-fetched to see both as instances of, and metaphors for, the union which the creative imagination itself effects. For that fusion is not logical; it apparently violates science and common sense; it welds together the discordant and the contradictory. Coleridge has of course given us the classic description of its nature and power. It 'reveals itself in the balance or reconcilement of opposite or discordant qualities: of sameness, with difference; of the general, with the concrete; the idea, with the image; the individual, with the representative; the sense of novelty and freshness, with old and familiar objects; a more than usual state of emotion, with more than usual order. . . .' It is a great and illuminating statement, but is a series of paradoxes. Apparently Coleridge could describe the effect of the imagination in no other way.

Shakespeare, in one of his poems, has given a description that oddly parallels that of Coleridge.

> Reason in it selfe confounded,
> Saw Division grow together,
> To themselves yet either neither,
> Simple were so well compounded.

I do not know what his 'The Phoenix and the Turtle' celebrates. Perhaps it *was* written to honor the marriage of Sir John Salisbury and Ursula Stanley; or perhaps the Phoenix is Lucy, Countess of Bedford; or perhaps the poem is merely an essay on Platonic love. But the scholars themselves are so uncertain, that I think we will do little violence to established habits of thinking, if we boldly pre-empt the poem for our own purposes. Certainly the poem is an instance of that magic power which Coleridge sought to describe. I propose that we take it for a moment as a poem about that power;

> So they loved as love in twaine,
> Had the essence but in one,
> Two distincts, Division none,
> Number there in love was slaine.

> Hearts remote, yet not asunder;
> Distance and no space was seene,
> Twixt this *Turtle* and his *Queene*;
> But in them it were a wonder. . . .

> Propertie was thus appalled,
> That the selfe was not the same;
> Single Natures double name,
> Neither two nor one was called.

Precisely! The nature is single, one, unified. But the name is double, and today with our multiplication of sciences, it is multiple. If the poet is to be true to his poetry, he must call it neither two nor one: the paradox is his only solution. The difficulty has intensified since Shakespeare's day: the timid poet, when confronted with the problem of 'Single Natures double name', has too often funked it. A history of poetry from Dryden's time to our own might bear as its subtitle 'The Half-Hearted Phoenix'.

In Shakespeare's poem, Reason is 'in it selfe confounded' at the union of the Phoenix and the Turtle; but it recovers to admit its own bankruptcy:

> Love hath Reason, Reason none,
> If what parts, can so remaine. . . .

and it is Reason which goes on to utter the beautiful threnos with which the poem concludes:

> Beautie, Truth, and Raritie,
> Grace in all simplicitie,
> Here enclosde, in cinders lie.
>
> Death is now the *Phoenix* nest,
> And the *Turtles* loyall brest,
> To eternitie doth rest. . . .
>
> Truth may seeme, but cannot be,
> Beautie bragge, but tis not she,
> Truth and Beautie buried be.
>
> To this urne let those repaire,
> That are either true or faire,
> For these dead Birds, sigh a prayer.

Having pre-empted the poem for our own purposes, it may not be too outrageous to go on to make one further observation. The urn to which we are summoned, the urn which holds the ashes of the phoenix, is like the well-wrought urn of Donne's 'Canonisation' which holds the phoenix-lovers' ashes: it is the poem itself. One is reminded of still another urn, Keats's Grecian urn, which contained for Keats, Truth and Beauty, as Shakespeare's urn encloses 'Beautie, Truth, and Raritie'. But there is a sense in which all such well-wrought urns contain the ashes of a phoenix. The urns are not meant for memorial purposes only, though that often seems to be their chief significance to the professors of literature. The phoenix rises from its ashes; or ought to rise; but it will not arise for all our mere sifting and measuring the ashes, or testing them for their chemical content. We must be prepared to accept the paradox of the imagination itself; else 'Beautie, Truth, and Raritie' remain enclosed in their cinders and we shall end with essential cinders, for all our pains.

SOURCE: ch. 1 of *The Well-Wrought Urn* (New York, 1947; London, 1949), pp. 3–20.

Helen Gardner (1949)

'POETS OF VISION'

. . . Mr Eliot has always been a poet of vision. His earlier poetry presented mainly what Wordsworth called a 'visionary dreariness'. He might indeed be accused in his early poetry, as Mary accused Harry, of attaching himself to loathing as others do to loving. The effort of every true poet is to unify his experience, and the development of every great poet is the extension of the amount of experience he can order into poetry. Mr Eliot could not have written *Four Quartets* if he had not earlier written 'Mr Eliot's Sunday Morning Service', where faith and hope and love are known in terms of their opposites. But the experience which lies behind *The Hollow Men* and *Ash Wednesday* compelled him to contemplate another vision; 'the visionary gleam, the glory and the dream', whose felt absence was his earlier subject. A deepening sense of the horror of life, something more terrible than dreariness, makes urgent the question; not why are we desolate, but why were we ever happy, or why did we ever expect happiness? Our wretchedness is not an illusion; was our joy, however transitory, perhaps equally real? After *The Waste Land* Mr Eliot's poetry becomes the attempt to find meaning in the whole of his experience, to include all that he has known. To do this, he enters into himself, finding within himself his own music and his own language.

English poetry is particularly rich in visionary poets: Langland, Vaughan, Traherne, Smart, Blake, Wordsworth. But these are not the poets we think of when we think of Mr Eliot. Although he shares with them the power to render 'unknown modes of Being', he differs from them in his attitude to the poet's task. His unique distinction among English poets is the balance he has maintained between the claims of his vision and the claims of his art. In his poetry he is neither a prophet nor a visionary primarily, but a poet, a great 'maker'. When we read *Four Quartets* we are left finally not with the thought of 'the transitory Being who beheld this vision', nor with the thought of the vision itself, but with the poem, beautiful, satisfying, self-contained, self-organised, complete. His master in this is not an English poet, but the greatest of European poets of vision: Dante. Although the range and scope of *The Divine Comedy* forbid us to make a comparison, yet there is a sense in which Mr Eliot can without impropriety be named with Dante. He too has found a 'dolce stil nuovo', and the origin of that style he could explain in Dante's words:

> Io mi son un che, quando
> amor mi spira, noto, ed a quel modo
> che ditta dentro, vo significando.

SOURCE: extract from *The Art of T. S. Eliot* (London, 1949; reissued 1968), pp. 184–6 in 1st edn.

T. R. Henn   (1950)

'THE TRADITIONAL MYRIAD-MINDEDNESS'

. . . There is some justice in Yeats's description of himself as of the last Romantics. His poetry is both traditional and intensely personal. Its rhythms are strongly accented, and in them there is implicit the half-chant of older poetry, and an intonation which, when he read his verse, seemed to give it a peculiar life of its own.[1] Those rhythms, and his idioms, are refreshed continually from common speech, from the book of the people, from the vulgar and tavern music of the street ballad; from Synge's brutality and violence and melancholy; from the strong and delicate cadences of the great Elizabethans. The poetry is built about a core of symbols, linked by history, or dream, or woman, or event, the 'images that waken in the blood', and which are the instruments of his thought. The symbols shape themselves into patterns within a framework determined by the poet-philosopher's view of time. And time involves the catastrophic interpretation of history, the great mutations of the world perceived in a dramatic foreshortening; for it is, perhaps, necessary that the romantic poet should be possessed by this sense of catastrophe or of regeneration to give urgency to his statement. Enrichment of the images springs from his own sense of his position in history. Reality crowded thickly about him; and it was living and vital because it was determined by the pressure of the past, implicit in the rhythms of history perceived and justified, from 1916 onwards, by the present. Visions were built on images, and the images, so far as his study of history, archaeology, and philosophy might give him certainty, were asserting their validity at every turn of political events. The funeral gleam of Troy, the burning roof and tower that marked the destruction of a great family; or the drunken soldiery of Byzantium or Clare-Galway, were images that caught fire backwards from the past into the present. Maud Gonne might be Laura, or Beatrice, or Helen, or Emer, but all drew a common life from the Great Memory. The poet as Renaissance man, painter, or politician, soldier or scholar or saint, justified his multiplicity by calling strong ghosts to stand by his bed. It did not matter that the statue of Cuchulain in the Post Office was a bad one; the epic of heroism and love and defeat drew its vitality from the identification with public and private history.

But in this poetry there is more than traditional romanticism. He had taken much of what was pertinent, his manner of thinking of love and death, but not of God, from the metaphysical poets. The passionate-dispassionate, the sinewy precision of words, the laminated metaphors, the redemption from the cynical or sordid by pride and steadfastness, are part of what he found and made his own. He found them and used them, not only because he refused to sacrifice his integrity as a dedicated poet, but because his instinct to understand remained alive to the end.

It is a final paradox that these qualities of balance and integrity should be related to a personality characteristically 'Romantic', in the best and worst senses. A poet who, by Chance or Choice, assumes the traditional myriad-mindedness, must play the parts that those roles demand; and he must study them, or he will fail to speak with conviction. Therefore he must posture, speak bravely, find that which is the prerogative of men of action, think himself into the heroes of mythology. Renaissance man, all that Hamlet and Lear stood for, might find its last emblem with Cuchulain's stand in the Post Office; as Robert Gregory's death as a fighter-pilot in Italy recalled the shade of Achilles:

> Though battle-joy may be so dear
> A memory, even to the dead. . . .

The end was to be gaiety, as Hamlet and Lear were gay, knowing John Synge's reality and joy, the bitter gaiety of defeat as the gyres ran on.

But there was no self-pity for the past, no blindness as to the present. Yeats was intensely aware of contemporary thought. His poetry is the outcome of a philosophy which, though he could think towards it only through the medium of the symbol, was yet unified, all detractions reckoned up, by a high and consistent purpose. That purpose is to be perceived in relation to Ireland; being, as Yeats saw it, at once the microcosm and the mirror of the world. Out of Ireland, whatever the hatred, whatever the momentary bitterness or perversity of the 'fanatic heart', would come the new and ordered society:

Preserve that which is living and help the two Irelands, Gaelic Ireland and Anglo-Ireland, so to unite that neither shall shed its pride. Study the great problems of the world, as they have been lived in our scenery, the re-birth of European spirituality in the mind of Berkeley, the restoration of European order in the mind of Burke. Every nation is the whole world in a mirror and our mirror has twice been very bright and clear. Do not be afraid to boast so long as the boast lays burdens on the boaster. Study the educational system of Italy, the creation of the philosopher Gentile, where even religion is studied not in the abstract but in the minds and lives of Italian saints and thinkers; it becomes at once part of Italian history.

As for the rest we wait till the world changes and its reflection changes in our mirror and an hieratical society returns, power descending from the few to the many, from the subtle to the gross, not because some man's policy has decreed it but because what is so overwhelming cannot be restrained. A new beginning, a new turn of the wheel.[2]

SOURCE: extract from *The Lonely Tower* (London, 1950), pp. 350–2.

NOTES

1. 'He stressed the rhythm till it almost became a chant; he went with speed, marking every beat and dwelling on his vowels': John Masefield, *Some Memories of W. B. Yeats* (London, 1940), p. 13. This, too, was his method of composition: chanting lines or half-lines aloud, wide gestures of the hands, till the words had obeyed his call.

2. *Explorations*, p. 337.

Northrop Frye (1957)

'THE UNIVERSE OF POETRY'

... The universe of poetry ... is a literary universe, and not a separate existential universe. Apocalypse means revelation, and when art becomes apocalyptic, it reveals. But it reveals only on its own terms, and in its own forms: it does not describe or represent a separate content of revelation. When poet and critic pass from the archetypal to the anagogic phase, they enter a phase of which only religion, or something as infinite in its range as religion, can possibly form an external goal. The poetic imagination, unless it disciplines itself in the particular way in which the imaginations of Hardy and Housman were disciplined, is apt to get claustrophobia when it is allowed to talk only about human nature and subhuman nature; and poets are happier as servants of religion than of politics, because the transcendental and apocalyptic perspective of religion comes as a tremendous emancipation of the imaginative mind. If men were compelled to make the melancholy choice between atheism and superstition, the scientist, as Bacon pointed out long ago, would be compelled to choose atheism, but the poet would be compelled to choose superstition, for even superstition, by its very confusion of values, gives his imagination more scope than a dogmatic denial of imaginative infinity does. But the loftiest religion, no less than the grossest superstition, comes to the poet, *qua* poet, only as the spirits came to Yeats, to give him metaphors for poetry.

The study of literature takes us toward seeing poetry as the imitation of infinite social action and infinite human thought, the mind of a man who is all men, the universal creative word which is all words. About this man and word we can, speaking as critics, say only one thing ontologically: we have no reason to suppose either that they exist or that they do not exist. We can call them divine if by divine we mean the unlimited or projected human. But the critic, *qua* critic, has nothing to say for or against the affirmations that a religion makes out of these conceptions. If Christianity wishes to identify the infinite Word and Man of the literary universe with the Word of God, the person of Christ, the historical Jesus, the Bible or church dogma, these identifications may be accepted by any poet or critic without injury to his work – the acceptance may even clarify and intensify his work, depending on his temperament and situation. But they can never be accepted by poetry as a whole, or by criticism as such. The literary critic, like the historian, is compelled to treat every religion in the same way that religions treat each other, as though it were a human hypothesis, whatever else he may in other contexts believe it to be. The discussion of the universal Word at the opening of the Chhandogya Upanishad (where it is symbolised by the sacred word 'Aum') is exactly as relevant and as irrelevant to literary criticism as the discussion at the opening of the Fourth Gospel. Coleridge was right in thinking that the 'Logos' was the goal of his work as a critic, but not right in thinking that his poetic Logos would so inevitably be absorbed into Christ as to make literary criticism a kind of natural theology.

The total Logos of criticism by itself can never become an object of faith or an ontological personality. The conception of a total Word is the postulate that there is such a thing as an order of words, and that the criticism which studies it makes, or could make, complete sense. Aristotle's *Physics* leads to the conception of an unmoved first mover at the circumference of the physical universe. This, in itself, means essentially that physics *has* a universe. The systematic study of motion would be impossible unless all phenomena of motion could be related to unifying principles, and those in their turn to a total unifying principle of movement which is not itself merely another phenomenon of motion. If theology identifies Aristotle's unmoved mover with a creating God, that is the business of theology; physics as physics will be unaffected by it. Christian critics may see their total Word as an analogy of Christ, as medieval critics did, but as literature itself may be accompanied in culture by any religion, criticism must detach itself accordingly. In short, the study of literature belongs to the 'humanities', and the humanities, as their name indicates, can take only the human view of the superhuman.

The close resemblance between the conceptions of anagogic criticism and those of religion has led many to assume that they can only be related by making one supreme and the other subordinate. Those who choose religion, like Coleridge, will, like him, try to make criticism a natural theology; those who choose culture, like Arnold, will try to reduce religion to objectified cultural myth. But for the purity of each the autonomy of each must be guaranteed. Culture interposes, between the ordinary and the religious life, a total vision of possibilities, and insists on its totality – for whatever is excluded from culture by religion or state will get its revenge somehow. Thus culture's essential service to a religion is to destroy intellectual idolatry, the recurrent tendency in religion to replace the object of its worship with its present understanding and forms of approach to that object. Just as no argument in favor of a religious or political doctrine is of any value unless it is an intellectually honest argument, and so guarantees the autonomy of logic, so no religious or political myth is either valuable or valid unless it assumes the autonomy of culture, which may be provisionally defined as the total body of imaginative hypothesis in a society and its tradition. To defend the autonomy of culture in this sense seems to me the social task of the 'intellectual' in the modern world: if so, to defend its subordination to a total synthesis of any kind, religious or political, would be the authentic form of the *trahison des clercs*.

Besides, it is of the essence of imaginative culture that it transcends the limits both of the naturally possible and of the morally acceptable.

The argument that there is no room for poets in any human society which is an end in itself remains unanswerable even when the society is the people of God. For religion is also a social institution, and so far as it is one, it imposes limitations on the arts just as a Marxist or Platonic state would do. Christian theology is no less of a revolutionary dialectic, or indissoluble union of theory and social practice. Religions, in spite of their enlarged perspective, cannot as social institutions *contain* an art of unlimited hypothesis. The arts in their turn cannot help releasing the powerful acids of satire, realism, ribaldry, and fantasy in their attempt to dissolve all the existential concretions that get in their way. The artist often enough has to find that, as God says in *Faust*, he 'muss als Teufel schaffen', which I suppose means rather more than that he has to work like the devil. Between religion's 'this is' and poetry's 'but suppose *this* is', there must always be some kind of tension, until the possible and the actual meet at infinity. Nobody wants a poet in the perfect human state, and, as even the poets tell us, nobody but God himself can tolerate a poltergeist in the City of God.

SOURCE: extract from *Anatomy of Criticism: Four Essays* (Princeton, N.J., 1957), pp. 125–8.

Frank Kermode (1957)

'THE SYMBOLISTS AND TRADITION'

. . . Symbolist criticism has always acknowledged – and without such an acknowledgement it is impossible to conceive of the success of a literary movement – the importance of the poetry of the past to the new poetry. The further admission . . . that discourse may be domesticated in the articulated symbolism of the works of art, automatically overthrows the doctrine of the supremacy of the short poem, and the modern novel further demonstrated the possibilities of complex symbolic relations in long works. The new step, perhaps, is to make available some of the poetry of the past which has been excluded by earlier Symbolist assumptions, and above all, to restore the long poem to the centre of activity. For the English this means Milton; and this fact alone justifies any attempt to kill the Symbolist historical doctrine of dissociation of sensibility as publicly as possible. The liberation of Milton – it has begun, but has not got far enough as yet – from that ban under which he has remained, at any rate in the eyes of many young poets, throughout the present century, is of extreme importance to the future. Spenser needs liberating, too; but Milton is more important. There are fewer flats among the elevations, far less 'binding-matter' in *Paradise Lost*, than is habitually assumed, even by people who read Milton. The time cannot be far off when it will be read once more as the most perfect achievement of English poetry, perhaps the richest and most intricately beautiful poem in the world. Then, perhaps, poets will marvel that it could have been done without so long; as easy, they will say, to imagine a Greek literature which abjured Homer.

There seems no good reason why this development should necessitate the end of the vogue for Donne and the Metaphysicals; yet there are signs already that it is ending, like the older taste for Jacobean drama. For this we must thank the Symbolist device of placing Donne and Milton on an historical see-saw. It is a great pity because at this moment it is possible – so fully has Grierson's work been supplemented – to read Donne more accurately than ever before; and because the chance of a significant revaluation of a great neglected poet like Jonson, and a fine neglected dramatist like Middleton, must go too. But these losses we will sustain more cheerfully if they are merely the price of Milton's restoration, if we can see him again as not an obstruction but a model. It may seem that I am calling up a ghastly rhetoric from the grave; but we are apt to be misled by Verlaine's remark. He too has his rhetoric, and as long as there is verbal communication there will be rhetorics; they are the means to order, and without that no lamp burns in the tower, no dancer spins. If poets turn back to Milton they will forget the old hatred of his rhetoric or his theology or (easiest, surely, of all) his life, and discover, if I may use the lines eulogistically, 'mere' now meaning 'pure', that

> He has found, after the manner of his kind,
> Mere images.

And by the time they have done that, the dissociation of sensibility, the great and in some ways noxious historical myth of Symbolism (though the attempt to see history in terms of the Image was noble) will be forgotten, except by historians crying their new categories and still unheard persuasions.

SOURCE: extract from *Romantic Image* (London, 1957), pp. 165–8.

Frank Kermode   (1966)

'THE IMAGINATION'S MERCIES'

. . . We have our vital interest in the structure of time, in the concords books arrange between beginning, middle and end; and as the Chicago critics, with a quite different emphasis, would agree, we lose something by pretending that we have not. Our geometries, in James's word, are required to measure change, since it is on change, between remote or imaginary origins and ends, that our interests are fixed. In our perpetual crisis we have, at the proper seasons, under the pressure perhaps of our own end, dizzying perspectives upon the past and the future, in a freedom which is the freedom of a discordant reality. Such a vision of chaos or absurdity may be more than we can easily bear. Philip Larkin, though he speaks quietly, speaks of something terrible:

> Truly, though our element is time,
> We are not suited to the long perspectives
> Open at each instant of our lives.
> They link us to our losses . . .

Merely to give order to these perspectives is to provide consolation, as De Quincey's opium did; and simple fictions are the opium of the people. But fictions too easy we call 'escapist'; we want them not only to console but to make discoveries of the hard truth here and now, in the middest. We do not feel they are doing this if we cannot see the shadow of the gable, or hear the discoveries of dissonance, the word set against the word. The books which seal off the long perspectives, which sever us from our losses, which represent the world of potency as a world of act, these are the books which, when the drug wears off, go on to the dump with the other empty bottles. Those that continue to interest us move through time to an end, an end we must sense even if we cannot know it; they live in change, until, which is never, *as* and *is* are one.

Naturally every such fiction will in some measure repeat others, but always with a difference, because of the changes in our reality. Stevens talks about the moment out of poverty as 'an *hour* / Filled with expressible bliss, in which I have / No need'. But the hour passes; the need, our interest in our loss, returns; and out of another experience of chaos grows another form – a form in time – that satisfies both by being a repetition and by being new. So two things seem to be true: first, that the poet is right to speak of his giant as 'ever changing, living in change'; and secondly, that he is right to say that 'the man-hero is not the exceptional monster, / But he that of repetition is most master'. Moreover, he is right about another thing, which for us who are not medium men, living in a reality which is always February, is the most important of all. If he were wrong here we should have to close up our books of poetry and read somebody on Necessity:

> Medium man
> In February hears the imagination's hymns
>   And sees its images, its motions
> And multitudes of motions
>
> And feels the imagination's mercies. . . .

SOURCE: extract from *Sense of an Ending: Studies in the Theory of Fiction* (New York, 1966), pp. 178–80.

C. S. Lewis   (1961)

'LITERATURE CONSIDERED AS LOGOS'

. . . It is no use trying to evade the question by locating the whole goodness of a literary work in its character as Poiema, for it is out of our various interests in the Logos that the Poiema is made.

The nearest I have ever yet got to an answer is that we seek an enlargement of our being. We want to be more than ourselves. . . .

Good reading, therefore, though it is not essentially an affectional or moral or intellectual activity, has something in common with all three. In love we escape from our self into one another. In the moral sphere, every act of justice or charity involves putting ourselves in the other person's place and thus transcending our own competitive particularity. In coming to understand anything we are rejecting the facts as they are for us in favour of the facts as they are. The primary impulse of each is to maintain and aggrandise himself. The secondary impulse is to go out of the self, to correct its provincialism and heal its loneliness. In love, in virtue, in the pursuit of knowledge, and in the reception of the arts, we are doing this. Obviously this process can be described either as an enlargement or as a temporary annihilation of the self. But that is an old paradox; 'he that loseth his life shall save it'.

We therefore delight to enter into other men's beliefs (those, say, of Lucretius or Lawrence) even though we think them untrue. And into their passions, though we think them depraved, like those, sometimes, of Marlowe or Carlyle. And also into their imaginations, though they lack all realism of content.

This must not be understood as if I were making the literature of power once more into a department within the literature of knowledge – a department which existed to gratify our rational curiosity about other people's psychology. It is not a question of knowing (in that sense) at all. It is *connaître* not *savoir*; it is *erleben*; we become these other selves. Not only nor chiefly in order to see what they are like but in order to see what they see, to occupy, for a while, their seat in the great theatre, to use their spectacles and be made free of whatever insights, joys, terrors, wonders or merriment those spectacles reveal. Hence it is irrelevant whether the mood expressed in a poem was truly and historically the poet's own or one that he also had imagined. What matters is his power to make us live it. I doubt whether Donne the man gave more than playful and dramatic harbourage to the mood expressed in *The Apparition*. I doubt still more whether the real Pope, save while he wrote it, or even then more than dramatically, felt what he expresses in the passage beginning 'Yes, I am proud'.[1] What does it matter?

This, so far as I can see, is the specific value or good of literature considered as Logos; it admits us to experiences other than our own. They are not, any more than our personal experiences, all equally worth having. Some, as we say, 'interest' us more than others. The causes of this interest are naturally extremely various and differ from one man to another; it may be the typical (and we say 'How true!') or the abnormal (and we say 'How strange!'); it may be the beautiful, the terrible, the awe-inspiring, the exhilarating, the pathetic, the comic, or the merely piquant. Literature gives the *entrée* to them all. Those of us who have been true readers all our life seldom fully realise the enormous extension of our being which we owe to authors. We realise it best when we talk with an unliterary friend. He may be full of goodness and good sense but he inhabits a tiny world. In it, we should be suffocated. The man who is contented to be only himself, and therefore less a self, is in prison. My own eyes are not enough for me, I will see through those of others. Reality, even seen through the eyes of many, is not enough. I will see what others have invented. Even the eyes of all humanity are not enough. I regret that the brutes cannot write books. Very gladly would I learn what face things present to a mouse or a bee; more gladly still would I perceive the olfactory world charged with all the information and emotion it carries for a dog.

Literary experience heals the wound, without undermining the privilege, of individuality. There are mass emotions which heal the wound; but they destroy the privilege. In them our separate selves are pooled and we sink back into sub-individuality. But in reading great literature I become a thousand men and yet remain myself. Like the night sky in the Greek poem, I see with a myriad eyes, but it is still I who see. Here, as in worship, in love, in moral action, and in knowing, I transcend myself; and am never more myself than when I do.

SOURCE: extracts from *An Experiment in Criticism* (Cambridge, 1961), pp. 137, 138–41.

NOTE

1. Pope, 'Epilogue', *The Satires*, dia. II, line 208.

Donald Hall   (1962)

'AMERICAN POETRY: NEW DIRECTIONS'

. . . Modern American poetry began in London shortly after the death of Queen Victoria. Ezra Pound recalls that Conrad Aiken told him that there was 'a guy at Harvard doing funny stuff. Mr Eliot turned up a year or so later.' Harriet Monroe founded *Poetry* in 1912, and discovered Mr Pound on her neck encouraging her to print Eliot, Frost and Yeats. But soon after the first successes of modernist poetry in America, when Amy Lowell was flying the flag of revolution, the modernists split into opposing camps. One side of this split became the orthodoxy that prevailed from, say, 1925 to 1955.

In the first decades of this century there were the expatriates and there were the poets who remained in the United States. Pound, Aiken and Eliot congregated in London, but things were also going on in New York. Poets and editors like Alfred Kreymbourg, Mina Loy, William Carlos Williams, Marianne Moore, Wallace Stevens, E. E. Cummings and Hart Crane mingled and established a domestic literary milieu. They shared little but liveliness and talent, but most of them also experimented with the use of common American speech, an indigenous language increasingly distinguishable from English. Even the frenchified Wallace Stevens and the rhetorical Hart Crane participated in this endeavour. And none of these New York poets

shared the concern with history which occupied Eliot and Pound, or
the erudition which this concern imposed.

Pound was the link between London and Greenwich Village, as
editor and publicist and even as poet. . . .

The new poets admired the forms of the sixteenth and seventeenth
centuries, and themselves attempted to write a symmetrical and
intellectual poetry which resembled Ralegh or Dryden more than
'Gerontion' or the *Cantos*. One can divide the chief poets of this time
into those who admired the tough density of Donne, and those who
preferred the wit of Marvell or the delicacy of Herrick. There were
Allen Tate and Yvor Winters on the one hand, and there was John
Crowe Ransom on the other. Late in the thirties another group of
poets took their departure most obviously from Auden – Karl Shapiro
and John Frederick Nims were the best, I think – but because their
poems were witty and formal they did not depart from the general
area of the orthodoxy.

Immediately after the war, two books were published which were
culminations of the twin strains of density and delicacy. Robert
Lowell's *Lord Weary's Castle* is a monument of the line of tough
rhetoricians; beyond this it was impossible to go. (The failure of John
Berryman's *Homage to Mistress Bradstreet*, as I see it, only proves my
point.) The effect of tremendous power under tremendous pressure
was a result of a constricted subject matter and a tense line, in which
the strict decasyllable was counterbalanced by eccentric caesura and
violent enjambement. In contrast was Richard Wilbur's *The Beautiful
Changes*, which was the peak of skilful elegance. Here was the ability to
shape an analogy, to perceive and develop comparisons, to display
etymological wit, and to pun six ways at once. It appealed to the mind
because it was intelligent, and to the sense of form because it was
intricate and shapely. It did not appeal to the passions and it did not
pretend to. These two poets, though they are not the oldest here, form
the real beginning of post-war American poetry because they are the
culmination of past poetries. . . .

The only contrary direction which endured throughout the
orthodoxy was the direction I will inadequately call the colloquial, or
the line of William Carlos Williams. Williams himself has been
admired by most new American poets, of whatever school, but the
poets of the orthodoxy have admired him for his descriptive powers,
they learned from him a conscience of the eye rather than a conscience
of the ear; for Williams the problem of native speech rhythm was of
first importance.

This poetry is no mere restriction of one's vocabulary. It wants to
use the language with the intimacy acquired in unrehearsed

unliterary speech. But it has other characteristics which are not linguistic. It is a poetry of experiences more than of ideas. The experience is presented often without comment, and the words of the description must supply the emotion which the experience generates, without generalisation or summary. Often too this poetry finds great pleasure in the world outside. It is the poetry of a man in the world, responding to what he sees: with disgust, with pleasure, in rant and in meditation. Naturally, this colloquial direction makes much of accuracy, of honest speech. 'Getting the tone right' is the poet's endeavour, not 'turning that metaphor neatly', or 'inventing a new stanza'. Conversely, when it fails most commonly it fails because the emotion does not sound true. . . .

. . . One thing is happening in American poetry, as I see it, which is genuinely new, and so new that I lack words for it. In lines like Robert Bly's:

> In small towns the houses are built right on the ground;
> The lamplight falls on all fours in the grass.

or Louis Simpson's:

> These houses built of wood sustain
> Colossal snows,
> And the light above the street is sick to death.

a new kind of imagination seems to be working. The vocabulary is mostly colloquial but the special quality of the lines has nothing to do with an area of diction; it is quality learned neither from T. S. Eliot nor William Carlos Williams. This imagination is irrational yet the poem is usually quiet and the language simple; there is no straining for apocalypse and no conscious pursuit of the unconscious. There is an inwardness to these images, a profound subjectivity. Yet they are not subjective in the autobiographical manner of *Life Studies* or *Heart's Needle*, which are confessional and particular. This new imagination reveals through images a subjective life which is *general*, and which corresponds to an old objective life of shared experience and knowledge.

The later poems of James Wright provide more examples of this new imagination. Among other poets [in the Penguin anthology edited by Hall] whose verse forms associate them with one or another poetical faction, I find the same quality scattered – an unacknowledged content. What I am trying to describe is not a school or a clique but a way of seeing and a way of feeling, and I believe they have grown by themselves from the complex earth of American writing and American experience.

SOURCE: extract from the Introduction to the anthology, *Contemporary American Poetry* (Harmondsworth, 1962), pp. 18, 19–20, 21–2, 24–5.

Harold Bloom   (1968)

'PERILOUS DIALECTIC'

... At the beginning of this essay I spoke of how little we understand the process by which one poet influences another, and I want to return to that mysterious process now as I close. In old-fashioned terms one can demonstrate that more lines of Yeats allude to or repeat more lines of Shelley than of any other poet, but all this would show us is that the memory does not easily lose the stores it has gathered up by a poet's twentieth year. Stylistically, late Yeats and Shelley have a great deal in common, though that must sound odd in the ears of anyone who is still much under the influence of recent aberrations of the history of taste. I cannot read the final stanzas of 'The Witch of Atlas' without thinking of the 'Byzantium' poems, and this is more than my own eccentricity. Yet the deepest influence of Shelley on Yeats is not in style but in something far more fundamental – Shelley's most characteristic poetry has the same relation to the lyrics of *The Tower* and *The Winding Stair* that the Japanese Noh drama has to Yeats's plays – the very idea of the act that is the Yeatsian poem is Shelley's. In Shelley when he is most himself – in the 'Ode to the West Wind', 'Adonais', 'The Triumph of Life' – one feels the entire weight of a poet's vocation and life veering on the destiny of the relational event that is the poem. When the poem breaks, as in Shelley it so frequently does out of sheer agnostic honesty, as in Yeats it sometimes does out of an extraordinary mixture of self-dramatisation and heroic desperation – then the very concept of a poet breaks with it, in a fitting imaginative gesture for a daimonic man, that man whose role it is to hold himself open to the unity of being. The Yeats of poems like 'A Dialogue of Self and Soul', 'Vacillation' and the haunting 'The Man and the Echo' is a very human, very Romantic and very Shelleyan Yeats, existing in the perilous dialectic that witnesses every object of desire disappearing into another experiential loss, that dares the true Romantic agony in which dialogue collapses towards monologue, and the confrontation of love expires into the crippling loneliness of enforced self-realisation. Yeats strove mightily to overcome the Shelleyan identity of his own youth, but I think it fortunate that he failed in the striving. We would have lost the poet who finally cast his own mythologies aside, to cry aloud in the perfect moment of agnostic confrontation in the poetry of our time, the very humanistic and Shelleyan cry of almost his last poem:

> O Rocky Voice
> Shall we in that great night rejoice?
> What do we know but that we face
> One another in this place?

SOURCE: extract from 'Yeats and the Romantics', in John Hollander (ed.), *Modern Poetry: Essays in Criticism* (Cambridge, 1968), pp. 519–20.

Geoffrey W. Hartman   (1970)

THE POET'S POLITICS

It is autumn of 1831, and a young writer goes to the big city to interest publishers in his work. We hear about his luck in a letter written by John Stuart Mill. 'Carlyle', reports Mill, 'intends staying in London all the winter . . . his object was to treat with booksellers about a work which he wishes to publish, but he has given this up for the present, finding that no bookseller will publish anything but a political pamphlet in the present state of excitement. In fact, literature is suspended; men neither read nor write.' Six months later, and shortly after the passage of the Reform Bill of 1832, Mill writes to the same correspondent:

One unspeakable blessing I now believe that we shall owe to the events of the last ten days; to whatever consummation the spirit which is now in the ascendent may conduct us, there is . . . a probability that we shall accomplish it through other means than anarchy and civil war. The irresistible strength of a unanimous people has been put forth, and has triumphed without bloodshed; it having been proved once for all that the people can carry their point by pacific means.

I start with the assumption that ours is a political age and even, as Napoleon said, that politics is destiny. What good, then, is poetry in this age? What claim does it have on our attention? It could be argued, of course, that all ages are political, that the crisis Mill records is a recurrent one. Indeed, as we look across literature, guided by present concerns, the idea of politics broadens itself. Every epic we know has a political, or cosmopolitical, subject. Men are drawn into a quarrel between clans of gods. Or a nation, as in the Bible, has to establish and then preserve its identity. Even in pastoral there are things to be gained and things to be lost: the pressures of the greater world are there for those who can recognise them. Those shepherds are highly competitive in their silly play, and Huizinga's *Homo Ludens* has taught us to recognise how play is related to mature conventions. One can make no special claim for poetry that startles us with its subject rather than with itself and confronts us by shouting: admire me, I am relevant! dote upon me, I am topical! Of the poems chosen for discussion, those of Wordsworth and Wallace Stevens seem at first completely apolitical. I have included them to suggest how much depends on our own consciousness, on contemporary experience pressing against poetry and precipitating its meaning.

In the unrest of the 1930s (there was unrest in the 1930s) an attempt was made to find criteria that would separate radically poetry from propaganda – that is to say, from the doctrines of religious sects or the ideologies of parties. Against militant critics who insisted that only a committed art was relevant, Cleanth Brooks and others wrote a defense of poetry, saying that art, however passionate or ideological its subject matter, had to be sophisticated enough to bear an ironical contemplation. The famous dictum 'A poem should not mean, but be' means cool it, play it cool, the poem is a play, a drama of attitudes testing the belief advanced. Much in this theory is important and right and still with us: the Beatles have learned a great deal from Mr Brooks. But in the contemporary unrest, a defense of poetry is needed that will stress once more Shelley's intuition that poets are unacknowledged legislators – unacknowledged, probably, because they talk imperatively to the whole of the human condition, not to a special element in it. So I begin with my real topic: the politics of poetry.

Purely ideological poetry lives and dies with the emotion, or social condition, that produced it. No one remembers now Don West's 'Southern Lullaby', a protest ballad of the 1930s:

> Eat little baby, eat well,
> A Bolshevik you'll be
> And hate this bosses' hell
> Sucking it in from me.
> Hate, little baby, hate deep.[1]

We can make up our own 1960s 'Northern Lullaby': 'Burn, baby, burn, / A militant you'll be', etc. This has nothing to do with great art, and yet great art has something to do with it. A first step toward understanding the relation of poetry and politics is to understand the interdependence of great art and popular art. I am reminded of a bad witticism in an experimental movie, where one character says to another: 'Go to Art, and tell him Pop sent you.' The consciousness that even highbrow art has a pop or folk basis arises strongly with the Romantics. Keats felt a double allegiance which marks all the greater poets of his period: 'Let us have the old poets, AND Robin Hood.' It's like saying today, let us have Eliot, Yeats, Stevens, AND Joan Baez. Wordsworth felt that Bishop Percy's *Reliques of Ancient English Poetry*, two small volumes of popular ballads and songs mainly from the sixteenth and seventeenth centuries, had 'absolutely redeemed the course of English poetry'. In Wordsworth's day, popular tales, political satire, and versified scandal about contemporary events still circulated in the form of broadsides hawked about on London streets. The streets themselves were a political cabaret. The older poets, too, the poets of the English Renaissance, were obviously in touch with popular sources – with legends, superstitions, romances. Chaucer is the first and clearest example; Shakespeare comes next. Even in Spenser and Milton popular elements remain: they are trying for a new type of sublimity, but it remains a vernacular sublime.

Yeats is concerned with the popular sources of art from the beginning of his career. He was an Irishman who used Celtic legend as a kind of public dream world. He did not want to be 'alone amid the obscure impressions of the senses' but sought a 'symbolic language reaching far into the past and associated with familiar names and conspicuous hills'. Chaucer, he once said, saved his imagination from abstraction. And in a late poem he counts himself among the Romantics because of this respect for traditions, learned or popular:

> We were the last romantics – chose for theme
> Traditional sanctity and loveliness;
> Whatever's written in what poets name
> The book of the people.

> ['Coole Park and Ballylee']

'The book of the people' – yet Yeats's poetry is far from plebeian. Though he uses simple forms and the ballad refrain as much as possible, his view of O'Leary and other Irish militants is not that of pure admiration. 'September 1913' is a ballad that begins by exalting

O'Leary and questioning, now that he's dead, the ability of the present generation to achieve his greatness of soul. But since poetry, as Yeats once said, comes out of a quarrel with oneself, as the ballad goes on it questions, almost despite its author, the noble dead. 'What, God help us, could they save?' (st. 2), 'that *delirium* of the brave' (st. 3, my italics). And the last verses suggest that it was delirium indeed, not a magnanimous passion for *rem publicam* but a carelessness for their own lives growing out of frustrated love: 'Some woman's yellow hair / Has maddened every mother's son.' In Romantic Ireland, private and public passions interacted. Personal frustrations became political ambitions. Yeats questions the motive of these Irish heroes, but not what the refrain insists on: 'Romantic Ireland's dead and gone.'

In 'Easter 1916' the eight line stanza with refrain becomes a more reflective sixteen- or twenty-four-line stanza. Yeats's questioning is now intense and complicated and almost purely a self-questioning – in 'September 1913' it had been a questioning of others. What has changed in the poet? He now acknowledges that Romantic Ireland is not dead, indeed that a new and terrible Romanticism is born. Terrible not only because associated with rebellion, violence, and death, but because Yeats fears to acknowledge it as an exemplary ethos, as a way of conducting one's life. His attitude had been that politics narrow the soul; politics are not magnanimous and magnanimity is all. He recurs to that thought anxiously in each succeeding stanza: this woman's voice grew shrill, that man was merely vainglorious, and all these 'Hearts with one purpose alone . . . Enchanted to a stone' sinned, by the obsessiveness of their purpose, against nature. Hatred, after love, fixed their heart. But if one passion, one idea, was like a stone in their heart, their example is now a stone in the poet's heart. His mind seems to have less room, in the way it turns around, in the way it worries and subtly repeats itself, than in the eight-line stanza of the previous ballad. Even though the upshot of the failed rebellion was simply to make us 'know their dream', it is a dream that weighs on us and cannot be shaken off. 'In dreams begin responsibilities', as he once said.

Around this time Yeats's whole attitude towards his own imagination changes. He elicits from it 'daemonic images' and tries to read them. This is clear in poems like 'The Second Coming' and 'Leda and the Swan'. He accepts, in other words, the romantic belief that the individual mind is in prophetic touch with the movement of history. The dream that sparked the Easter rebellion cannot be dismissed by criticising its aim or the mixed motives of those who participated in it: the 'terrible beauty' born of the dream announces a new era which he tries to face in 'A Prayer for my Daughter' (1919). In this poem there are intimations of the 'blood-dimmed tide' that will drown the 'ceremony of innocence' he evokes at the end. A storm comes, like an omen of the future, out of the 'murderous innocence' of the sea – where 'murderous innocence' suggests both the impersonality of fate, of historical evolution, and the 'terrible beauty' of historical revolution, its Dionysian element, the purging of private emotions in the suffering, communion and greatness of collective action. Yet in a new type of eight-line stanza which will inform some of his best poems, Yeats reasserts his older ideal of magnanimity, which excludes intellectual hatred and soul-narrowing politics. He prays in a sense against his own imagination, and what he prays for is that his daughter should be out of phase with history and able to preserve an older order. Her birth and the natural hopes it arouses are set movingly and precariously against that other, revolutionary, birth of terrible beauty:

> How but in custom and in ceremony
> Are innocence and beauty born?
> Ceremony's a name for the rich horn,
> And custom for the spreading laurel tree.

Thus Yeats is gradually forced to contrast the book of his mind with the book of the people. The masterful images of the latter no longer jibe with the demonic images of the former. The courteous romanticism of Spenser (that famous Irishman!) is not the terrible romanticism of MacDonagh, MacBride, Connolly, and Pearse, whom he formally names at the end of 'Easter, 1916' – though their names, inserted in this way, remain proper nouns, casual and idiosyncratic, instead of permanent and symbolic through long association:

> I write it out in a verse –
> MacDonagh and MacBride
> And Connolly and Pearse
> Now and in time to be,
> Wherever green is worn,
> Are changed, changed utterly:
> A terrible beauty is born.

In Wordsworth there are no glittering emblems and only a few masterful images. The poet does not begin with a symbol – that is to say, an event or myth from the 'book of the people' – but with an ordinary sight, a daily thing that seems to have no connection with the march of history or politics. This ordinary sight grows on the poet's consciousness until it attains an almost visionary intensity:

> The little hedgerow birds,
> That peck along the road, regard him not.
> He travels on, and in his face, his step,
> His gait, is one expression: every limb,
> His look and bending figure, all bespeak
> A man who does not move with pain, but moves
> With thought. – He is insensibly subdued
> To settled quiet: he is one by whom
> All effort seems forgotten; one to whom
> Long patience hath such mild composure given,
> That patience now doth seem a thing of which
> He hath no need. He is by nature led
> To peace so perfect that the young behold
> With envy, what the Old Man hardly feels.
> – I asked him whither he was bound, and what
> The object of his journey; he replied
> 'Sir! I am going many miles to take
> A last leave of my son, a mariner,
> Who from a sea-fight has been brought to Falmouth,
> And there is dying in an hospital. –'

> ['Old Man Travelling']

Though we are not given – as in Yeats – the poet's inner discourse, the poet in the act of questioning the strong image or event, we feel his mind turning around, puzzling, reflecting on the experience. The more intensely Wordsworth thinks, the more the Old Man grows on his imagination: thought increases, instead of resolving, a mystery. Is the strange patience of this man a sign of animal vigor or of religious faith? Does it express deeply working sources of life or mere feebleness and animal persistence in that feebleness? Here is someone moving his slow thighs toward a strange, if ordinary, destination.

In the first part of the poem (the first 14 lines) this destination seems to be nature – the Old Man is journeying back to the source. He moves so slowly, he is so much part of the landscape, that even the hedgerow birds regard him not. But the second part of the poem shows that his destination lies elsewhere. The patient, organic development suggested to us by his tranquility opens, with those four concluding lines of simple yet stately speech, into the opposite image of early and unnatural death, of a life cut off before maturation – one might almost say, naturation.

This quiet contrast, this inversion of the natural order of things (one could expect the young man to be traveling to the old man's death bed), is heightened to the point of visionary fear when we realise that all intermediate stages between the longevity of the old man and the premature death of his son have dropped out. A leap forward is suggested, as if Wordsworth's era, the era of the French Revolution and of the Napoleonic wars of which the son dying at Falmouth is a victim, were moving history along at so fast a pace it had become unnatural. We are again, as in Yeats, caught between two worlds, or standing at a fatal crossroads in the development of humanity: while the old order (essentially agrarian, slow-changing, in tune with nature) is dying, the new moves in so fast that nothing seems to be able to grow, to have the proper time for development. 'A multitude of causes unknown to former times', writes Wordsworth in the preface to *Lyrical Ballads* (1800), 'are now acting . . . to blunt the discriminating powers of the mind. . . . The most effective of these causes are the great national events which are daily taking place [war with France], and the increasing accumulation of men in cities [the Industrial Revolution], where the uniformity of their occupations produces a craving for extraordinary incident, which the rapid communication of intelligence [journalism] hourly gratifies.' To counteract this 'degrading thirst after outrageous stimulation', Wordsworth wrote his *lyrical* ballads. 'Old Man Travelling' shows how a poet can penetrate the crisis of his time without bold symbols or violent poetic effects.

With Robert Lowell we are back not only in the realm of direct political poetry but also that of masterful images:

> The old South Boston Aquarium stands
> in a Sahara of snow now. Its broken windows are boarded.
> The bronze weathervane cod has lost half its scales.
> The airy tanks are dry.
>
> Once my nose crawled like a snail on the glass;
> my hand tingled
> to burst the bubbles
> drifting from the noses of the cowed, compliant fish.
>
> My hand draws back. I often sigh still
> for the dark downward and vegetating kingdom
> of the fish and reptile. One morning last March,
> I pressed against the new barbed and galvanized
>
> fence on the Boston Common. Behind their cage,
> yellow dinosaur steamshovels were grunting
> as they cropped up tons of mush and grass
> to gouge their underworld garage.

['For the Union Dead']

There is something strange, however, as well as strong about these images. Like a dream we cannot quite follow, but in which every sight is overcharged, the continuity of Lowell's poem is casual to the point of discontinuity, as each stanza flashes an aggressive picture onto the screen of the mind. This forces us to question the character of the organising consciousness: what kind of a mind must one have to see like this? While in Wordsworth we hardly feel contrasts, here they become crass juxtaposition: the 'service' mentioned in the epigraph ('Relinquunt Omnia Servare Rem Publicam') and the 'servility' of the last stanza ('a savage servility / slides by on grease'); the Boston Aquarium in a Sahara of snow (st. 1); the fish in the air (st. 1); the air in the tanks (st. 1); the bubbles rising from the fish (st. 2) and the drained faces of negro children rising like balloons; bubbles and Colonel Shaw on his bubble; the nose-snail of the child and the nose of the fish (st. 2); the child pressing against the glass of the Boston Aquarium (st. 2) and the man Lowell pressing against the fence of Boston Common (sts. 3, 4). In a pun two meanings try to occupy one word; in this poem all things press ominously to occupy the same place. The personal past, the personal present, the historical past, the historical present, space relations, and time relations – all these come 'nearer', mass like storm clouds on our sight. While each stanza, practically, offers us a new emblem, nothing happens. The last stanza, contrasted with the first, reveals merely another complex apocalyptic emblem, suggesting that the men who think they have mastered nature are really being mastered by it: the waters of the Aquarium have flooded our world without our noticing, and servile nature is secretly in control:

> The Aquarium is gone. Everywhere,
> giant finned cars nose forward like fish;
> a savage servility
> slides by on grease.

What kind of a mind, then, has constructed this curious machine of which all the parts are visionary, yet which moves so elusively? We have called Lowell's images emblems, but they are clearly infected by the crudity of pop art and are more like cartoons or topsy-turvy, promiscuous advertisements: the Mosler Safe advertises the atom bomb (or vice versa); Colonel Shaw (in the penultimate stanza) rides on his bubble, like Superman or Colonel Glenn. The poet's mind cannot escape the infection of the age, and perhaps that is the point. Lowell's poem intensifies our sense of inverted values, disorder, and crisis. It expresses the situated individual who confronts all this not only out there but also in himself. This makes all the poets chosen here intensely modern. Though Lowell is closest to Yeats in the way he elicits yet draws back from ominous images, Wordsworth too is forced to face the problem of the prophetic mind, of the darkness which it senses, from which it draws back (like Lowell's hand in st. 3), yet which it must meet in some way. In this natural, daily facing of omens, the reflective mind can have no outside aid: no other force than mind defends the mind against itself.

It is a virtue of Stevens's 'The Snowman' to catch consciousness in the act, to depict by one exemplary movement (which is the poem) this defense against overthink, against our relentless mental pollution of nature. I use the word *pollution* advisedly. What Lowell needs more than anything is the perspective of the snowman:

> One must have a mind of winter
> To regard the frost and the boughs
> Of the pinetrees crusted with snow;
>
> And have been cold a long time
> To behold the junipers shagged with ice,
> The spruces rough in the distant glitter
>
> Of the January sun; and not to think
> Of any misery in the sound of the wind,
> In the sound of a few leaves,
>
> Which is the sound of the land
> Full of the same wind
> That is blowing in the same bare place
>
> For the listener, who listens in the snow,
> And, nothing himself, beholds
> Nothing that is not there and the nothing that is.

The hygiene, the cleansing power of this wintery mind is clear, whether or not we understand the poem. Steven's poetry is, in fact, so difficult to understand because our mind is not wintery enough. It tends to be too spiritual, or too fictional, or simply eager for thought. The surface and subject matter of 'The Snowman' are so slippery that mind cannot take hold: the poem consists of one propositional sentence that, in fulfilling itself, also cancels itself out. Complete in line 7 (at the semicolon), the proposition ironically does not suffice the mind which proposed it and which now, running on, begins to defend itself against the very idea of ideas by a 'structured and mounting negation' (Sigurd Burkhardt). This kind of poetry does not wish to become thought or afterthought. It is happy to be 'the cry of its occasion', something heard, or at best something that cleanses the doors of the senses.

'The great poems of heaven and hell have been written', said Stevens, 'the great poem of the earth remains to be written.' His poetry, like Wordsworth's, is prelusive of that unwritten epic. The earth is all before him. He writes of ordinary evenings and dawns, of seasons and weathers, of sun and snow.

> How clean the sun when seen in its idea
> Washed in the remotest cleanliness of a heaven
> That has expelled us and our images.
>
> ['Notes toward a Supreme Fiction']

To see winter, one must have a mind of winter; to see the sun one must have a sunny mind. But if we pollute our environment by 'meanings', by pathetic fictions, we see merely ourselves in nature when our real desire is to see nature. Stevens asks us, therefore, to reverse ourselves and become what we see instead of seeing what we are. Since we have remade nature in our image – and behold, it is not good – now the link between us and the earth should no longer be balanced in our favor, even imaginatively. Unless we stop occupying nature with our ideas and anxieties we shall be in the dilemma . . . expressed by Theodor Adorno. 'I cannot look at nature', said Adorno, 'I cannot look at the shadow of trees without the shadow of Buchenwald interposing.' The woods of Arcady are dead indeed. What man has made of man and what man has made of nature are intimately joined, yet through the politics of poetry we may still open a chink in this claustrophobic mind and see 'Nothing that is not there and the nothing that is'. To quote Stevens a last time:

> You must become an ignorant man again
> And see the sun again with an ignorant eye
> And see it clearly in the idea of it.
>
> ['Notes towards a Supreme Fiction']

SOURCE: essay in *Beyond Formalism: Literary Essays, 1957–70* (New Haven, Conn., 1970), pp. 247–57.

NOTE

1. Don West's 'Southern Lullaby' is quoted in Cleanth Brooks, *Modern Poetry and the Tradition* (Chapel Hill, N.C., 1939), p. 51.

124

A. E. Dyson   (1972)

. . . I can best illustrate my own feelings about the union of worlds in literature through a reference to the Symbolist phrase, 'All art aspires to the condition of music'. While listening to music, we know beyond argument that the emotional content cannot be paraphrased or transposed. It can, of course, be talked about – but this is discourse of a different kind. We apprehend moments of nostalgia, heroism, exuberance, exquisite tenderness, and can record or discuss these in general terms. But however much Wagner's *Ring* or Mahler's symphonies flood us with such feelings, we value these works chiefly for themselves. If they disappeared from the world, nothing could replace them; something would be missing beyond recall. The component feelings would still exist, and so would other splendid embodiments, but a most valued experience would be no more. The clarinet entry in the slow movement of Brahms's Second Piano Concerto is irreplaceable. There are other manifestations of piercing beauty, revelatory tenderness, but there is nothing else like that. Music is full of tragic heroism, apocalyptic revelation, but there is only one Immolation of Brünnhilde, only one proclamation of 'Hostias' in Verdi's Requiem, only one Beethoven Ninth.

On such matters there can be no argument, and certainly none that jumps back from art to 'life'. We value music, great paintings, King's College Chapel, not only for the beauty and life inherent in them but, more particularly, for what they are. They may convey sharply to us other fine experiences, but the experience we value most is themselves. In this, they are as irreplaceable as people, and as unique in their power to move us to love.

It is a disadvantage, peculiar among the arts to literature, that this supreme and prime truth so often gets lost. We can fall into the error of assuming that a poem or novel is important only as one among many expressions of, or pieces of evidence from, 'life', and not at all or only very marginally for itself. Literature can be mistaken for raw material of history or sociology, so that those who love it – the real students of literature – might even find themselves abused for their pains. To assert that *Death in Venice* is a unique and precious masterpiece is to risk being accused of 'aestheticism' in some disabling sense. But this is not a mistake that could be made about anyone who claimed in this manner to value Bach's Mass or the 'Mona Lisa', which are instantly seen to be perfect and durable in themselves. We may value them in part for the new things they show us about the Christian Mass or about a certain kind of face smiling, but clearly we do not value them simply for this.

For this reason, my approach to art is essentially formalist, and it is the forms themselves that I value most. Because works of art incarnate and yet also transform their creator's consciousness, they are among life's ends as well as its means. In this sense they are symbols of humanity, and symbols which may influence our philosophy, and indeed our religion itself. . . .

. . . The artists do indeed achieve what they covet: aiming at beauty, they create beauty; aiming at order, they create artefacts wonderfully balanced and controlled. Since such works of art unite the soul of man with the world outside him, they are more substantial than mere fictions, or mere lies. They exist as symbols, apart from their makers; they belong, with nature itself, in the world outside.

The world of art is not spun out of a man as a spider's web is spun; it is not merely a report from the prison house. The soul of man is joined with the soul of form outside himself; and the transmutations of structure tug towards, not away from, truth. I agree with Coleridge in believing that successful works of art incarnate the human mind and spirit much as Nature incarnates the Mind and Spirit of God.

The essential aspect is that all revelation is enigmatic; there can be no simple union of the timeless with time. We live in a universe which bombards us with impressions, the most powerful and compelling of which are beauty, goodness and truth. These intimations reach us in a darkened form, in union with transience and suffering, and we move as strangers and pilgrims through their path. Always the spiritual qualities co-exist with mutability and enigma – not only in the world of nature, and of human creation, but in the supreme revelation in the Word. For a Christian, this is the quintessence of Incarnation, that God is really, if mysteriously, revealed in mortal flesh. The world of nature falls into place as lesser revelation; the world of art as the distinctive contribution of man. . . .

When the soul of man quickens to creation, it produces symbols: authentic and durable intimations of truth. . . .

SOURCE: extracts from *Between Two Worlds: Aspects of Literary Form* (London, 1972), pp. 10–12, 151, 152.

Richard Ellmann　　(1976)

[Ellmann is discussing the work and influence of Eliot, Frost, Pound, Stevens and Williams.] . . . At first the influence of Eliot was by far the strongest. The gloom of *The Waste Land* could be recognised in every language, and for years the latest poem in Urdu or Swahili or Japanese was more likely to resemble that poem than to resemble previous poems written in those languages. But if young poets began by imitating Eliot, their next task was not to imitate him, to avoid his cadences and to see life without his spectacles. Poets like Hart Crane labored splendidly to free themselves. As for Pound, his influence was at first more personal than poetic. A generous man outside of politics, he aided a great many other writers to find themselves and then to find publishers. Only gradually did his influence, and that of Williams, prove to be more helpful guides for the young than that of Eliot.

In view of Eliot's decision to be naturalised a British subject and to be received in the Anglican Church, his status as American poet may seem jeopardised. Still, some claim to him may be made by the land where he was born and spent his first twenty-four years, especially since his later poetry draws heavily upon the Mississippi River and the Dry Salvages off Cape Ann just as his early poetry is often set in Boston. (W. H. Auden, though he became an American citizen as Eliot a British one, seems English to the bone.) More largely, Eliot's break with traditional forms was a much more conspicuous feature of American than of English poets of the time, and the same could be said of his attempt at radical criticism and large-scale synthesis.

These five poets, and several others, lesser perhaps but of exceptional ability, such as Robinson Jeffers, Marianne Moore, John Crowe Ransom, E. E. Cummings, and Hart Crane, were dominant into the fifties and sixties. Stevens died in 1953, Frost and Williams ten years later, Eliot in 1965, and Pound in 1972. New reputations were slow to form in their shadow. Some poets in later generations died before their seniors, several of them by their own hand. It seemed for a time that the great eminences of twentieth-century poetry were to be followed by low-lying plains. But as the century progressed, it became clear that younger poets had found their own recourse.

This began with a suspicion or even distaste for eminences. The immense conceptions of their predecessors seized large truths at the expense of small ones. The presuppositions which had been common about art, about poetry itself, now appeared to be dubiously élitist. The institution of literature was itself called into question. Black poets contended against artifact poems as though they were irremediably associated with white poets, but most white poets, disobligingly, now came to evince a similar bias. There was a sense that the earlier poets of the century had aimed to become modern classics, and in so doing had lost touch with the immediate and the unkempt, with the authentic and the imperfect, with the contemporary pungency.

The labels which many recent poets have adopted, such as Black Mountain, projectivist, New York, beat, are not likely to survive. Two directions have, however, become conspicuous in much recent poetry. One takes its point of departure from a late change in Eliot's conception of verse. Originally he insisted upon its impersonality, and found the test of a successful work to be the author's skill in finding an objective correlative for feelings. In later life, however, he acknowledged with needless embarrassment and humility that *The Waste Land* was for him only a 'personal and wholly insignificant grouse against life.' It was no longer impersonal, then. In his last work, *Four Quartets*, he wished to be understood as speaking in his own voice. Ezra Pound's *Cantos* went through a similar development, the earlier ones held away from the poet, the later ones sporadically autobiographical: 'From the wreckage of Europe ego scriptor.' The possibility of a more explicit autobiographical poetry, verging sometimes on confession, has attracted many recent poets. Robert Lowell's *Life Studies* in 1959, sacrificing many of the elaborations of his early verse for the sake of candor, marked a turn. But a similar development occurred in Berryman, Merwin, and others. If Allen Ginsberg was attempting to outconfess confession, in the service of new forms of ecstatic realisation, these other poets had also their motives beyond autobiography. Sylvia Plath gathers the world into her account of private incidents and feelings. If Eliot and Pound were covertly autobiographical when they pretended not to be, their more autobiographical descendants were covertly archetypal, as if the universe were confessing through them.

Another and almost opposite emphasis in much contemporary verse might be seen as a development from Pound and Williams, though averse to acknowledge the derivation. These poets mostly shun personality as egoistic, and seem concerned to extend the boundaries of verse by incorporating a surrealist strangeness into the familiar. Pound had spoken of a 'consciousness disjunct,' but Pound was not greatly interested in the unconscious or in the disjunctiveness between it and the conscious mind. For some poets this unconscious is rather the archaic survivals into the present: Olson justifies considering the geological remains that form Gloucester, as Snyder sees the temper of Oxford and Cambridge in terms of the strata that underlie them. Other poets, such as Denise Levertov, seek out the 'authentic' in the casual, or like Robert Duncan, the magical in the natural, and move toward a secular mysticism. Poets such as Robert Bly and John Ashbery find a certain logic, or at least a concord of discords, in disconnected or uncanny images. And of course there are excellent poets who successfully resist even these general classifications.

SOURCE: extract from the Introduction to *The New Oxford Book of American Verse* (London, 1976), pp. *xxvii–xxx*.

PART TWO

The Poet as Critic & Artist

1. KEY STATEMENTS, 1860–1920

Richard Wagner (1860)

. . . The influence of the two leading German poets, Goethe and Schiller, peculiar, new and unprecedented as it was in art-history, shows itself in this – that now for the first time this problem of an ideal, purely human art-form in its fullest meaning became the object of investigation; and the search for this form was almost the most important element of their labours. Rebelling against the force of that method of expression that still passed for a law among the Latin nations, they succeeded . . . in going back from it to the origin of all European art-form – the Greek. . . .

In order to gain a proper conception of [the] part to be taken by the poet – a part so important for the influence of the whole; in order to conceive of it as a voluntary one, and as wished for by the poet himself, I considered first of all those repeated and earnestly expressed hopes and wishes of great poets, such as I have already mentioned, to see in the opera an ideal branch of art. I sought to explain to myself the motive of this wish, and thought I found it in that natural desire of the poet, which decides him, in conception as well as in form, to use language, the materialisation of abstract ideas, in such a way as to work immediately upon the feelings themselves. As this tendency is a controlling one even in the *invention* of the poetic subject, and only that life-picture of humanity is called poetic in which all motives attributable to abstract reason disappear in favor of the representation of motives of pure human feeling, so it is also the only criterion for the *form* and *expression* of the poetic recital. The poet seeks, in his language, to make the abstract, conventional meaning of words subordinate to their original, sensible one; and to secure, by rhythmic order, as well as by the almost musical dressing of words in versification, an effect for his phraseology which shall gain possession of and influence the feelings as though by enchantment.

In this course of the poet, so necessary to his very nature, we see him finally come to the limits of his branch of art, where it already seems to touch music; and thus the most successful work of the poet must be, for us, that which should be, in its perfection, entirely musical. . . .

Beethoven received the rich and promising heritage of both these masters [sc. Goethe and Schiller – Ed.]. He developed the symphonic form to such a comprehensive breadth, and filled it with contents of such unprecedentedly various and ravishing melody, that we stand to-day before the symphony of Beethoven as before the stone that marks the boundary of an entirely new period in the general history of art; for in it there came into the world a phenomenon, nothing even approaching which is to be found in the art of any age or any nation.

For in this symphony there is spoken by musical instruments a language of which no one in any preceding age had any knowledge, inasmuch as the pure musical expression in it enchains the hearer with a lasting effect hitherto unknown, in the most inconceivably varied shades of tone, and moves his inmost nature with a strength unattainable by any other art; revealing to him in its variety so free and audacious a regularity, that it must seem to us more powerful than all logical sequence, yet without in the least containing in itself the laws of logic. Indeed, that purely logical mental process which followed the guidance of cause and effect, finds nothing here to cling to. The symphony must needs appear to us a revelation from another world; and in very truth it does discover to us a connection between the phenomena of existence, which differs entirely from the ordinary logical *nexus*, and in regard to which one thing is undeniable – that it forces itself upon us in the most overwhelmingly convincing manner, and takes possession of our feelings with such positiveness that the reasoning faculty is entirely confused and disarmed by it.

The metaphysical necessity for the discovery of this entirely new power of language precisely in our own age, seems to me to lie in the increasingly conventional development of modern tongues. If we look more closely at the development of these languages, we shall find in the so-called roots of words an origin which shows us distinctly how in its first beginning the formation of the *idea* from the *thing*, was almost entirely coincident with the subjective conception with regard to the latter; and the assumption that the first language of mankind must have had a great resemblance to singing, need not perhaps appear ridiculous.

Human speech certainly developed from a purely sensuous, subjectively-felt signification of words, into a more abstract sense, in such a way that at length these words had only a conventional meaning left, which deprived the feelings of all part in the understanding of them, and made their very connection and construction entirely dependent on certain rules that could be learned. Conventionality developed in language, in necessary accord with the moral development of the race; a conventionality whose laws were no longer comprehensible to the purely natural feelings, but were incorporated in rules of education intelligible only to the reflective powers. And since the modern European languages, further divided into different classes, began to follow their purely conventional development with an increasingly obvious tendency, music has developed, on the other hand, into a hitherto unknown capability of expression. . . .

SOURCE: extracts from 'The Music of the Future' (1860), reproduced in *Art, Life and Theories of Richard Wagner*, trans. Edward L. Burlingham (2nd edn, New York, 1889), reprinted in R. Ellmann and C. Feidelson Jnr, *The Modern Tradition* (New York, 1965), pp. 104–6.

Charles Baudelaire   (1861)

. . . There is another heresy, an error which has a more persistent life: I mean the heresy of didacticism, with its inevitable corollaries, the heresies of passion, truth and morality. Most people assume that the object of poetry is some kind of teaching, that it must now fortify conscience, now perfect manners, now, in sum, demonstrate something useful. Poetry, however little one descends into oneself, interrogates one's soul, recalls one's memories of enthusiasm, has no object but itself: it can have no other, and no poem will be so great, so noble, so truly worthy of the name of poem as that which has been written solely for the pleasure of writing a poem.

I do not mean that poetry may not ennoble manners – let this be understood – or that its final result may not be to raise men above the level of common interests; that would be an obvious absurdity. I say that if the poet has pursued a moral end, he has diminished his poetical power; and it is not risky to bet that his work will be poor. Poetry cannot, on pain of death or dethronement, be assimilated into science or morality; it does not have truth for its objects, but only itself. The means of demonstrating truths are altogether different. Truth has nothing to do with songs. Everything that makes a song charming, gracious, irresistible, would steal from truth its authority and power. Cold, calm, and impassive, the spirit of demonstration rebuffs the Muse's diamonds and flowers, and so is the exact contrary of the poetical temper.

Pure intellect aims at truth, taste discloses beauty to us, and the moral sense teaches us duty. It is true that the mean has connections with both extremes, and is separated from the moral sense by only a slight difference which Aristotle has not hesitated to number among the several virtues of its delicate operations. Moreover, what particularly exasperates the man of taste in the spectacle of vice is its deformity, its disproportion. Vice strikes a blow against the right and true, and revolts the intellect and conscience; but as an outrage to harmony, as a dissonance, it will especially offend certain poetical natures; and I do not think it would be scandalising to consider every infraction of morality, of moral beauty, as an offence against universal rhythm and prosody.

This is the admirable, immortal instinct of beauty which makes us consider the earth and its sights as a glimpse of heaven, a correspondence with it. The unquenchable thirst for everything that is beyond and everything that life reveals, is the most living proof of our immortality. It is at once through poetry and *across* poetry, through music and *across* music, that the soul catches a glimpse of the splendours situated beyond the tomb; and when an exquisite poem brings tears to the eyelids, these tears are not proof of an excess of joy, but witness rather of a roused melancholy, of nervous strain, of a nature, exiled in the imperfect, which would like to take possession at once, on this very earth, of a heaven that has been made manifest.

So the first principle of poetry is, strictly and simply, the human aspiration towards a superior beauty, and the principle declares itself in an enthusiasm, a carrying off of the soul; enthusiasm quite independent of passion, which is the heart's drunkenness, and of truth, which is the reason's pasture. For passion is a natural thing, too natural not to introduce a marring, discordant tone into the domain of pure beauty; too intimate and too violent not to scandalise the pure desires, gracious melancholies, and noble despairs which dwell in the supernatural regions of poetry. . . .

SOURCE: extract from 'Théophile Gautier' (1861), included in *L'Art romantique* (1868); reproduced in *Oeuvres complètes*, ed. Jacques Crépet (Paris, 1925), III, pp. 157–60; English trans. in Ellmann and Feidelson, op. cit., pp. 101–2.

Stéphane Mallarmé   (1895)

. . . Language, in the hands of the mob, leads to the same facility and directness as does money. But, in the Poet's hands, it is turned, above all, to dream and song; and, by the constituent virtue and necessity of an art which lives on fiction, it achieves its full efficacy.

Out of a number of words, poetry fashions a single new word which is total in itself and foreign to the language – a kind of incantation. Thus the desired isolation of language is effected; and chance (which might still have governed these elements, despite their artful and alternating renewal through meaning and sound) is thereby instantly and thoroughly abolished. Then we realise, to our amazement, that we had never truly heard this or that ordinary poetic fragment; and, at the same time, our recollection of the object thus conjured up bathes in a totally new atmosphere. . . .

SOURCE: extract from 'Crisis in Poetry' (1895), included in *Stéphane Mallarmé: Selected Prose Poems, Essays and Letters*, trans. Bradford Cook (Baltimore, Md, 1956) pp. 42–3.

D. H. Lawrence   (1912)

Georgian Poetry is an anthology of verse which has been published during the reign of our present king, George V. It contains one poem of my own, but this fact will not, I hope, preclude my reviewing the book.

This collection is like a big breath taken when we are waking up after a night of oppressive dreams. The nihilists, the intellectual, hopeless people – Ibsen, Flaubert, Thomas Hardy – represent the dream we are waking from. It was a dream of demolition. Nothing was, but was nothing. Everything was taken from us. And now our lungs are full of new air, and our eyes see it is morning, but we have not forgotten the terror of the night. We dreamed we were falling through space into nothingness, and the anguish of it leaves us rather eager.

But we are awake again, our lungs are full of new air, our eyes of morning. The first song is nearly a cry, fear and the pain of remembrance sharpening away the pure music. And that is this book.

The last years have been years of demolition. Because faith and belief were getting pot-bound, and the Temple was made a place to barter sacrifices, therefore faith and belief and the Temple must be broken. This time art fought the battle, rather than science or any new religious faction. And art has been demolishing for us: Nietzsche, the Christian religion as it stood; Hardy, our faith in our own endeavour; Flaubert, our belief in love. Now, for us, it is all smashed, we can see the whole again. We were in prison, peeping at the sky through loop-holes. The great prisoners smashed at the loop-holes, for lying to us. And behold, out of the ruins leaps the whole sky.

It is we who see it and breathe in it for joy. God is there, faith, belief, love, everything. We are drunk with the joy of it, having got away from the fear. In almost every poem in the book comes this note of exultation after fear, the exultation in the vast freedom, the illimitable wealth that we have suddenly got.

> But send desire often forth to scan
> The immense night that is thy greater soul,

says Mr Abercrombie. His deadly sin is Prudence, that will not risk to avail itself of the new freedom. Mr Bottomley exults to find men for ever building religions which yet can never compass all.

> Yet the yielding sky
> Invincible vacancy was there discovered.

Mr Rupert Brooke sees

> every glint
> Posture and jest and thought and tint
> Freed from the mask of transiency,
> Triumphant in eternity,
> Immote, immortal.

and this at Afternoon Tea. Mr John Drinkwater sings:

> We cherish every hour that strays
> Adown the cataract of days:
> We see the clear, untroubled skies,
> We see the glory of the rose –

Mr Wilfrid Wilson Gibson hears the 'terror turned to tenderness', then

> I watched the mother sing to rest
> The baby snuggling on her breast.

And to Mr Masefield:

When men count
Those hours of life that were a bursting fount
Sparkling the dusty heart with living springs,
There seems a world, beyond our earthly things,
Gated by golden moments.

It is all the same – hope, and religious joy. Nothing is really wrong. Every new religion is a waste-product from the last, and every religion stands for us for ever. We love Christianity for what it has brought us, now that we are no longer upon the cross.

The great liberation gives us an overwhelming sene of joy, *joie d'être, joie de vivre*. This sense of exceeding keen relish and appreciation of life makes romance. I think I could say every poem in the book is romantic, tinged with a love of the marvellous, a joy of natural things, as if the poet were a child for the first time on the seashore, finding treasures. 'Best trust the happy moments', says Mr Masefield, who seems nearest to the black dream behind us. There is Mr W. H. Davies's lovely joy, Mr De La Mare's perfect appreciation of life at still moments, Mr Rupert Brooke's brightness, when he 'lived from laugh to laugh', Mr Edmund Beale Sargant's pure, excited happiness in the woodland – it is all the same, keen zest in life found wonderful. In Mr Gordon Bottomley it is the zest of activity, of hurrying, labouring men, or the zest of the utter stillness of long snows. It is a bookful of Romance that has not quite got clear of the terror of realism.

There is no *carpe diem* touch. The joy is sure and fast. It is not the falling rose, but the rose for ever rising to bud and falling to fruit that gives us joy. We have faith in the vastness of life's wealth. We are always rich: rich in buds and in shed blossoms. There is no winter that we fear. Life is like an orange tree, always in leaf and bud, in blossom and fruit.

And we ourselves, in each of us, have everything. Somebody said: 'The Georgian poets are not love poets. The influence of Swinburne has gone.' But I should say the Georgian poets are just ripening to be love poets. Swinburne was no love poet. What are the Georgian poets, nearly all, but just bursting into a thick blaze of being? They are not poets of passion, perhaps, but they are essentially passionate poets. The time to be impersonal has gone. We start from the joy we have in being ourselves, and everything must take colour from that joy. It is the return of the blood, that has been held back, as when the heart's action is arrested by fear. Now the warmth of blood is in everything, quick, healthy, passionate blood. I look at my hands as I write and know they are mine, with red blood running its way, sleuthing out Truth and pursuing it to eternity, and I am full of awe for this flesh and blood that holds this pen. Everything that ever was thought and ever will be thought, lies in this body of mine. This flesh and blood sitting here writing, the great impersonal flesh and blood, greater than me, which I am proud to belong to, contains all the future. What is it but the quick of all growth, the seed of all harvest, this body of mine? And grapes and corn and birds and rocks and visions, all are in my fingers. I am so full of wonder at my own miracle of flesh and blood that I could not contain myself, if I did not remember we are all alive, have all of us living bodies. And that is a joy greater than any dream of immortality in the spirit, to me. It reminds me of Rupert Brooke's moment triumphant in its eternality; and of Michelangelo, who is also the moment triumphant in its eternality; just the opposite from Corot, who is the eternal triumphing over the moment, at the moment, at the very point of sweeping it into the flow.

Of all love poets, we are the love poets. For our religion is loving. To love passionately, but completely, is our one desire.

What is 'The Hare' but a complete love poem, with none of the hackneyed 'But a bitter blossom was born' about it, nor yet the Yeats, 'Never give all the heart'. Love is the greatest of all things, no 'bitter blossom' nor such-like. It is sex-passion, so separated, in which we do not believe. The *Carmen* and *Tosca* sort of passion is not interesting any longer, because it can't progress. Its goal and aim is possession, whereas possession in love is only a means to love. And because passion cannot go beyond possession, the passionate heroes and heroines – Tristans and what-not – must die. We believe in the love that is happy ever after, progressive as life itself.

I worship Christ, I worship Jehovah, I worship Pan, I worship Aphrodite. But I do not worship hands nailed and running with blood upon a cross, nor licentiousness, nor lust. I want them all, all the gods. They are all God. But I must serve in real love. If I take my whole, passionate, spiritual and physical love to the woman who in return loves me, that is how I serve God. And my hymn and my game of joy is my work. All of which I read in the anthology of *Georgian Poetry*.

SOURCE: review of *Georgian Poetry, 1911–1912* (London, 1912), reprinted in *Phoenix* (London, 1936; reprinted 1961), pp. 304–7.

Guillaume Apollinaire   (1913)

... It is the social function of great poets and artists to renew continually the appearance nature has for the eyes of men.

Without poets, without artists, men would soon weary of nature's monotony. The sublime idea men have of the universe would collapse with dizzying speed. The order which we find in nature, and which is only an effect of art, would at once vanish. Everything would break up in chaos. There would be no seasons, no civilisation, no thought, no humanity; even life would give way, and the impotent void would reign everywhere.

Poets and artists plot the characteristics of their epoch, and the future docilely falls in with their desires.

The general form of an Egyptian mummy is in conformity with the figures drawn by Egyptian artists, and yet ancient Egyptians were far from being all alike. They simply conformed to the art of their time. ...

SOURCE: extract from 'On Painting' (1913), reproduced in *Cubist Painters: Aesthetic Meditations*, trans. Lionel Abel (New York, 1944), p. 117.

Ezra Pound   (1913, 1916)

I   A FEW DON'TS BY AN IMAGISTE

An 'Image' is that which presents an intellectual and emotional complex in an instant of time. I use the term 'complex' rather in the technical sense employed by the new psychologists, such as Hart, though we might not agree absolutely in our application.

It is in the presentation of such a 'complex' instantaneously which gives that sense of sudden liberation; that sense of freedom from time limits and space limits; that sense of sudden growth which we experience in the presence of the greatest works of art.

It is better to present one Image in a lifetime than to produce voluminous works.

All this, however, some may consider open to debate. The

immediate necessity is to tabulate A LIST OF DON'TS for those beginning to write verses. But I can not put all of them into Mosaic negative.

To begin with, consider the three rules recorded by Mr Flint, not as dogma – never consider anything as dogma – but as the result of long contemplation, which, even if it is some one else's contemplation, may be worth consideration.

Pay no attention to the criticism of men who have never themselves written a notable work. Consider the discrepancies between the actual writing of the Greek poets and dramatists, and the theories of the Graeco-Roman grammarians, concocted to explain their metres.

Language

Use no superfluous word, no adjective, which does not reveal something.

Don't use such an expression as 'dim land *of peace*'. It dulls the image. It mixes an abstraction with the concrete. It comes from the writer's not realising that the natural object is always the *adequate* symbol.

Go in fear of abstractions. Don't retell in mediocre verse what has already been done in good prose. Don't think any intelligent person is going to be deceived when you try to shirk all the difficulties of the unspeakably difficult art of good prose by chopping your composition into line lengths.

What the expert is tired of today the public will be tired of tomorrow.

Don't imagine that the art of poetry is any simpler than the art of music, or that you can please the expert before you have spent at least as much effort on the art of verse as the average piano teacher spends on the art of music.

Be influenced by as many great artists as you can, but have the decency either to acknowledge the debt outright, or to try to conceal it.

Don't allow 'influence' to mean merely that you mop up the particular decorative vocabulary of some one or two poets whom you happen to admire. A Turkish war correspondent was recently caught red-handed babbling in his despatches of 'dove-grey' hills, or else it was 'pearl-pale', I can not remember.

Use either no ornament or good ornament.

Rhythm and Rhyme

Let the candidate fill hs mind with the finest cadences he can discover, preferably in a foreign language,* so that the meaning of the words

* This is for rhythm; his vocabulary must of course be found in his native tongue.

may be less likely to divert his attention from the movement; e.g. Saxon charms, Hebridean Folk Songs, the verse of Dante, and the lyrics of Shakespeare – if he can dissociate the vocabulary from the cadence. Let him dissect the lyrics of Goethe coldly into their component sound values, syllables long and short, stressed and unstressed, into vowels and consonants.

It is not necessary that a poem should rely on its music, but if it does rely on its music that music must be such as will delight the expert.

Let the neophyte know assonance and alliteration, rhyme immediate and delayed, simple and polyphonic, as a musician would expect to know harmony and counterpoint and all the minutiae of his craft. No time is too great to give to these matters or to any one of them, even if the artist seldom have need of them.

Don't imagine that a thing will 'go' in verse just because it's too dull to go in prose.

Don't be 'viewy' – leave that to the writers of pretty little philosophical essays. Don't be descriptive; remember that the painter can describe a landscape much better than you can, and that he has to know a deal more about it.

When Shakespeare talks of the 'Dawn in russet mantle clad' he presents something which the painter does not present. There is in this line of his nothing that one can call description; he presents.

Consider the way of the scientist rather than the way of an advertising agency for a new soap.

The scientist does not expect to be acclaimed as a great scientist until he has *discovered* something. He begins by learning what has been discovered already. He goes from that point onward. He does not bank on being a charming fellow personally. He does not expect his friends to applaud the results of his freshman class work. Freshmen in poetry are unfortunately not confined to a definite and recognisable class room. They are 'all over the shop'. Is it any wonder 'the public is indifferent to poetry'?

Don't chop your stuff into separate *iambs*. Don't make each line stop dead at the end, and then begin every next line with a heave. Let the beginning of the next line catch the rise of the rhythm wave, unless you want a definite longish pause.

In short, behave as a musician, a good musician, when dealing with that phase of your art which has exact parallels in music. The same laws govern, and you are bound by no others.

Naturally, your rhythmic structure should not destroy the shape of your words, or their natural sound, or their meaning. It is improbable that, at the start, you will be able to get a rhythm-structure strong enough to affect them very much, though you may fall a victim to all sorts of false stopping due to line ends and caesurae.

The musician can rely on pitch and the volume of the orchestra. You can not. The term harmony is misapplied in poetry; it refers to simultaneous sounds of different pitch. There is, however, in the best verse a sort of residue of sound which remains in the ear of the hearer and acts more or less as an organ-base.

A rhyme must have in it some slight element of surprise if it is to give pleasure; it need not be bizarre or curious, but it must be well used if at all.

Vide further Vildrac and Duhamel's notes on rhyme in *Technique Poétique*.

That part of your poetry which strikes upon the imaginative eye of the reader will lose nothing by translation into a foreign tongue; that which appeals to the ear can reach only those who can take it in the original.

Consider the definiteness of Dante's presentation, as compared with Milton's rhetoric. Read as much of Wordsworth as does not seem unutterably dull.

If you want the gist of the matter go to Sappho, Catullus, Villon, Heine when he is in the vein, Gautier when he is not too frigid; or, if you have not the tongues, seek out the leisurely Chaucer. Good prose will do you no harm, and there is good discipline to be had by trying to write it. . . .

SOURCE: extract from article in *Poetry* (March 1913); reproduced in Peter Jones (ed.), *Imagist Poetry* (Harmondsworth, 1972), pp. 130–3.

II 'A VORTEX'

. . . The image is not an idea. It is a radiant node or cluster; it is what I can, and must perforce, call a VORTEX, from which, and through which, and into which, ideas are constantly rushing. In decency one can only call it a VORTEX. And from this necessity came the name 'vorticism'. *Nomina sunt consequentia rerum*, and never was that statement of Aquinas more true than in the case of the vorticist movement. . . .

Note: I am often asked whether there can be a long imagiste or vorticist poem. The Japanese, who evolved the *hokku*, evolved also the Noh plays. In the best 'Noh' the whole play may consist of one image. I mean it is gathered about one image. Its unity consists in one image, enforced by movement and music. I see nothing against a long vorticist poem.

On the other hand, no artist can possibly get a vortex into every poem or picture he does. One would like to do so, but it is beyond one. Certain things seem to demand metrical expression, or expression in a rhythm more agitated than the rhythms acceptable to prose, and these subjects, though they do not contain a vortex, may have some interest, an interest as 'criticism of life' or of art. It is natural to express these things, and a vorticist or imagiste writer may be justified in presenting a certain amount of work which is not vorticism or imagisme, just as he might be justified in printing a purely didactic prose article. Unfinished sketches and drawings have a similar interest; they are trials and attempts toward a vortex. . . .

SOURCE: extracts from essay on 'Vorticism', included in Pound's *Gaudier Brzeska: A Memoir* (1916; rev. edn 1959), pp. 106, 109; reproduced in Ellmann and Feidelson, op. cit., p. 152.

Anonymous   (1915, 1916)

I   'THE ESSENTIALS OF ALL GREAT POETRY'

. . . The poets in this volume do not represent a clique. Several of them are unknown to the others, but they are united by certain common principles, arrived at independently. These principles are not new; they have fallen into desuetude. They are the essentials of all great poetry, indeed of all great literature, and they are simply these:

1. To use the language of common speech, but to employ always the *exact* word, not the nearly-exact, nor the merely decorative word.

2. To create new rhythms – as the expression of new moods – and not to copy old rhythms, which merely echo old moods. We do not insist upon 'free-verse' as the only method of writing poetry. We fight for it as for a principle of liberty. We believe that the individuality of a poet may often be better expressed in free-verse than in conventional forms. In poetry, a new cadence means a new idea.

3. To allow absolute freedom in the choice of subject. It is not good art to write badly about aeroplanes and automobiles; nor is it necessarily bad art to write well about the past. We believe passionately in the artistic value of modern life, but we wish to point

out that there is nothing so uninspiring nor so old-fashioned as an aeroplane in the year 1911.

4. To present an image (hence the name 'Imagist'). We are not a school of painters, but we believe that poetry should render particulars exactly and not deal in vague generalities, however magnificent and sonorous. It is for this reason that we oppose the cosmic poet, who seems to us to shirk the real difficulties of his art.

5. To produce poetry that is hard and clear, never blurred nor indefinite.

6. Finally, most of us believe that concentration is of the very essence of poetry. . . .

II 'FROM POET TO READER'

. . . In the first place, 'Imagism' does not mean merely the presentation of pictures. 'Imagism' refers to the manner of presentation, not to the subject. It means a clear presentation of whatever the author wishes to convey. Now he may wish to convey a mood of indecision, in which case the poem should be indecisive; he may wish to bring before his reader the commonly shifting and changing lights over a landscape, or the varying attitudes of mind of a person under strong emotion, then his poem must shift and change to present this clearly. The 'exact' word does not mean the word which exactly describes the object in itself, it means the 'exact' word which brings the effect of that object before the reader as it presented itself to the poet's mind at the time of writing the poem. Imagists deal but little with similes, although much of their poetry is metaphorical. The reason for this is that, while acknowledging the figure to be an integral part of all poetry, they feel that the constant imposing of one figure upon another in the same poem blurs the central effect.

The great French critic, Rémy de Gourmont, wrote last Summer in *La France* that the Imagists were the descendants of the French *Symbolistes*. In the Preface to his *Livre des Masques* M. de Gourmont has thus described *Symbolisme*: 'Individualism in literature, liberty of art, abandonment of existing forms. . . . The sole excuse which a man can have for writing is to write down himself, to unveil for others the sort of world which mirrors itself in his individual glass. . . . He should create his own aesthetics – and we should admit as many aesthetics as there are original minds, and judge them for what they are and not what they are not.' In this sense the Imagists are descendants of the *Symbolistes*; they are individualists.

The only reason that Imagism has seemed so anarchaic and

strange to English and American reviewers is that their minds do not easily and quickly suggest the steps by which modern art has arrived at its present position. Its immediate prototype cannot be found in English or American literature, we must turn to Europe for it. With Debussy and Stravinsky in music, and Gauguin and Matisse in painting, it should have been evident to every one that art was entering upon an era of change. But music and painting are universal languages, so we have become accustomed to new idioms in them, while we still find it hard to recognise a changed idiom in literature. . . .

SOURCE: extracts from the Prefaces to the 1915 and 1916 issues of *Some Imagist Poets* (published in London and Boston, Mass.); texts reproduced in Peter Jones (ed.), op. cit.: I (1915), p. 135; II (1916), pp. 136–7.

The authorship of these Prefaces (and that of the third and last issue, in 1917) is not specified. The chief mover of *Some Imagist Poets* as anthologies was the American poet Amy Lowell, but her fellow-American Hilda Doolittle and the English poet Richard Aldington were closely involved in the project, and the Prefaces may have been collaborative statements. Ezra Pound, it is certain, had no part in the anthology-project, having distanced himself by 1915 from Amy Lowell's interpretation of the Imagist theory. See Jones, op. cit., 'Introduction', pp. 20–4. [Ed.]

Rainer Maria Rilke   (1920)

Oh, Dear, how many times in my life – and never so much as now – have I told myself that Art, as I conceive it, is a movement contrary to nature. No doubt God never foresaw that any one of us would turn inwards upon himself in this way, which can only be permitted to the Saint because he seeks to besiege his God by attacking him from this unexpected and badly defended quarter. But for the rest of us, whom do we approach when we turn our back on events, on our future even, in order to throw ourselves into the abyss of our being, which would engulf us were it not for the sort of trustfulness that we bring to it, and which seems stronger even than the gravitation of our nature? If the meaning of sacrifice is that the moment of greatest danger coincides with that when one is saved, then certainly nothing resembles sacrifice more than this terrible will to Art. How tenacious it is, how insensate! All that the rest forget in order to make their life possible, we are always bent on discovering, on magnifying even; it is we who are the real awakeners of our monsters, to which we are not hostile enough to become their conquerors; for in a certain sense we are at one with them; it is they, the monsters, that hold the surplus strength which is indispensable to those that must surpass themselves. Unless one assigns to the act of victory a mysterious and far deeper meaning, it is not for us to consider ourselves the tamers of our internal lions. But suddenly we feel ourselves walking beside them, as in a Triumph, without being able to remember the exact moment when this inconceivable reconciliation took place (bridge barely curved that connects the terrible with the tender . . .).

SOURCE: extract from a letter of 1920, reproduced in *Rilke: Letters to Merline*, trans. Violet M. Macdonald (London, 1952), p. 47.

2. THREE MASTERS: A SELECTION OF CRITICISM & COMMENTARY

W. B. Yeats

I

. . . There are some doubters even in the western villages. One woman told me last Christmas that she did not believe either in Hell or in ghosts. Hell was an invention got up by the priests to keep people good; and ghosts would not be permitted, she held, to go 'traipsin' about the earth' at their own free will; 'but there are faeries and little leprechauns, and water horses, and fall angels'. I have met also a man with a Mohawk Indian tattooed upon his arm, who held exactly similar beliefs and disbeliefs. . . . No matter what one doubts, one never doubts the faeries, for, as the man with the Mohawk Indian on his arm said, 'they stand to reason'.   ['Belief and Unbelief', 1893]

. . . A young man . . . had written many poems and painted many mystical designs since we met last, but latterly had neither written nor painted, for his whole heart was set upon making his character vigorous and calm, and the emotional life of the artist was bad for him, he feared. . . . The poetry he resisted was full of his nature and his visions. . . . The poems were all endeavours to capture some high, impalpable mood in a net of obscure images. There were fine passages in all, but these were often embedded in thoughts which have evidently a special value to his mind, but are to other men the counters of an unknown coinage. . . .   ['A Visionary', 1893]

[Yeats is speaking to the queen of the faeries, through a seeress.] I then asked her whether it was true that she and her people carried away mortals, and if so, whether they put in another soul in the place of the one they had taken. 'We change the bodies', was her answer. 'Are any of you ever born into mortal life?' 'Yes.' 'Do I know any who were among your people before birth?' 'You do.' 'Who are they?' 'It would not be lawful for you to know.' I then asked her whether she and her people were not 'dramatisations of our moods'? 'She does not understand', said my friend, 'but says that her people are much like human beings and do most of the things humans do'. I asked her other questions, as to her nature and her purpose in the universe, but only seemed to puzzle her. . . . ['Regina, Regina Pigmeorum, Veni', 1893]

[An old man is speaking to Yeats.] 'I have sought through all my life to find the secret of life. I was not happy in my youth, for I knew that it would pass, and I was not happy in my manhood, for I knew that age was coming; and so I gave myself, in youth and manhood and age, to the search for the Great Secret. I longed for a life whose abundance would fill centuries, I scorned the life of fourscore winters. I would be – no, I *will* be – like the ancient gods of the land.' . . .   ['The Heart of the Spring', 1897]

. . . It may be that in a few years Fable, who changes mortalities to immortalities in her cauldron, will have changed Mary Haynes and Raftery to perfect symbols of the sorrow of beauty and of the magnificence and penury of dreams. . . .   ['Dust Hath Closed Helen's Eyes', 1900]

. . . That night, I awoke lying upon my back and hearing a voice speaking above me and saying, 'No human soul is like any other human soul, and therefore the love of God for any human soul is infinite, for no other soul can satisfy the same need in God'. . . .   ['A Voice', 1902]

. . . We make out of the quarrel with others, rhetoric, but of the quarrel with ourselves, poetry. . . . Nor has any poet I have read of or heard of or met been a sentimentalist. The other self, the anti-self or the antithetical self, as one may choose to name it, comes but to those who are no longer deceived, whose passion is reality. . . .
. . . When life puts away her conjuring tricks one by one, those that deceive us longest may well be the wine cup and the sensual kiss, for our Chambers of Commerce and of Commons have not the divine architecture of the body, nor has their frenzy been ripened by the sun. . . .
. . . It is not permitted to a man who takes up pen or chisel, to seek originality, for passion is his only business, and he cannot but mould or sing after a new fashion, because no disaster is like another. . . .   ['Anima Hominis', 1917]

SOURCE: excerpts from essays published at various times and collected finally in *Mythologies* (London, and New York, 1959), pp. 7; 11–12; 56; 173; 30; 68; 331, 332, 339.

II

... we must learn that beauty and truth are always justified of themselves, and that their creation is a greater service to our country than writing that compromises either in the seeming service of a cause. ...

... Literature is, to my mind, the great teaching power of the world, the ultimate creator of all values, and it is this, not only in the sacred books whose power everybody acknowledges, but by every movement of imagination in song or story or drama that height of intensity and sincerity has made literature at all. Literature must take the responsibility of its power, and keep all its freedom: it must be like the spirit and like the wind that blows where it listeth; it must claim its right to pierce through every crevice of human nature, and to describe the relation of the soul and the heart to the facts of life and of law, and to describe that relation as it is, not as we would have it be; and in so far as it fails to do this it fails to give us that foundation of understanding and charity for whose lack our moral sense can be but cruelty. ...   [1904]

... Literature is always personal, always one man's vision of the world, one man's experience, and it can only be popular when men are ready to welcome the visions of others. A community that is opinion-ridden, even when those opinions are in themselves noble, is likely to put its creative minds into some sort of prison. ...   [1904]

... It is one of the most inexplicable things about human nature that a writer, with a strange temperament, an Edgar Allen Poe, let us say, made what he is by conditions which never existed before, can create personages and lyric emotions which startle us by being at once bizarre and an image of our own secret thoughts. ...

... Every argument carries us backwards to some religious conception, and in the end the creative energy of men depends upon their believing that they have, within themselves, something immortal and imperishable, and that all else is but an image in a looking-glass. So long as that belief is not a formal thing, a man will create out of a joyful energy, seeking little for any external test of an impulse that may be sacred, and looking for no foundation outside life itself. ...

... art, in its highest moments, is not a deliberate creation, but the creation of intense feeling, of pure life; and every feeling is the child of all past ages and would be different if even a moment had been left out. Indeed, is it not that delight in beauty which tells an artist that he has imagined what may never die, itself but a delight in the permanent yet ever-changing form of life, in her very limbs and lineaments? . . .

. . . We call certain minds creative because they are among the moulders of their nation and they are not made upon its mould, and they resemble one another in this only – they have never been foreknown or fulfilled an expectation. . . .

. . . A feeling for the form of life, for the graciousness of life, for the dignity of life, for the moving limbs of life, for the nobleness of life, for all that cannot be written in codes, has always been among the great gifts of literature to mankind. . . .   [1904]

. . . Art delights in the exception, for it delights in the soul expressing itself according to its own laws and arranging the world about it in its own pattern, as sand strewn upon a drum will change itself into different patterns, according to the notes of music that are sung or played to it. But the average man is average because he has not attained to freedom. Habit, routine, fear of public opinion, fear of punishment here or hereafter, a myriad of things that are 'something other than human life', something less than flame, work their will upon his soul and trundle his body there and there. . . .

. . . The arts are at their greatest when they seek for a life growing always more scornful of everything that it is not itself and passing into its own fulness, as it were, ever more completely as all that is created out of the passing mode of society slips from it; and attaining that fulness, perfectly it may be – and from this is tragic joy and the perfectness of tragedy – when the world itself has slipped away in death. We, who are believers, cannot see reality anywhere but in the soul itself, and seeing it there we cannot do other than rejoice in every energy, whether of gesture, or of action, or of speech, coming out of the personality, the soul's image, even though the very laws of Nature seem as unimportant as did the laws of Rome to Coriolanus when his pride was upon him. Has not the long decline of the arts been but the shadow of declining faith in an unseen reality?

> If the sun and moon should doubt,
> They'd immediately go out.   . . .   [1904]

. . . All good art is extravagant, vehement, impetuous, shaking the dust of time from its feet, as it were, and beating against the walls of the world. . . .

. . . All art is founded upon personal vision, and the greater the art the more surprising the vision; and all bad art is founded upon impersonal types and images, accepted by average men and women out of imaginative poverty and timidity, or the exhaustion that comes from labour. . . .   [1904]

. . . If they are to read poetry at all, if they are to enjoy beautiful rhythm, if they are to get from poetry anything but what it has in common with prose, they must hear it spoken by men who have music in their voices and a learned understanding of its sound. There is no poem so great that a fine speaker cannot make it greater or that a bad ear cannot make it nothing. . . .   [1904]

. . . I desire a mysterious art, always reminding and half-reminding those who understand it of dearly loved things, doing its work by suggestion, not by direct statement, a complexity of rhythm, colour, gesture, not space-pervading like the intellect, but a memory and a prophecy: a mode of drama Shelley and Keats could have used without ceasing to be themselves, for which even Blake in the mood of *The Book of Thel* might not have been too obscure. . . .   [1919]

SOURCE: extracts from *Samhain* (1904), collected in *Explorations* (London, 1962), pp. 107, 117; 115; 144, 151, 152–3, 158–9; 164, 169–70; 193, 194; 212; and extract from 'A People's Theatre' (1919), also collected in *Explorations*, p. 255.

III

. . . When I was a boy in Dublin . . . I thought, so far as I can recollect my thoughts after so many years, that if a powerful and benevolent spirit has shaped the destiny of this world, we can better discover that destiny from the words that have gathered up the heart's desire of the world, than from historical records, or from speculations, wherein the heart withers. Since then I have observed dreams and visions very carefully, and am now certain that the imagination has some way of lighting on the truth that the reason has not, and that its commandments, delivered when the body is still and the reason silent, are the most binding we can ever know. . . .
    . . . It is only by ancient symbols, by symbols that have numberless meanings besides the one or two the writer lays an emphasis upon, or the half-score he knows of, that any highly subjective art can escape from the barrenness and shallowness of a too conscious arrangement,

into the abundance and depth of Nature. . . .   ['The Philosophy of Shelley's Poetry', 1900]

. . . Everything that can be seen, touched, measured, explained, understood, argued over, is to the imaginative artist nothing more than a means, for he belongs to the invisible life, and delivers its ever new and ever ancient revelation. We hear much of his need for the restraints of reason, but the only restraint he can obey is the mysterious instinct that has made him an artist, and that teaches him to discover immortal moods in mortal desires, an undecaying hope in our trivial ambitions, a divine love in sexual passion. . . .   ['The Moods', 1895]

. . . The more a poet rids his verses of heterogeneous knowledge and irrelevant analysis, and purifies his mind with elaborate art, the more does the little ritual of his verse resemble the great ritual of Nature, and become mysterious and inscrutable. He becomes, as all the great mystics have believed, a vessel of the creative power of God; and whether he be a great poet or a small poet, we can praise the poems, which seem to be his, with the extremity of praise that we give this great ritual which is but copies from the same eternal model. . . .   ['The Return of Ulysses', 1896]

. . . Three types of men have made beautiful things. Aristocracies have made beautiful manners, because their place in the world puts them above the fear of life, and the countrymen have made beautiful stories and beliefs, because they have nothing to lose and so do not fear, and the artists have made the rest, because Providence has filled them with recklessness. . . .
     . . . In life courtesy and self-possession, and in the arts style, are the sensible impressions of the free mind, for both arise out of a deliberate shaping of all things, and from never being swept away, whatever the emotion, into confusion or dullness. . . . the nobleness of the arts is the mingling of contraries, the extremity of sorrow, the extremity of joy, perfection of personality, the perfection of its surrender, overflowing turbulent energy, and marmorean stillness; and its red rose opens at the meeting of the two beams of the cross, and at the trysting-place of mortal and immortal, time and eternity. . . .   ['Poetry and Tradition', 1907]

. . . Art bids us touch and taste and hear and see the world, and shrinks from what Blake calls mathematical form, from every abstract thing, from all that is of the brain only, from all that is not a fountain jetting from the entire hopes, memories, and sensations of the body. Its morality is personal, knows little of any general law. . . .   ['Discoveries', 1906]

. . . Only that which does not teach, which does not cry out, which does not persuade, which does not condescend, which does not explain, is irresistible. It is made by men who expressed themselves to the full, and it works through the best minds; whereas the external and picturesque and declamatory writers, that they may create kilts and bagpipes and newspapers and guide-books, leave the best minds empty. . . .   ['J. M. Synge and the Ireland of His Time', 1910]

. . . works of art are always begotten by previous works of art, and every masterpiece becomes the Abraham of a chosen people. When we delight in a spring day there mixes, perhaps, with our personal emotion an emotion Chaucer found in Guillaume de Lorris, who had it from the poetry of Provence; we celebrate our draughty May with an enthusiasm made ripe by more meridian suns; and all our art has its image in the Mass that would lack authority if not descended from savage ceremonies taught amid what perils and by what spirits to naked savages. The old images, the old emotions, awakened again to overwhelming life, like the gods Heine tells of, by the belief and passion of some new soul, are the only masterpieces. . . .   ['Art and Ideas', 1913]

. . . We know that we must at last forsake the world, and we are accustomed in moments of weariness or exaltation to consider a voluntary forsaking; but how can we, who have read so much poetry, seen so many paintings, listened to so much music, where the cry of the flesh and the cry of the soul seems one, forsake it harshly and rudely? . . .   ['Gitanjali', 1912]

[Yeats on his earlier self, in the Rhymers' Club days.] I remember praying that I might get my imagination fixed on life itself, like the imagination of Chaucer. In those days I was a convinced ascetic, yet I envied Dowson his dissipated life. . . .
    [Yeats reflecting on poets more recent than himself.] I think profound philosophy must come from terror. An abyss opens under our feet; inherited convictions, the presuppositions of our thoughts, those Fathers of the Church Lionel Johnson expounded, drop into the abyss. Whether we will or not we must ask the ancient questions: Is there reality anywhere? Is there a God? Is there a Soul? We cry with the Indian Sacred Book: 'They have put a golden stopper into the

neck of the bottle; pull it! Let out reality!' . . .   ['Modern Poetry:
A Broadcast', 1936]

. . . A poet writes always of his personal life, in his finest work out of its
tragedy, whatever it be, remorse, lost love, or mere loneliness; he
never speaks directly as to someone at the breakfast table, there is
always a phantasmagoria. . . .
    . . . I hated and still hate with an ever growing hatred the literature
of the point of view. I wanted, if my ignorance permitted, to get back
to Homer, to those that fed at his table. I wanted to cry as all men
cried, to laugh as all men laugh. . . .
    . . . I planned to write short lyrics or poetic dramas where every
speech would be short or concentrated, knit by dramatic tension. . . .
Then, and in this English poetry has followed my lead, I tried to make
the language of poetry coincide with that of passionate, normal
speech. I wanted to write in whatever language comes most naturally
when we soliloquise, as I do all day long, upon the events of our own
lives or of any life where we can see ourselves for the moment. . . . It
was a long time before I had made a language to my liking. I began to
make it when I discovered some twenty years ago that I must seek, not
as Wordsworth thought, words in common use, but a powerful and
passionate syntax, and a complete coincidence between period and
stanza. Because I need a passionate syntax for passionate subject-
matter'I compel myself to accept those traditional metres that have
developed with the language. Ezra Pound, Turner, Lawrence wrote
admirable free verse: I could not. I would lose myself, become
joyless. . . . If I wrote amid all its accidence, I would be full of
self-contempt because of my egotism and indiscretion, and foresee the
boredom of my reader. I must choose a traditional stanza, even what I
alter must seem traditional. . . .
    . . . I once boasted, copying the phrase from a letter of my father's,
that I would write a poem 'cold and passionate as the
dawn'. . . .   ['A General Introduction to My Work', 1937] *Essays
and Introductions* (1961), pp. 509, 511, 521–2, 523.

. . . I have spent my life in clearing out of poetry every phrase written
for the eye, and bringing back to syntax all that is for the ear
alone. . . . As I altered my syntax I altered my intellect. . . . I had
begun to get rid of everything that is not, whether in lyric or dramatic
poetry, in some sense character in action; a pause in the midst of an
action perhaps, but action always its end and theme. 'Write for the
ear', I thought, so that you may be instantly understood as when actor
or folk singer stands before an audience. I delight in active men,

taking the same delight in soldier and craftsman; I would have poetry turn its back on all that is modish curiosity, psychology – the poetic theme has always been present. I recall an Indian tale: certain men said to the greatest of the sages, 'Who are your Masters?' And he replied, 'The wind and the harlot, the virgin and the child, the lion and the eagle.' . . .   ['An Introduction for My Plays', 1937]

SOURCE: extracts from essays etc. published at various times and collected finally in *Essays and Introductions* (London, 1961), pp. 65, 87; 195; 202; 253, 255; 292–3; 341; 352–3; 392; 492, 502–3; 509, 511, 521–2; 523; 529–30.

IV

. . . But Muses resemble women who creep out at night and give themselves to unknown sailors and return to talk of Chinese porcelain – porcelain is best made, a Japanese critic has said, where the conditions of life are hard – or of the Ninth Symphony – virginity renews itself like the moon – except that the Muses sometimes form in those low haunts their most lasting attachments. . . .

. . . an early conviction of mine, that the creative power of the lyric poet depends upon his accepting some one of the few traditional attitudes, lover, sage, hero, scorner of life. They bring us back to the spiritual norm. . . .

. . . I think if I could be given a month of Antiquity and leave to spend it where I chose, I would spend it in Byzantium a little before Justinian opened St Sophia and closed the Academy of Plato. I think I could find in some little wine-shop some philosophical worker in mosaic who could answer all my questions, the supernatural descending nearer to him than to Plotinus even, for the pride of his delicate skill would make what was an instrument of power to princes and clerics, a murderous madness in the mob, show as a lovely flexible presence like that of a perfect human body.

I think that in early Byzantium, maybe never before or since in recorded history, religious, aesthetic and practical life were one, that architects and artificers – though not, it may be, poets, for language had been the instrument of controversy and must have grown abstract – spoke to the multitude and to the few alike. The painter, the mosaic worker, the worker in gold and silver, the illuminator of sacred books, were almost impersonal, almost perhaps without the consciousness of individual design, absorbed in their subject-matter and that the vision of a whole people. They could copy out of old Gospel books those pictures that seemed as sacred as the text, and yet weave all into a vast design, the work of many that seemed the work of one, that made building, picture, pattern, metal-work of rail and lamp, seem but a single image; and this vision, this proclamation of their invisible master, had the Greek nobility. Satan, always still half-divine, never the horned scarecrow of the didactic Middle Ages. . . .

SOURCE: extracts from the revised edition of *A Vision* (London, 1937), pp. 24, 234, 279–80.

V

. . . I ceased to read modern books that were not books of imagination, and if some philosophic idea interested me, I tried to trace it back to its earliest use, believing that there must be a tradition of belief older than any European Church, and founded on the experience of the world before the modern bias. It was this search for a tradition that urged George Pollexfen and myself to study the visions and thoughts of the countrypeople, and some country conversation, repeated by one or the other, gave us a day's discussion. . . .   ['Hodos Chamelionton', 1922]

. . . I go to the first performance of Alfred Jarry's *Ubu Roi*. . . . Feeling bound to support the most spirited party, we have shouted for the play, but that night . . . I am very sad, for comedy, objectivity, has displayed its growing power once more. I say: 'After Stéphane Mallarmé, after Paul Verlaine, after Gustave Moreau, after Puvis de Chavannes, after all our subtle colour and nervous rhythm, after the faint mixed tints of Condor, what more is possible? After us the Savage God.' . . .   ['The Tragic Generation', 1922]

. . . We artists suffer in our art if we do not love most of all life at peace with itself and doing without forethought what its humanity bids it and therefore happily. We are, as seen from life, an artifice, an emphasis, an uncomplete arc perhaps. Those who it is our business to cherish and celebrate are complete arcs. Because the life man sees is not the final end of things, the moment we attain to greatness of any kind by personal labour and will we become fragmentary, and find no task in active life which can use our finest facilities. We are compelled to think and express and not to do. . . .   ['Estrangement', 1909]

. . . Am I going against nature in my constant attempt to fill my life with work? Is my mind as rich as in idle days? Is not perhaps the poet's labour a mere rejection? If he seeks purity – the ridding of his life of all but poetry – will not inspiration come? Can one reach God by toil? He gives Himself to the pure in heart. He asks nothing but attention. . . .   ['The Death of Synge', 1909]

Source: extracts from *Autobiographies* (revised edition, London, 1955), pp. 265, 348–9, 475, 522.

T. S. Eliot

I

. . . No poet, no artist of any art, has his complete meaning alone. His significance, his appreciation is the appreciation of his relation to the dead poets and artists. You cannot value him alone; you must set him, for contrast and comparison, among the dead. I mean this as a principle of aesthetic, not merely historical, criticism. The necessity that he shall conform, that he shall cohere, is not onesided; what happens when a new work of art is created is something that happens simultaneously to all the works of art which preceded it. The existing monuments form an ideal order among themselves, which is modified by the introduction of the new (the really new) work of art among them. The existing order is complete before the new work arrives; for order to persist after the supervention of novelty, the *whole* existing order must be, if ever so slightly, altered; and so the relations, proportions, values of each work of art toward the whole are readjusted; and this is conformity between the old and the new. Whoever has approved this idea of order, of the form of European, of English literature will not find it preposterous that the past should be altered by the present as much as the present is directed by the past. And the poet who is aware of this will be aware of great difficulties and responsibilities.

In a peculiar sense he will be aware also that he must inevitably be judged by the standards of the past. I say judged, not amputated, by them; not judged to be as good as, or worse or better than, the dead; and certainly not judged by the canons of dead critics. It is a judgment, a comparison, in which two things are measured by each other. To conform merely would be for the new work not really to conform at all; it would not be new, and would therefore not be a work of art. And we do not quite say that the new is more valuable because it fits in; but its fitting in is a test of its value – a test, it is true, which can only be slowly and cautiously applied, for we are none of us infallible judges of conformity. We say: it appears to conform, and is perhaps individual, or it appears individual, and may conform; but we are hardly likely to find that it is one and not the other. . . .   ['Tradition and the Individual Talent', 1919]

. . . The only way of expressing emotion in the form of art is by finding an 'objective correlative'; in other words, a set of objects, a situation, a chain of events which shall be the formula of that *particular* emotion; such that when the external facts, which must terminate in sensory experience, are given, the emotion is immediately invoked. . . .   ['Hamlet', 1919]

. . . It might seem to be intimated . . . that the work of Swinburne can be shown to be a sham, just as bad verse is a sham. It would only be so if you could produce or suggest something that it pretends to be and is not. The world of Swinburne does not depend upon some other world which it simulates; it has the necessary completeness and self-sufficiency for justification and permanence. It is impersonal, and no one else could have made it. The deductions are true to the postulates. It is indestructible. None of the obvious complaints that were or might have been brought to bear upon the first *Poems and Ballads* holds good. The poetry is not morbid, it is not erotic, it is not destructive. These are adjectives which can be applied to the material, the human feelings, which in Swinburne's case do not exist. The morbidity is not of human feeling but of language. Language in a healthy state presents the object, is so close to the object that the two are identified.

They are identified in the verse of Swinburne solely because the object has ceased to exist, because the meaning is merely the hallucination of meaning, because language, uprooted, has adapted itself to an independent life of atmospheric nourishment. In Swinburne, for example, we see the word 'weary' flourishing in this way independent of the particular and actual weariness of flesh or spirit. The bad poet dwells partly in a world of objects and partly in a world of words, and he never can get them to fit. Only a man of genius could dwell so exclusively and consistently among words as Swinburne. His language is not, like the language of bad poetry, dead. It is very much alive, with this singular life of its own. But the language which is more important to us is that which is struggling to digest and express new objects, new groups of objects, new feelings, new aspects, as, for instance, the prose of Mr James Joyce or the earlier Conrad. . . .   ['Swinburne as Poet', 1920]

. . . The difference is not simply a difference of degree between poets. It is something which had happened to the mind of England between the time of Donne or Lord Herbert of Cherbury and the time of Tennyson or Browning; it is the difference between the intellectual poet and the reflective poet. Tennyson and Browning are poets, and they think; but they do not feel their thought as immediately as the odour of a rose. A thought to Donne was an experience; it modified his sensibility. When a poet's mind is perfectly equipped for its work, it is constantly amalgamating disparate experience; the ordinary man's experience is chaotic, irregular, fragmentary. The latter falls in love, or reads Spinoza, and these two experiences have nothing to do with each other, or with the noise of the typewriter or the smell of cooking; in the mind of the poet these experiences are always forming new wholes.

We may express the difference by the following theory: The poets of the seventeenth century, the successors of the dramatists of the sixteenth, possessed a mechanism of sensibility which could devour any kind of experience. They are simple, artificial, difficult, or fantastic, as their predecessors were; no less nor more than Dante, Guido Cavalcanti, Guinicelli, or Cino. In the seventeenth century a dissociation of sensibility set in, from which we have never recovered, and this dissociation, as is natural, was aggravated by the influence of the two most powerful poets of the century, Milton and Dryden. Each of these men performed certain poetic functions so magnificently well that the magnitude of the effect concealed the absence of others. The language went on and in some respects improved; the best verse of Collins, Gray, Johnson, and even Goldsmith satisfies some of our fastidious demands better than that of Donne or Marvell or King. But while the language became more refined, the feeling became more crude. . . .   ['The Metaphysical Poets', 1921]

. . . The story of Ulysses, as told by Dante, reads like a straight-forward piece of romance, a well-told seaman's yarn. . . .

It is worth pointing out again how very right was Dante to introduce among his historical characters at least one character who even to him could hardly have been more than a fiction. For the *Inferno* is relieved from any question of pettiness or arbitrariness in Dante's selection of damned. It reminds us that Hell is not a place but a *state*; that man is damned or blessed in the creatures of his imagination as well as in men who have actually lived; and that Hell, though a state, is a state which can only be thought of, and perhaps only experienced, by the projection of sensory images: and that the resurrection of the body has perhaps a deeper meaning than we understand. But these are such thoughts as come only after many readings; they are not necessary for the first poetic enjoyment.

The experience of a poem is the experience both of a moment and of a lifetime. It is very much like our intenser experiences of other human beings. There is a first, or an early moment which is unique, of shock and surprise, even of terror (*Ego dominus tuus*); a moment which can never be forgotten, but which is never repeated integrally; and yet which would become destitute of significance if it did not survive in a larger whole of experience; which survives inside a deeper and a calmer feeling. The majority of poems one outgrows and outlives, as one outgrows and outlives the majority of human passions: Dante's is one of those which one can only just hope to grow up to at the end of life. . . .   ['Dante', 1929]

. . . It is, in my opinion, in *In Memoriam*, that Tennyson finds full expression. Its technical merit alone is enough to ensure its perpetuity. While Tennyson's technical competence is everywhere masterly and satisfying, *In Memoriam* is the most unapproachable of all his poems. Here are 132 passages, each of several quatrains in the same form, and never monotony or repetition. And the poem has to be comprehended as a whole. We may not memorize a few passages, we cannot find a 'fair sample'; we have to comprehend the whole of a poem which is essentially the length that it is. We may choose to remember:

> Dark house, by which once more I stand
>   Here in the long unlovely street,
>   Doors, where my heart was used to beat
> So quickly, waiting for a hand,
>
> A hand that can be clasp'd no more –
>   Behold me, for I cannot sleep,
>   And like a guilty thing I creep
> At earliest morning to the door.
>
> He is not here; but far away
>   The noise of life begins again,
>   And ghastly thro' the drizzling rain
> On the bald street breaks the blank day.

This is a great poetry, economical of words, a universal emotion related to a particular place; and it gives me the shudder that I fail to get from anything in *Maud*. But such a passage, by itself, is not *In Memoriam*: *In Memoriam* is the whole poem. It is unique: it is a long poem made by putting together lyrics, which have only the unity and continuity of a diary, the concentrated diary of a man confessing himself. It is a diary of which we have to read every word. . . .   ['*In Memoriam*', 1936]

SOURCE: extracts from essays subsequently collected in *Selected Essays* (3rd enlarged edn, London, 1951), pp. 15–16; 145; 327; 287–8; 250–1, 333–4.

II

. . . There is first the probability that this imagery had some personal saturation value, so to speak, for Seneca; another for Chapman, and another for myself, who have borrowed it twice from Chapman. I suggest that what gives it such intensity as it has in each case is its saturation – I will not say with 'associations', for I do not want to revert to Hartley – but with feelings too obscure for the authors even to know quite what they were. And of course only a part of an author's imagery comes from his reading. It comes from the whole of his sensitive life since early childhood. Why, for all of us, out of all that we have heard, seen, felt, in a lifetime, do certain images recur, charged with emotion, rather than others? The song of one bird, the leap of one fish, at a particular place and time, the scent of one flower, an old woman on a German mountain path, six ruffians seen through an open window playing cards at night at a small French railway junction where there was a water-mill: such memories may have symbolic value, but of what we cannot tell, for they come to represent the depths of feeling into which we cannot peer. We might just as well ask why, when we try to recall visually some period in the past, we find in our memory just the few meagre arbitrarily chosen set of snapshots that we do find there, the faded poor souvenirs of passionate moments. . . .

. . . [As to] the question of obscurity: when all exceptions have been made, and after admitting the possible existence of minor 'difficult' poets whose public must always be small, I believe that the poet naturally prefers to write for as large and miscellaneous an audience as possible, and that it is the half-educated and ill-educated, rather than the uneducated, who stand in his way: I myself should like an audience which could neither read nor write. The most useful poetry, socially, would be one which could cut across all the present stratifications of public taste – stratifications which are perhaps a sign of social disintegration. The ideal medium for poetry, to my mind, and the most direct means of social 'usefulness' for poetry, is the theatre. In a play of Shakespeare you get several levels of significance. For the simplest auditors there is the plot, for the more thoughtful the character and conflict of character, for the more literary the words and phrasing, for the more musically sensitive the rhythm, and for auditors of greater sensitiveness and understanding a meaning which reveals itself gradually. And I do not believe that the classification of audience is so clear-cut as this; but rather that the sensitiveness of every auditor is acted upon by all these elements at once, though in different degrees of consciousness. . . .

SOURCE: extracts from *The Use of Poetry and the Use of Criticism* (London, 1933), pp. 147–8; 152–3.

III

. . .

The soul of Man must quicken to creation.
Out of the formless stone, when the artist unites himself with stone,
Spring always new forms of life, from the soul of man that is joined
    to the soul of stone;
Out of the meaningless practical shapes of all that is living or
    lifeless
Joined with the artist's eye, new life, new form, new colour.
Out of the sea of sound the life of music,
Out of the slimy mud of words, out of the sleet and hail of verbal
    imprecisions,
Approximate thoughts and feelings, words that have taken the
    place of thoughts and feelings,
There spring the perfect order of speech, and the beauty of
    incantation.
. . .

SOURCE: extract from Choruses from 'The Rock' (1934): IX, lines 16–24.

IV

. . .

Time present and time past

Are both perhaps contained in time future
And time future contained in time past.
If all time is eternally present
All time is unredeemable.
What might have been is an abstraction
Remaining a perpetual possibility
Only in a world of speculation.
What might have been and what has been
Point to one end, which is always present.
Footfalls echo in the memory
Down the passage which we did not take
Towards the door we never opened
Into the rose-garden. My words echo
Thus, in your mind.
                    But to what purpose
Disturbing the dust on a bowl of rose-leaves
I do not know.
                    Other echoes
Inhabit the garden. Shall we follow?
Quick, said the bird, find them, find them,
Round the corner. Through the first gate,
Into our first world, shall we follow
The deception of the thrush? Into our first world.
There they were, dignified, invisible,
Moving without pressure, over the dead leaves,
In the autumn heat, through the vibrant air,
And the bird called, in response to
The unheard music hidden in the shrubbery,
And the unseen eyebeam crossed, for the roses
Had the look of flowers that are looked at.
There they were as our guests, accepted and accepting.
So we moved, and they, in a formal pattern,
Along the empty alley, into the box circle,
To look down into the drained pool.
Dry the pool, dry concrete, brown edged,
And the pool was filled with water out of sunlight,
And the lotos rose, quietly, quietly,
The surface glittered out of heart of light,
And they were behind us, reflected in the pool.
Then a cloud passed, and the pool was empty.
Go, said the bird, for the leaves were full of children,
Hidden excitedly, containing laughter.
Go, go, go, said the bird: human kind

Cannot bear very much reality.
Time past and time future
What might have been and what has been
Point to one end, which is always present.
. . .

SOURCE: opening section of *Burnt Norton* (1935), subsequently included in *Four Quartets* (London, 1943).

V

. . . I have, in early essays, extolled what I called impersonality in art, and it may seem that, in giving as a reason for the superiority of Yeats's later work the greater expression of personality in it, I am contradicting myself. It may be that I expressed myself badly, or that I had only an adolescent grasp of that idea – as I can never bear to re-read my own prose writings, I am willing to leave the point unsettled – but I think now, at least, that the truth of the matter is as follows. There are two forms of impersonality: that which is natural to the mere skilful craftsman, and that which is more and more achieved by the maturing artist. The first is that of what I have called the 'anthology piece', of a lyric by Lovelace or Suckling, or of Campion, a finer poet than either. The second impersonality is that of the poet who, out of intense and personal experience, is able to express a general truth; retaining all the particularity of his experience, to make of it a general symbol. And the strange thing is that Yeats, having been a great craftsman in the first kind, became a great poet in the second. It is not that he became a different man, for, as I have hinted, one feels sure that the intense experience of youth had been lived through – and indeed, without this early experience he could never have attained anything of the wisdom which appears in his later writing. But he had to wait for a later maturity to find expression of early experience; and this makes him, I think, a unique and especially interesting poet. . . .

There was much also for Yeats to work out of himself, even in technique. To be a younger member of a group of poets, none of them certainly of anything like his stature, but further developed in their limited path, may arrest for a time a man's development of idiom. Then again, the weight of the pre-Raphaelite prestige must have been tremendous. The Yeats of the Celtic twilight – who seems to me to have been more the Yeats of the pre-Raphaelite twilight – uses Celtic folklore almost as William Morris uses Scandinavian folklore. His

longer narrative poems bear the mark of Morris. Indeed, in the
pre-Raphaelite phase, Yeats is by no means the least of the
pre-Raphaelites. I may be mistaken, but the play, *The Shadowy Waters*,
seems to me one of the most perfect expressions of the vague
enchanted beauty of that school: yet it strikes me – this may be an
impertinence on my part – as the western seas descried through the
back window of a house in Kensington, an Irish myth for the
Kelmscott Press; and when I try to visualize the speakers in the play,
they have the great dim, dreamy eyes of the knights and ladies of
Burne-Jones. I think that the phase in which he treated Irish legend in
the manner of Rossetti or Morris is a phase of confusion. He did not
master this legend until he made it a vehicle for his own creation of
character – not, really, until he began to write the *Plays for Dancers*.
The point is, that in becoming more Irish, not in subject-matter but in
expression, he became at the same time universal.

The points that I particularly wish to make about Yeats's
development are two. The first, on which I have already touched, is
that to have accomplished what Yeats did in the middle and later
years is a great and permanent example – which poets-to-come
should study with reverence – of what I have called Character of the
Artist: a kind of moral, as well as intellectual, excellence. The second
point, which follows naturally after what I have said in criticism of the
lack of complete emotional expression in his early work, is that Yeats
is pre-eminently the poet of middle age. By this I am far from meaning
that he is a poet only for middle-aged readers: the attitude towards
him of younger poets who write in English, the world over, is enough
evidence to the contrary. Now, in theory, there is no reason why a
poet's inspiration or material should fail, in middle age or at any time
before senility. For a man who is capable of experience finds himself in
a different world in every decade of his life; as he sees it with different
eyes, the material of his art is continually renewed. But in fact, very
few poets have shown this capacity of adaptation to the years. It
requires, indeed, an exceptional honesty and courage to face the
change. Most men either cling to the experiences of youth, so that
their writing becomes an insincere mimicry of their earlier work, or
they leave their passion behind, and write only from the head, with a
hollow and wasted virtuosity. There is another and even worse
temptation: that of becoming dignified, of becoming public figures
with only a public existence – coat-racks hung with decorations and
distinctions, doing, saying, and even thinking and feeling only what
they believe the public expects of them. Yeats was not that kind of
poet: and it is, perhaps, a reason why young men should find his later
poetry more acceptable than older men easily can. For the young can

see him as a poet who in his work remained in the best sense always young, who even in one sense became young as he aged. But the old, unless they are stirred to something of the honesty with oneself expressed in the poetry, will be shocked by such a revelation of what a man really is and remains. They will refuse to believe that *they* are like that:

> You think it horrible that lust and rage
> Should dance attendance upon my old age;
> They were not such a plague when I was young:
> What else have I to spur me into song?

These lines are very impressive and not very pleasant, and the sentiment has recently been criticized by an English critic whom I generally respect. But I think he misread them. I do not read them as a personal confession of a man who differed from other men, but of a man who was essentially the same as most other men; the only difference is in the greater clarity, honesty and vigour. To what honest man, old enough, can these sentiments be entirely alien? They can be subdued and disciplined by religion, but who can say that they are dead? Only those to whom the maxim of La Rochefoucauld applies: 'Quand les vices nous quittent, nous nous flattons de la créance que c'est nous qui les quittons.' The tragedy of Yeats's epigram is all in the last line. . . .   ['Yeats', 1940]

. . . It may appear strange, that when I profess to be talking about the 'music' of poetry, I put such emphasis upon conversation. But I would remind you, first, that the music of poetry is not something which exists apart from the meaning. Otherwise, we could have poetry of great musical beauty which made no sense, and I have never come across such poetry. The apparent exceptions only show a difference of degree: there are poems in which we are moved by the music and take the sense for granted, just as there are poems in which we attend to the sense and are moved by the music without noticing it. Take an apparently extreme example – the nonsense verse of Edward Lear. His non-sense is not vacuity of sense: it is a parody of sense, and that is the sense of it. *The Jumblies* is a poem of adventure, and of nostalgia for the romance of foreign voyage and exploration; *The Yongy-Bongy Bo* and *The Dong with a Luminous Nose* are poems of unrequited passion – 'blues' in fact. We enjoy the music, which is of a high order, and we enjoy the feeling of irresponsibility towards the sense. Or take a poem of another type, the *Blue Closet* of William Morris. It is a delightful poem, though I cannot explain what it means and I doubt whether the author could have explained it. It has an

effect somewhat like that of a rune or charm, but runes and charms
are very practical formulae designed to produce definite results, such
as getting a cow out of a bog. But its obvious intention (and I think the
author succeeds) is to produce the effect of a dream. It is not
necessary, in order to enjoy the poem, to know what the dream means;
but human beings have an unshakeable belief that dreams mean
something: they used to believe – and many still believe – that dreams
disclose the secrets of the future; the orthodox modern faith is that
they reveal the secrets – or at least the more horrid secrets – of the
past. It is a commonplace to observe that the meaning of a poem may
wholly escape paraphrase. It is not quite so commonplace to observe
that the meaning of a poem may be something larger than its author's
conscious purpose, and something remote from its origins. One of the
more obscure of modern poets was the French writer Stéphane
Mallarmé, of whom the French sometimes say that his language is so
peculiar that it can be understood only by foreigners. The late Roger
Fry, and his friend Charles Mauron, published an English translation
with notes to unriddle the meanings: when I learn that a difficult
sonnet was inspired by seeing a painting on the ceiling reflected on the
polished top of a table, or by seeing the light reflected from the foam
on a glass of beer, I can only say that this may be a correct
embryology, but it is not the meaning. If we are moved by a poem, it
has meant something, perhaps something important, to us; if we are
not moved, then it is, as poetry, meaningless. We can be deeply stirred
by hearing the recitation of a poem in a language of which we
understand no word; but if we are then told that the poem is gibberish
and has no meaning, we shall consider that we have been deluded –
this was no poem, it was merely an imitation of instrumental music.
If, as we are aware, only a part of the meaning can be conveyed by
paraphrase, that is because the poet is occupied with frontiers of
consciousness beyond which words fail, though meanings still exist. A
poem may appear to mean very different things to different readers,
and all of these meanings may be different from what the author
thought he meant. For instance, the author may have been writing
some peculiar personal experience, which he saw quite unrelated to
anything outside; yet for the reader the poem may become the
expression of a general situation, as well as of some private experience
of his own. The reader's interpretation may differ from the author's
and be equally valid – it may even be better. There may be much more
in a poem than the author was aware of. The different interpretations
may all be partial formulations of one thing; the ambiguities may be
due to the fact that the poem means more, not less, than ordinary
speech can communicate.

So, while poetry attempts to convey something beyond what can be conveyed in prose rhythms, it remains, all the same, one person talking to another; and this is just as true if you sing it, for singing is another way of talking. The immediacy of poetry to conversation is not a matter on which we can lay down exact laws. Every revolution in poetry is apt to be, and sometimes to announce itself to be a return to common speech. That is the revolution which Wordsworth announced in his prefaces, and he was right: but the same revolution had been carried out a century before by Oldham, Waller, Denham and Dryden; and the same revolution was due again something over a century later. The followers of a revolution develop the new poetic idiom in one direction or another; they polish or perfect it; meanwhile the spoken language goes on changing, and the poetic idiom goes out of date. Perhaps we do not realize how natural the speech of Dryden must have sounded to the most sensitive of his contemporaries. No poetry, of course, is ever exactly the same speech that the poet talks and hears: but it has to be in such a relation to the speech of his time that the listener or reader can say 'that is how I should talk if I could talk poetry'. This is the reason why the best contemporary poetry can give us a feeling of excitement and a sense of fulfilment different from any sentiment aroused by even very much greater poetry of a past age.

The music of poetry, then, must be a music latent in the common speech of its time. And that means also that it must be latent in the common speech of the poet's *place*. It would not be to my present purpose to inveigh against the ubiquity of standardized, or 'B.B.C.' English. If we all came to talk alike there would no longer be any point in our not writing alike: but until that time comes – and I hope it may be long postponed – it is the poet's business to use the speech which he finds about him, that with which he is most familiar. I shall always remember the impression of W. B. Yeats reading poetry aloud. To hear him read his own works was to be made to recognize how much the Irish way of speech is needed to bring out the beauties of Irish poetry: to hear Yeats reading William Blake was an experience of a different kind, more astonishing than satisfying. Of course, we do not want the poet merely to reproduce exactly the conversational idiom of himself, his family, his friends and his particular district; but what he finds there is the material out of which he must make his poetry. He must, like the sculptor, be faithful to the material in which he works; it is out of sounds that he has heard that he must make his melody and harmony.

It would be a mistake, however, to assume that all poetry ought to be melodious, or that melody is more than one of the components of the music of words. Some poetry is meant to be sung; most poetry, in modern times, is meant to be spoken – and there are many other things to be spoken of besides the murmur of innumerable bees or the moan of doves in immemorial elms. Dissonance, even cacophony, has its place: just as, in a poem of any length, there must be transitions between passages of greater and less intensity, to give a rhythm of fluctuating emotion essential to the musical structure of the whole; and the passages of less intensity will be, in relation to the level on which the total poem operates, prosaic – so that, in the sense implied by that context, it may be said that no poet can write a poem of amplitude unless he is a master of the prosaic.

What matters, in short, is the whole poem: and if the whole poem need not be, and often should not be, wholly melodious, it follows that a poem is not made only out of 'beautiful words'. I doubt whether, from the point of view of *sound* alone, any word is more or less beautiful than another – within its own language, for the question whether some languages are not more beautiful than others is quite another question. The ugly words are the words not fitted for the company in which they find themselves; there are words which are ugly because of rawness or because of antiquation; there are words which are ugly because of foreignness or ill-breeding (e.g. *television*): but I do not believe that any word well-established in its own language is either beautiful or ugly. The music of a word is, so to speak, at a point of intersection: it arises from its relation first to the words immediately preceding and following it, and indefinitely to the rest of its context; and from another relation, that of its immediate meaning in that context to all the other meanings which it has had in other contexts, to its greater or less wealth of association. Not all words, obviously, are equally rich and well-connected: it is part of the business of the poet to dispose the richer among the poorer, at the right points, and we cannot afford to load a poem too heavily with the former – for it is only at certain moments that a word can be made to insinuate the whole history of a language and a civilization. This is an 'allusiveness' which is not the fashion or eccentricity of a peculiar type of poetry; but an allusiveness which is in the nature of words, and which is equally the concern of every kind of poet. My purpose here is to insist that a 'musical poem' is a poem which has a musical pattern of sound and a musical pattern of the secondary meanings of the words which compose it, and that these two patterns are indissoluble and one. And if you object that it is only the pure sound, apart from the sense, to which the adjective 'musical' can be rightly applied, I can only

reaffirm my previous assertion that the sound of a poem is as much an abstraction from the poem as is the sense.   ['The Music of Poetry', 1942]

SOURCE: extracts from essays subsequently collected in *On Poetry and Poets* (London, 1957), pp. 255–8; 29–33.

W. H. Auden

I

... A poet is, before anything else, a person who is passionately in love with language. Whether this love is a sign of his poetic gift or the gift itself – for falling in love is given not chosen – I don't know, but it is certainly the sign by which one recognises whether a young man is potentially a poet or not.

'Why do you want to write poetry?' If the young man answers: 'I have important things I want to say', then he is not a poet. If he answers: 'I like hanging around words listening to what they say', then maybe he is going to be a poet.

As T. S. Eliot has said in one of his essays, the sign of promise in a young writer is not originality of idea or emotion, but technical competence. The subject matter of promising juvenilia is as a rule slight and unimportant, the style derivative, but this slight derivative thing is completely said.

In the first stages of his development, before he has found his distinctive style, the poet is, as it were, engaged to language and, like any young man who is courting, it is right and proper that he should play the chivalrous servant, carry parcels, submit to tests and humiliations, wait hours at street corners, and defer to his beloved's slightest whims, but once he has proved his love and been accepted, then it is another matter. Once he is married, he must be master in his own house and be responsible for their relationship.

The poet is the father who begets the poem which the language bears. At first sight this would seem to give the poet too little to do and the language too much till one remembers that, as the husband, it is he, not the language, who is responsible for the success of their marriage which differs from natural marriage in that in this relationship there is no loveless lovemaking, no accidental pregnancies.

Poets, like husbands, are good, bad and indifferent. Some are Victorian tyrants who treat language like a doormat, some are dreadfully hen-pecked, some bored, some unfaithful. For all of them, there are periods of tension, brawls, sulky silences, and, for many, divorce after a few passionate years. . . .

SOURCE: extract from 'Squares and Oblongs', in Charles D. Abbott (ed.), *Poets at Work* (New York, 1948), excerpted from pp. 171–81.

II

. . . Great changes in artistic style always reflect some alteration in the frontier between the sacred and profane in the imagination of a society. Thus, to take an architectural example, a seventeenth-century monarch had the same function as that of a modern State official – he had to govern. But in designing his palace, the Baroque architect did not aim, as a modern architect aims when designing a government building, at making an office in which the king could govern as easily and efficiently as possible; he was trying to make a home fit for God's earthly representative to inhabit; in so far as he thought at all about what the king would do in it as a ruler, he thought of his ceremonial not his practical actions.

Even today few people find a functionally furnished living room beautiful because, to most of us, a sitting room is not merely a place to sit in; it is also a shrine for father's chair.

Thanks to the social nature of language, a poet can relate any one sacred being or event to any other. The relation may be harmonious, an ironic contrast or a tragic contradiction like the great man, or the beloved, and death; he can relate them to every other concern of the mind, the demands of desire, reason and conscience, and he can bring them into contact and contrast with the profane. Again the consequences can be happy, ironic, tragic and, in relation to the profane, comic. How many poems have been written, for example, upon one of these three themes:

This was sacred but now it is profane. Alas, or thank goodness!
This is sacred but ought it to be?
This is sacred but is that so important?

But it is from the sacred encounters of his imagination that a poet's impulse to write a poem arises. Thanks to the language, he need not name them directly unless he wishes; he can describe one in terms of another and translate those that are private or irrational or socially unacceptable into such as are acceptable to reason and society. Some poems are directly *about* the sacred beings they were written *for*: others are not, and in that case no reader can tell what was the original encounter which provided the impulse for the poem. Nor, probably, can the poet himself. Every poem he writes involves his whole past. Every love poem, for instance, is hung with trophies of lovers gone, and among these may be some very peculiar objects indeed. The lovely lady of the present may number among her predecessors an overshot waterwheel. But the encounter, be it novel or renewed by recollection from the past, must be suffered by a poet before he can write a genuine poem.

Whatever its actual content and overt interest, every poem is rooted in imaginative awe. Poetry can do a hundred and one things, delight, sadden, disturb, amuse, instruct – it may express every possible shade of emotion, and describe every conceivable kind of event, but there is only one thing that all poetry must do; it must praise all it can for being and for happening. . . .   ['Knowing, Making and Judging']

In our age, the mere making of a work of art is itself a political act. So long as artists exist, making what they please and think they ought to make, even if it is not terribly good, even if it appeals to only a handful of people, they remind the Management of something managers need to be reminded of, namely, that the managed are people with faces, not anonymous members, that *Homo Laborans* is also *Homo Ludens*.

If a poet meets an illiterate peasant, they may not be able to say much to each other, but if they both meet a public official, they share the same feeling of suspicion; neither will trust one further than he can throw a grand piano. If they enter a government building, both share the same feeling of apprehension; perhaps they will never get out again. Whatever the cultural differences between them, they both sniff in any official world the smell of an unreality in which persons are treated as statistics. The peasant may play cards in the evening while the poet writes verses, but there is one political principle to which they both subscribe, namely, that among the half dozen or so things for which a man of honour should be prepared, if necessary, to die, the right to play, the right to frivolity, is not the least. . . .   ['The Poet and the City']

The artist, the man who makes, is less important to mankind, for good or evil, than the apostle, the man with a message. Without a religion, a philosophy, a code of behaviour, call it what you will, men cannot live at all; what they believe may be absurd or revolting, but they have to believe something. On the other hand, however much the arts may mean to us, it is possible to imagine our lives without them.

As a human being, every artist holds some set of beliefs or other but, as a rule, these are not of his own invention; his public knows this and judges his work without reference to them. We read Dante for his poetry not for his theology because we have already met the theology elsewhere.

There are a few writers, however, like Blake and D. H. Lawrence, who are both artists and apostles and this makes a just estimation of their work difficult to arrive at. Readers who find something of value in their message will attach unique importance to their writings because they cannot find it anywhere else. But this importance may be shortlived; once I have learned his message, I cease to be interested in a messenger and, should I later come to think his message false or misleading, I shall remember him with resentment and distaste. Even if I try to ignore the message and read him again as if he were only an artist, I shall probably feel disappointed because I cannot recapture the excitement I felt when I first read him.

When I first read Lawrence in the late Twenties, it was his message which made the greatest impression on me, so that it was his 'think' books like *Fantasia of the Unconscious* rather than his fiction which I read most avidly. As for his poetry, when I first tried to read it, I did not like it; despite my admiration for him, it offended my notions of what poetry should be. Today my notions of what poetry should be are still, in all essentials, what they were then and hostile to his, yet there are a number of his poems which I have come to admire enormously. When a poet who holds views about the nature of poetry which we believe to be false writes a poem we like, we are apt to think: 'This time he has forgotten his theory and is writing according to ours.' But what fascinates me about the poems of Lawrence's which I like is that I must admit he could never have written them had he held the kind of views about poetry of which I approve.

Man is a history-making creature who can neither repeat his past nor leave it behind; at every moment he adds to and thereby modifies everything that had previously happened to him. Hence the difficulty of finding a single image which can stand as an adequate symbol for man's kind of existence. If we think of his ever-open future, then the natural image is of a single pilgrim walking along an unending road into hitherto unexplored country; if we think of his never-forgettable past, then the natural image is of a great crowded city, built in every style of architecture, in which the dead are as active citizens as the living. The only feature common to both images is that both are purposive; a road goes in a certain direction, a city is built to endure and be a home. The animals, who live in the present, have neither cities nor roads and do not miss them; they are at home in the wilderness and at most, if they are social, set up camps for a single generation. But man requires both; the image of a city with no roads leading away from it suggests a prison, the image of a road that starts from nowhere in particular, an animal spoor.

Every man is both a citizen and a pilgrim, but most men are predominantly one or the other and in Lawrence the pilgrim almost obliterated the citizen. It is only natural, therefore, that he should have admired Whitman so much, both for his matter and his manner.

Whitman's essential message was the Open Road. The leaving of the soul free unto herself, the leaving of his fate to her and to the loom of the open road. . . . The true democracy . . . where all journey down the open road. And where a soul is known at once in its going. Not by its clothes or appearance. Not by its family name. Not even by its reputation. Not by works at all. The soul passing unenhanced, passing on foot, and being no more than itself.

In his introduction to *New Poems,* Lawrence tries to explain the difference between traditional verse and the free verse which Whitman was the first to write.

The poetry of the beginning and the poetry of the end must have that exquisite finality, perfection which belongs to all that is far off. It is in the realm of all that is perfect . . . the finality and perfection are conveyed in exquisite form: the perfect symmetry, the rhythm which returns upon itself like a dance where the hands link and loosen and link for the supreme moment of the end . . . But there is another kind of poetry, the poetry of that which is at hand: the immediate present. . . . Life, the ever present, knows no finality, no finished crystallisation. . . . It is obvious that the poetry of the instant present cannot have the same body or the same motions as the poetry of the before and after. It can never submit to the same conditions, it is never finished. . . . Much has been written about free verse. But all that can be said, first and last, is that free verse is, or should be, direct utterance from the instant whole man. It is the soul and body surging at once, nothing left out. . . . It has no finish. It has no satisfying stability. It does not want to get anywhere. It just takes place.

It would be easy to make fun of this passage, to ask Lawrence, for example, to tell us exactly how long an instant is, or how it would be physically possible for the poet to express it in writing before it had become past. But it is obvious that Lawrence is struggling to say something which he believes to be important. Very few statements which poets make about poetry, even when they appear to be quite lucid, are understandable except in their polemic context. To understand them, we need to know what they are directed against, what the poet who made them considered the principal enemies of genuine poetry.

In Lawrence's case, one enemy was the conventional response, the laziness or fear which makes people prefer secondhand experience to the shock of looking and listening for themselves.

Man fixes some wonderful erection of his own between himself and the wild chaos, and gradually goes bleached and stifled under his parasol. Then comes a poet, enemy of convention, and makes a slit in the umbrella; and lo! the glimpse of chaos is a vision, a window to the sun. But after a while, getting used to the vision, and not liking the genuine draft from chaos, commonplace man daubs a simulacrum of the window that opens into chaos and patches the umbrella with the painted patch of the simulacrum. That is, he gets used to the vision; it is part of his house decoration.

Lawrence's justified dislike of the conventional response leads him into a false identification of the genuine with the novel. The image of the slit in the umbrella is misleading because what you can see through it will always be the same. But a genuine work of art is one in which every generation finds something new. A genuine work of art remains an example of what being genuine means, so that it can stimulate later artists to be genuine in their turn. Stimulate, not compel; if a playwright in the twentieth century chooses to write a play in a pastiche of Shakespearian blank verse, the fault is his, not Shakespeare's. Those who are afraid of firsthand experience would find means of avoiding it if all the art of the past were destroyed.

However, theory aside. Lawrence did care passionately about genuineness of feeling. He wrote little criticism about other poets who were his contemporaries, but, when he did, he was quick to pounce on any phoniness of emotion. About Ralph Hodgson's lines

> The sky was lit,
> The sky was stars all over it,
> I stood, I knew not why

he writes, 'No one should say *I knew not why* any more. It is as meaningless as *Yours truly* at the end of a letter', and, after quoting an American poetess

> Why do I think of stairways
> With a rush of hurt surprise?

he remarks, 'Heaven knows, my dear, unless you once fell down'. Whatever faults his own poetry may have, it never puts on an act. Even when Lawrence talks nonsense, as when he asserts that the moon is made of phosphorous or radium, one is convinced that it is nonsense in which he sincerely believed. This is more than can be said

176   W. H. AUDEN

of some poets much greater than he. When Yeats assures me, in a
stanza of the utmost magnificence, that after death he wants to
become a mechanical bird, I feel that he is telling what my nanny
would have called 'A story'.   ['D. H. Lawrence']

SOURCE: extracts from essays subsequently collected in *The Dyer's Hand*
(London, 1963), pp. 59–60; 88–9; 277–8.

3. KEY STATEMENTS, 1930–75

Conrad Aiken   (1931, 1940)

I

. . . what I think the poetry of the future can most valuably give us [is] a complete intellectual integrity. We are complex creatures living in a kind of chaos. We live and die by question. What certainties we are born with do not survive us; our faiths are doubtful, our doubts are almost of necessity faiths. If we are good animals, we are courageous in this world of flux, and immensely enjoy it: we can learn, if we are intelligent and sensitive, to enjoy even our suffering. And it is the poet, in this situation, from whom we can learn most. It is he who is equipped to dive with full consciousness into this splendid Gehenna. We do not want him any longer to prettify, whether it be a sunset or a flower or a man's sense of evil. What we want from him is intensity, both in the analytic and *af*fective parts of language; a complete honesty in seeing life as a kaleidoscopic series of incandescent instants – sometimes apparently meaningless, sometimes profound; that he should be religious, without religion; skeptic, without dogma; and should have tasted truth in all its inconsistencies of form. 'It is the acme of life' – to quote . . . from Mr Santayana – 'to understand life. The height of poetry is to speak the language of the gods.' . . . Or perhaps better – dare I suggest? – to speak the full language of man. . . .   ['The Future of Poetry, 1931]

II

Language is a living thing and it won't [lie] down: suppress it as you will, starve or stifle it no matter for how long, mutilate or amputate it as brutally as you like, it will nevertheless, eventually, in some new and unexpected spokesman, vividly and violently revenge itself. For the roots of language are sensory and sensuous. Without that rich and basic and sensitive tactilism, it is not properly itself, nor properly our speech: and if for the little moment of a generation it may submit, apparently, to the artifices of too severe or narrow a culture, or permit a merely 'social' selection of its resources, enduring a regimentation of whatever sort, this will invariably prove to be temporary. Sooner or later will come again those fellows who love language for itself because they live it. Not for these the paler and drier and more abstract of its virtues, useful as these too may be – rather, the full tumult of it at its animal and sensual best, language at its most vascular and vital. The creative chaos of perceptions and feelings is come again. And the conventual excellences die, as it were, in sunlight.

Mr Dylan Thomas is a restorer and re-creator of this sort, and the more welcome for being so overdue. For nearly twenty years, poetry has been increasingly the victim of a kind of monkish snobbism: at the mercy of intellectual and aesthetic dandies on the one hand – effeminates, castrates – and theorists – and of hysterical social fanatics on the other, it is no wonder that it has become itself a sort of *castrato*. Eliot and Pound were good poets, but devastating influences. Themselves 'on the shrink', and acidly defensive, they were predestined shrivellers and wizeners of others; there was precious little of tolerance or generosity in them; nor can it be said that the generation which succeeded them a decade ago did much to improve matters. Here again was the acid defense – a shade more dilute, but essentially the same thing. The acid defense, with a note of amused self-deprecation and apology added – in fact, poetry ashamed to be poetry. . . . And Mr Thomas, a born language-lover and language-juggler, a poet with an unmistakable genius for the affective values of language and prosody, who has the air, like a necromancer, of keeping a thousand words on the wing at once, undoes all this sterile mischief as if it were simplicity itself. Rhetoric, and eloquence – ? Of course, and why not? And all the rest of the poet's bag of tricks. He says right off, and emphatically, and unashamedly –

> Now stamp the Lord's prayer on a grain of rice,
> A Bible-leaved of all the written words
> Strip to this tree: a rocking alphabet,
> Genesis in the root, the scarecrow word,
> And one light's language in the book of trees;
> Doom on deniers at the wind-turned statement.

And he proceeds to pour out such a glitter of magic – magic by itself and for its own sake – as we have not seen since Wallace Stevens published *Harmonium*. It is the answer, and the right answer, to all the jejune precisionism, and dreary ironic defeatism, of the past generation: it is the return of the gift of the gab, and let us celebrate it. If Mr Thomas does nothing else – difficult as that may be to believe – he has already given us something priceless by breaking open this door. And by offering us, as if it were the most natural thing in the world, another murex. . . .   ['Dylan Thomas', 1940]

Source: extracts from articles subsequently republished in *Collected Criticism* (Oxford, 1968 – in earlier form entitled *A Reviewer's ABC*), pp. 82; 370–1.

Michael Roberts   (1936)

. . . the critical theory appropriate to such poetry [i.e., that dealing in dream or myth imagery] is not new. Hints of its method are found in the older critics, and in Shelley. 'Poetry', said Shelley, 'differs in this respect from logic, that it is not subject to the control of the active powers of the mind, and that its birth and recurrence have no necessary connexion with the consciousness or will.' Sometimes the reason for the order of the images of such poems and the cause of their effectiveness are fairly obvious. Their power and order may come from casual memory, or from the make-up of the mind, from the deep impressions of early childhood, or from the influence of the birth trauma, or from the structure of the language itself. The meaning of a word is never a simple thing, a 'standing-for' an object or relation: it is the whole complex set of grammatical habits and associations of ideas which have grown up from our first hearing of it, and the poet exploits this symbolism of words as he exploits the more directly 'psychological' symbolism or substitution value of images. It is possible, therefore, for a poem to be professedly realistic and yet to have the vigour and insistence of a dream or nightmare. Good poetry always has something of this quality, but the nightmare may be directly verbal, rather than visual. Robert Graves is, I think, a poet whose poetry is mainly verbal. That is to say, although there is often a visual picture corresponding to his poems, the effect of the poem depends upon the direct evocative effect of the words, not on the visual stimulus.

Among the poems which deliberately free themselves from logic there are not only the joke-poems, which are simply an exercise of poetic energy showing the word-sense of the poet; but also the relaxation-poems, which range from those in which words associate themselves mainly according to relations and similarities of sound (as in Miss Sitwell's *Hornpipe*), to those which are day-dream narratives. . . .

In some poems, the dream-quality is exaggerated and the structure which is believed to characterise the fantasies of the deeper levels in sleep is deliberately made the model for the structure of the poem. The *Parade Virtues for a Dying Gladiator* of Sacheverell Sitwell is of that kind, and so, too, are the poems which the Surrealists, and their English admirer, David Gascoyne, aim at producing. Such poems, if they are the product of a normal mind, may become fascinating when we get over their initial strangeness; but the 'order' of such poems is not necessarily identical with the 'imaginative order' of myth and legend. The poem may be a good one without being socially important, or it may be fascinating without being specifically poetic. It might, for example, be more effective as a film than it is in printed words. . . .

To myths, rather than to dreams, many poets still turn for the content of their poems, and the researches of Sir James Frazer and other anthropologists have provided the *motif* of a few good poems and many bad ones. Myths are more than fumbling attempts to explain historical and scientific facts: they control and organise the feeling, thought and action of a people: their function is symbolic as well as significant. But often the stories have become the conventional material of second-rate poetry, and have become perverted so that the symbolism has been lost, and we are left with the mere husk of a story, a story easily discredited by scientific and historical research. When Mr Yeats turned to the myth as a means of giving shape and significance to his vision of the world, he was returning to the essential purpose of the myth and setting an example which Mr Eliot, among others, has followed. But the modern reader cannot be expected to be influenced by a myth whose plain narrative sense is counter to his everyday beliefs. Either the poet must break away from any such direct narrative, or he must attempt, as I think Mr Day Lewis has attempted in his *Flight* poem, to present a story credible in the ordinary everyday sense. If the poet turns to an existing myth or legend, however shop-soiled, and sees in it a profound significance, he will see the legend itself exemplified and symbolised in the world about him. . . .

If a poet is to give new life to a legend, if indeed he is to write good poetry at all, he must charge each word to its maximum poetic value. It must appeal concurrently to all the various levels of evocation and interpretation: experiments in new rhythms and new images, if they are not used in this specifically poetic way, are of no more than technical interest. In discussing new technical devices a distinction must be drawn between those which produce an effect upon the reader even before he has noticed them, and those which, like some of the devices of Mr Cummings, attract the reader's attention and lead him to infer, by ordinary reasoning, what effect the poet intended to produce. There are, I think, many examples of the first kind in this book, and of the many auditory devices of this kind, none, perhaps, are more effective, or have had greater effect upon later poets, than those of Wilfred Owen.

In Owen's poetry, the use of half-rhymes is not merely the result of an attempt to escape from the over-obviousness of rhyme-led poetry, though Owen probably discovered its possibilities in that way. His innovations are important because his sound-effects directly reinforce the general effect which he is trying to produce. In Owen's war poetry, the half-rhymes almost invariably fall from a vowel of high pitch to one of low pitch, producing an effect of frustration, disappointment, hopelessness. In other poets, rising half-rhymes are used, which produce the opposite effect, without reaching out to the full heartiness of rhyme. Full end-rhyme itself is felt by many modern poets to be too arbitrary and too noisy for serious poetry, unless modified, as Hopkins modifies it, by taking some of the stress off the last syllable of the line either by stressing earlier syllables, or by placing the emphasis of meaning, as distinct from metre, elsewhere. If they use end-rhymes at all, it is often for satiric purposes, or in a modified form, rhyming stressed with unstressed syllables, as Sacheverell Sitwell has done, and thus producing an uncertain, tentative, hesitating effect in keeping with the poet's purpose.

Nevertheless rhyme, like meaning and metre, is one of the possible elements in a verbal pattern, and few poets abandon it entirely. The sense of order in complication is part of the fascination of poetry, and often, as in the poetry of C. Day Lewis, internal rhymes, carefully but not obviously placed, are used to produce a pattern running counter to sense and rhythm and to add that intricacy and richness which marks the difference between part-song and unison. . . .

Modern poets have been decreasingly concerned with sound-effects as independent entities, and today the auditory rhetoric of poetry is dictated, not by its own rules, but by the central impulse of the poem. Perhaps for this reason, no adequate study of auditory rhetoric exists. Prosody is little more than an enumeration and naming of all the possible combinations of stressed and unstressed syllables. It takes no account of the variety of stresses, or of the quantitative patterns interwoven with accentual patterns, and it ignores the 'laws' of consonant and vowel sequences. It becomes useless if it loses sight of its original purpose and erects itself into a system of unchanging orthodoxy. In criticism all general rules and classifications are elucidatory: and new discoveries or the introduction of matters previously thought to be irrelevant may compel us to amend them or admit their limitations. . . .

Sometimes it is argued that readers, too, must leave the judgment of contemporary literature to posterity; but the judgment of posterity is only another name for the accumulated judgments of those who read most carefully and with least prejudice and preconception. To read merely to concur in the judgments of our ancestors is to inhibit all spontaneous response and to miss the pleasure of that reading which moulds the opinions, tastes and actions of our time. The first important thing about contemporary literature is that it *is* contemporary: it is speaking to us and for us, here, now. Judgment can only follow an act of sympathy and understanding, and to let our appreciation grow outwards from that which immediately appeals to us is both wiser and more enjoyable than to echo the judgments of others or to restrict and sour our appreciation by hastily attacking anything which at first seems difficult or irritating.

SOURCE: extracts from Introduction to *Faber Book of Modern Verse* (London, 1936; 13th impression).

Wallace Stevens   (1937, 1942)

The Man with the Blue Guitar

I

The man bent over his guitar,
A shearsman of sorts. The day was green.

They said, 'You have a blue guitar,
You do not play things as they are.'

The man replied, 'Things as they are
Are changed upon the blue guitar.'

And they said then, 'But play, you must,
A tune beyond us, yet ourselves,

A tune upon the blue guitar
Of things exactly as they are.'

II

I cannot bring a world quite round,
Although I patch it as I can.

I sing a hero's head, large eye
And bearded bronze, but not a man

Although I patch him as I can
And reach through him almost to man.

If to serenade almost to man
Is to miss, by that, things as they are,

Say that it is the serenade
Of a man that plays a blue guitar.

III

Ah, but to play man number one,
To drive the dagger in his heart,

To lay his brain upon the board
And pick the acrid colours out,

To nail his thought across the door,
Its wings spread wide to rain and snow,

To strike his living hi and ho,
To tick it, tock it, turn it true,

To bang it from a savage blue,
Jangling the metal of the strings . . .

IV

So that's life, then: things as they are?
It picks its way on the blue guitar.

A million people on one string?
And all their manner in the thing,

And all their manner, right and wrong,
And all their manner, weak and strong?

The feelings crazily, craftily call,
Like a buzzing of flies in the autumn air,

And that's life, then: things as they are,
This buzzing of the blue guitar.

V

Do not speak to us of the greatness of poetry,
Of the torches wisping in the underground,

Of the structure of vaults upon a point of light.
There are no shadows in our sun,

Day is desire and night is sleep.
There are no shadows anywhere.

The earth, for us, is flat and bare
There are no shadows. Poetry

Exceeding music must take the place
Of empty heaven and its hymns,

Ourselves in poetry must take their place,
Even in the chattering of your guitar.

VI

A tune beyond us as we are,
Yet nothing changed by the blue guitar;

Ourselves in the tune as if in space,
Yet nothing changed, except the place

Of things as they are and only the place
As you play them, on the blue guitar,

Placed, so, beyond the compass of change,
Perceived in a final atmosphere;

For a moment final, in the way
The thinking of art seems final when

The thinking of god is smoky dew.
The tune is space. The blue guitar

Becomes the place of things as they are,
A composing of senses of the guitar.

VII

It is the sun that shares our works.
The moon shares nothing. It is a sea.

When shall I come to say of the sun,
It is a sea; it shares nothing;

The sun no longer shares our works
And the earth is alive with creeping men,

Mechanical beetles never quite warm?
And shall I then stand in the sun, as now

I stand in the moon, and call it good,
The immaculate, the merciful good,

Detached from us, from things as they are?
Not to be part of the sun? To stand

Remote and call it merciful?
The strings are cold on the blue guitar.

. . .

SOURCE: first 7 stanza-sections of the poem, first published in the eponymous volume (1937) and included in *Collected Poems* (New York and London, 1965).

★

. . . The truth is that the social obligation so closely urged is a phase of the pressure of reality which a poet (in the absence of dramatic poets) is bound to resist or evade today. Dante in Purgatory and Paradise was still the voice of the Middle Ages but not through fulfilling any social obligation. Since that is the role most frequently urged, if that role is eliminated, and if a possible poet is left facing life without any categorical exactions upon him, what then? What is his function? Certainly it is not to lead people out of the confusion in which they find themselves. Nor is it, I think, to comfort them while they follow their readers to and fro. I think that his function is to make his imagination become the light in the minds of others. His role, in short, is to help people to live their lives. Time and time again it has been said that he may not address himself to an élite. I think he may. There is not a poet whom we prize living today that does not address himself to an élite. The poet will continue to do this: to address himself to an élite even in a classless society, unless, perhaps, this exposes him to imprisonment or exile. In that event he is likely not to address himself to anyone at all. He may, like Shostakovich, content himself with pretence. He will, nevertheless, still be addressing himself to an élite, for all poets address themselves to someone and it is of the essence of that instinct, and it seems to amount to an instinct, that it should be to an élite, not to a drab but to a woman with the hair of a pythoness, not to a chamber of commerce but to a gallery of one's own, if there are enough of one's own to fill a gallery. And that élite, if it responds, not out of complaisance, but because the poet has quickened it, because he has educed from that for which it was searching in itself and in the life around it and which it had not yet quite found, will thereafter do for the poet what he cannot do for himself, that is to say, receive his poetry.

I repeat that his role is to help people to live their lives. He has had immensely to do with giving life whatever savor it possesses. He has had to do with whatever the imagination and the senses have made of the world. He has, in fact, had to do with life except as the intellect has had to do with it and, as to that, no one is needed to tell us that poetry and philosophy are akin. . . .

. . . There is, in fact, a world of poetry indistinguishable from the world in which we live, or, I ought to say, no doubt, from the world in which we shall come to live, since what makes the poet the potent figure that he is, or was, or ought to be, is that he creates the world to which we turn incessantly and without knowing it and that he gives to life the supreme fictions without which we are unable to conceive of it.

SOURCE: extract from *The Noble Rider and the Sound of Words* (New York and London, 1942), taken from pp. 27–33.

Hermann Hesse (1943)

Soap Bubbles

From years of study and of contemplation
An old man brews a work of clarity,
A gay and involuted dissertation
Discoursing on sweet wisdom playfully.

An eager student bent on storming heights
Has delved in archives and in libraries,
But adds the touch of genius when he writes
A first book full of deepest subtleties.

A boy, with bowl and straw, sits and blows
Filling with breath the bubbles from the bowl.
Each praises like a hymn, and each one glows;
Into the filmy beads he blows his soul.

Old man, student, boy, all these three
Out of the Maya-foam of the universe
Create illusions. None is better or worse.
But in each of them the Light of Eternity
Sees its reflection, and burns more joyfully.

SOURCE: one of the supposed poems of the young Joseph Knecht in *Magister Ludi* (1943), translated from the original German by Richard and Clara Winston under the title *The Glass Bead Game* (New York, 1960; London, 1970; paperback edn, Harmondsworth, 1972). Other translations of the work retain the original (preferable) title.

Robert Frost   (1949)

Abstraction is an old story with the philosophers, but it has been like a new toy in the hands of the artists of our day. Why can't we have any one quality of poetry we choose by itself? We can have it in thought. Then it will go hard if we can't in practice. Our lives for it.

Granted no one but a humanist much cares how sound a poem is if it is only *a* sound. The sound is the gold in the ore. Then we will have the sound out alone and dispense with the inessential. We do till we make the discovery that the object in writing poetry is to make all poems sound as different as possible from each other, and the resources for that of vowels, consonants, punctuation, syntax, words, sentences, meter are not enough. We need the help of context – meaning – subject matter. That is the greatest help towards variety. All that can be done with words is soon told. So also with meters – particularly in our language where there are virtually but two, strict iambic and loose iambic. The ancients with many were still poor if they depended on meters for all tune. It is painful to watch our sprung-rhythmists straining at the point of omitting one short from a foot for relief from monotony. The possibilities for tune from the dramatic tones of meaning struck across the rigidity of a limited meter are endless. And we are back in poetry as merely one more art of having something to say, sound or unsound. Probably better if sound, because deeper and from wider experience.

Then there is this wildness whereof it is spoken. Granted again that it has an equal claim with sound to being a poem's better half. If it is a wild tune, it is a poem. Our problem then is, as modern abstractionists, to have the wildness pure; to be wild with nothing to be wild about. We bring up as aberrationists, giving way to undirected associations and kicking ourselves from one chance suggestion to another in all directions as of a hot afternoon in the life of a grasshopper. Theme alone can steady us down. Just as the first mystery was how a poem could have a tune in such a straightness as meter, so the second mystery is how a poem can have wildness and at the same time a subject that shall be fulfilled.

It should be of the pleasure of a poem itself to tell how it can. The figure a poem makes. It begins in delight and ends in wisdom. The figure is the same as for love. No one can really hold that the ecstasy should be static and stand still in one place. It begins in delight, it inclines to the impulse, it assumes direction with the first line laid down, it runs a course of lucky events, and ends in a clarification of life – not necessarily a great clarification, such as sects and cults are founded on, but in a momentary stay against confusion. It has denouement. It has an outcome that though unforseen was predestined from the first image of the original mood – and indeed from the very mood. It is but a trick poem and no poem at all if the best of it was thought of first and saved for the last. It finds its own name as it goes and discovers the best waiting for it in some final phrase at once wise and sad – the happy-sad blend of the drinking song.

No tears in the writer, no tears in the reader. No surprise for the writer, no surprise for the reader. For me the initial delight is in the surprise of remembering something I didn't know I knew. I am in a place, in a situation, as if I had materialised from cloud or risen out of the ground. There is a glad recognition of the long lost and the rest follows. Step by step the wonder of unexpected supply keeps growing. The impressions most useful to my purpose seem always those I was unaware of and so made no note of at the time when taken, and the conclusion is come to that like giants we are always hurling experience ahead of us to pave the future with against the day when we may want to strike a line of purpose across it for somewhere. The line will have the more charm for not being mechanically straight. We enjoy the straight crookedness of a good walking stick. Modern instruments of precision are being used to make things crooked as if by eye and hand in the old days. . . .

More than once I should have lost my soul to radicalism if it had been the originality it was mistaken for by its young converts. Originality and initiative are what I ask for my country. For myself the originality need be no more than the freshness of a poem run in the way I have described: from delight to wisdom. The figure is the same as for love. Like a piece of ice on a hot stove the poem must ride on its own melting. A poem may be worked over once it is in being, but may not be worried into being. Its most precious quality will remain its having run itself and carried away the poet with it. Read it a hundred times: it will forever keep its freshness as a metal keeps its fragrance. It can never lose its sense of a meaning that once unfolded by surprise as it went.

SOURCE: extracts from 'The Figure a Poem Makes', in *Collected Poems* (New York, and London, 1949), pp. 54–5, 56–7.

Dylan Thomas   (1951)

You want to know why and how I just began to write poetry, and which poems or kinds of poetry I was first moved and influenced by.

To answer the first part of this question, I should say I wanted to write poetry in the beginning because I had fallen in love with words. The first poems I knew were nursery rhymes, and before I could read them for myself I had come to love just the words of them, the words alone. What the words stood for, symbolised, or meant, was of very secondary importance. What mattered was the *sound* of them as I heard them for the first time on the lips of the remote and incomprehensible grown-ups who seemed, for some reason, to be living in my world. And these words were, to me, as the notes of bells, the sounds of musical instruments, the noises of wind, sea and rain, the rattle of milkcarts, the clopping of hooves on cobbles, the fingering of branches on a window pane, might be to someone, deaf from birth, who has miraculously found his hearing. I did not care what the words said, overmuch, nor what happened to Jack and Jill and the Mother Goose rest of them; I cared for the shape of sound that their names, and the words describing their actions, made in my ears; I cared for the colours the words cast on my eyes. I realise that I may be, as I think back all that way, romanticising my reactions to the simple and beautiful words of those pure poems; but that is all I can honestly remember, however much time might have falsified my memory. I fell in love – that is the only expression I can think of – at once, and am still at the mercy of words, though sometimes now, knowing a little of their behaviour very well, I think I can influence them slightly and have even learned to beat them now and then, which they appear to enjoy. I tumbled for words at once. And when I began to read the nursery rhymes for myself, and, later, to read other verses and ballads, I knew that I had discovered the most important things, to me, that could be ever. There they were, seemingly lifeless, made only of black and white, but out of them, out of their own being, came love and terror and pity and pain and wonder and all the other vague abstractions that make our ephemeral lives dangerous, great and bearable. Out of them came the gusts and grunts and hiccups and hee-haws of the common fun of the earth; and though what the words meant was, in its own way, often deliciously funny enough, so much funnier seemed to me, at that almost forgotten time, the shape and shade and size and noise of the words as they hummed, strummed, jugged and galloped along. That was the time of innocence; words burst upon me, unencumbered by trivial or portentous association; words were their spring-like selves, fresh with Eden's dew, as they flew out of the air. They made their own original associations as they sprang and shone. The words, 'Ride a cock-horse to Banbury Cross', were as haunting to me, who did not know then what a cock-horse was nor cared a damn where Banbury Cross might be, as, much later, were such lines as John Donne's, 'Go and catch a falling star. Get with child a mandrake root', which also I could not understand when I first read them. And as I read more and more, and it was not all verse, by any means, my love for the real life of words increased until I knew that I must live *with* them and *in* them always. I knew, in fact, that I must be a writer of words, and nothing else. The first thing was to feel and know their sound and substance; what I was going to do with those words, what use I was going to make of them, what I was going to *say* through them, would come later. I knew I had to know them most intimately in all their forms and moods, their ups and downs, their chops and changes, their needs and demands. (Here, I am afraid, I am beginning to talk too vaguely. I do not like writing *about* words, because then I often use bad and wrong and stale and woolly words. What I like to do is to treat words as a craftsman does his wood or stone or what-have-you, to hew, carve, mould, coil, polish and plane them into patterns, sequences, sculptures, fugues of sound expressing some lyrical impulse, some spiritual doubt or conviction, some dimly-realised truth I must try to reach and realise). It was when I was very young, and just at school, that, in my father's study, before homework that was never done, I began to know one kind of writing from another, one kind of goodness, one kind of badness. My first, and greatest, liberty was that of being able to read everything and anything I cared to. I read indiscriminately, and with my eyes hanging out. I could never have dreamt that there were such goings-on in the world between the covers of books, such sand-storms and ice-blasts of words, such slashing of humbug, and humbug too, such staggering peace, such enormous laughter, such and so many blinding bright lights breaking across the just-awaking wits and splashing all over the pages in a million bits and pieces all of which were words, words, words, and each of which was alive forever in its own delight and glory and oddity and light (I must try not to make these supposedly helpful notes as confusing as my poems themselves.) I wrote endless imitations, though I never thought them to be imitations but, rather, wonderfully original things, like eggs laid by tigers. They were imitations of anything I happened to be reading at the time: Sir Thomas Browne, de Quincey, Henry Newbolt, the Ballads, Blake, Baroness Orczy, Marlowe, Chums, the Imagists, the Bible, Poe, Keats, Lawrence, Anon., and Shakespeare. A mixed lot, as you see, and randomly remembered. I tried my callow hand at almost every poetical form. How could I learn the tricks of a trade unless I tried to do them myself? I learned that the bad tricks come easily; and the good ones, which help you to say what you think you wish to say in the most meaningful, moving way, I am still learning. (But in earnest company you must call these tricks by other names, such as technical devices, prosodic experiments, etc.)

The writers, then, who influenced my earliest poems and stories were, quite simply and truthfully, all the writers I was reading at the time, and, as you see from a specimen list higher up the page, they ranged from writers of schoolboy adventure yarns to incomparable and inimitable masters like Blake. That is, when I began, bad writing had as much influence on my stuff as good. The bad influences I tried to remove and renounce bit by bit, shadow by shadow, echo by echo, through trial and error, through delight and disgust and misgiving, as I came to love words more and to hate the heavy hands that knocked them about, the thick tongues that [had] no feel for their multitudinous tastes, the dull and botching hacks who flattened them out into a colourless and insipid paste, the pedants who made them moribund and pompous as themselves. Let me say that the things that first made me love language and want to work *in* it and *for* it were nursery rhymes and folk tales, the Scottish Ballads, a few lines of hymns, the most famous Bible stories and the rhythms of the Bible, Blake's Songs of Innocence, and the quite incomprehensible magical majesty and nonsense of Shakespeare heard, read, and near-murdered in the first forms of my school. . . .

Source: from Notes (written in summer 1951) answering a student's questions at Laugharne, first published as 'Notes on the Art of Poetry' in *Texas Quarterly* (1961).

Robert Conquest   (1957, 1963)

In the late 1920s a group of poets were starting to write who were to be the typical poets of the 1930s. Towards the end of the 1930s a group of writers with quite different attitudes began to emerge, who were to dominate the 1940s. Each of these groups was, if not launched, at any rate presented to public fire by anthologies which took up definite positions. It is a notable fact that no anthology of this sort has appeared in this country for more than ten years.

It is in the belief that a general tendency has once again set in, and that genuine and healthy poetry of the new period has established itself, that this collection [sc. *New Lines*] has been made.

In the 1940s the mistake was made of giving the Id – a sound player on the percussion side under a strict conductor – too much of a say in the doings of the orchestra as a whole. As it turned out, it could only manage the simpler part of melody and rhythm, and was completely out of its depth with harmony and orchestration. This led to a rapid collapse of public taste, from which we have not yet recovered. . . .

The most glaring fault awaiting correction when the new period opened was the omission of the necessary intellectual component from poetry. It cannot be denied that this has led, to some extent, to a tendency to over-intellectualise. Some years ago Mr John Wain advocated the methods of Mr William Empson in poetry. Other writers revived eighteenth-century forms. And soon a number of young poets were following Empsonian and similar academic principles and often producing verse of notable aridity. As a starting-point for Mr Wain and others this was a not unreasonable way of learning the first lesson – that a poem needs an intellectual backbone. But that it became merely a fashionable formula among the young is unfortunate. Intellectual frameworks can be filled out with bad materials as well as good, and Empsonianism has been almost as much a vehicle for unpleasant exhibitionism and sentimentality as the trends it was designed to correct. The second lesson, that an intellectual skeleton is not worth much unless it is given the flesh of humanity, irony, passion or sanity, was not always learnt.

This is perhaps only to say that any forthright lead will find its followers and imitators among young writers. And at least the

Empsonian fashion is an improvement on its predecessors – in reading the poorer five-finger exercises one is always consoled by the thought of how much worse they used to be when other less restrained styles were in vogue.

Still it is noticeable that the writings of that group are admirable almost exactly in inverse ratio to their reliance on formulae. . . .

The connoisseur of influences would probably find that the general recognition of Yeats as the great poet of the century is reflected in a considerable debt of matter and method among the poets in this book. Writers such as Robert Graves and Edwin Muir also have their echoes. It is a question not merely of technical influence, but of the example of these poets' unabashed and untheoretical eye to visual and emotional events, which their sometimes eccentric views cannot obscure. Auden, too, casts an obvious shadow here and there: who can escape that large and rational talent? But, in his case, it is mainly a matter of technical influence. There is little of the Auden tendency to turn abstractions into beings in their own right. . . .

'THE MOVEMENT': II

. . . The crux, perhaps, of all attitudes destructive to poetry is overweening pharisaism, a conscious notion of poetry as a means of improving those unfortunate enough not to have the sensitivity, or the rectitude, or the dedicatedness, of the poet. This is, in practice, to dehumanise poetry. For the pleasure of poetry is not the pleasure of thinking 'how clever I am', or 'how moral I am', or 'how mature I am', but the objective non-egotistical pleasure, 'I like the effect'. Of course, poetry, like any other good, has intellectual and ethical implications whose nature is a suitable field of enquiry for philosophers. But the essential is the direct employment, not indulgence of the comfortable feeling, 'the author and I are one up on you peasants'.

How this last arose is well described by Mr Philip Larkin:

Poetry has lost its old audience, and gained a new one. This has been caused by the consequences of a cunning merger between poet, literary critic and academic critic (three classes now notoriously indistinguishable): it is hardly an exaggeration to say that the poet has gained the happy position wherein he can praise his own poetry in the press and explain it in the class-room, and the reader has been bullied into giving up the consumer's power to say *I don't like this, bring me something different*. . . . The cash customers of poetry, therefore, who used to put down their money in the sure and certain hope of enjoyment as if at a theatre or concert hall, were quick to move elsewhere. Poetry was no longer a pleasure. They have been replaced by a humbler squad, whose aim is not pleasure but self-improvement, and who have uncritically accepted the contention that they cannot appreciate poetry without preliminary investment in the intellectual equipment which, by the merest chance, their tutor happens to have about him. . . . But at bottom poetry, like all art, is inextricably bound up with giving pleasure, and if a poet loses his pleasure-seeking audience he has lost the only audience worth having, for which the dutiful mob that signs on every September is no substitute. . . . if the medium is in fact to be rescued from among our duties and restored to our pleasures, I can only think that a large-scale revaluation has got to set in against present notions.

This idea of being a priesthood (or better, inquisition) devoted to preserving the immaculateness of art, and of converting a culture to their high professions, is of course ridiculous. But it has also naturally and fortunately produced the 'revulsion' of which Mr Larkin speaks.

Meanwhile, one almost never sees criticism of the professional type which shows any sign of a study of the nature of logical discourse. Even the best often gives the impression of skilled and sophisticated argument in the scholastic tradition – unaware, though, of developments since the time of Duns Scotus. Almost all criticism, good and bad, is in fact concerned with value judgement. The jargon and the expertise now so widely employed are simply devices to make such judgement appear objective, to make it seem to derive rigorously from the nature of the poem discussed. The real way to get any objectivity into value judgements is not to conceal them in this fashion, but to recognise them. This is not automatically to lessen their significance: it depends on the critic! Leading critics of our time, and with them their supposed systems, are refuted not on their own ground, but by their actual choice (sometimes absurd almost beyond controversy) among contemporary poetry.

'Systematic' criticism is almost always not basically interested in the poem itself, but either in its 'impulse', 'values', morality – in fact Content – or in its language, structure, 'strategy' – in fact Form. Such preoccupations must distract the analyser's attention to the crudest, because most discussible, elements even of Form and Content. But, in any case, one never sees anything about either which could not be said equally of a good or a bad poem of any particular type under discussion.

The more scientific sounding the jargon employed, the more involuted the phraseology, the less meaning it has conveyed even at its own particular level. A. E. Housman, a formidable mind indeed, could criticise a contributor to *The Cambridge History of English Literature* for writing that certain instances in Wordsworth 'tend to prove that his poetry is not identical with his habitual teaching'. Housman says: 'one asks oneself what the writer can possibly mean by poetry. How can any poetry be identical with any teaching?' The remark is just. It is true that, though it goes deep and concerns the very nature of literature, it could perhaps be answered by the claim that the writer should have used a word other than 'identical', that although there is a certain vagueness in the style yet a meaning of sorts can be detected. But the subject is refractory enough already without the gratuitous misuse of language. And the odd instances that Housman detected even in 1915 have now become more or less ordinary usage. For example: 'If poetry is to continue to be worth the effort in the present time, it must be a concentration of experience, not a diffusion of it'. And again, 'We call a poem convincing if its mode of enactment relates to what we already know'.

As far as can be seen, what the last writer intended to convey could have been expressed in English. What advantage comes from doing otherwise? Only one: an air of ceremonious certainty, which the opinions could not justify, is conveyed instead by the vocabulary. A well-known mathematician once said, 'The consuming hunger of the uncritical mind for what it imagines to be certainty or finality impels it to feast upon shadows in the prevailing famine of substance'. Is not the key word 'uncritical'? Critic and all the words based on it derive etymologically from (and are associated more substantially still with), the idea of judgement. The Meccano set of supposed principles is an abdication of judgement in favour of something else.

As has often been pointed out, poets very seldom hold an extreme 'irrational', inspirational, view of the writing of poetry. Nevertheless, they are well aware of the complexity of it, both technically and psychologically. All attempts so far made to reduce the operation to a clearly conceptualised and self-conscious process have been failures. And so, similarly, have the equivalent attempts to analyse verse after it has been written. It is in this doomed attempt to achieve 'rigour', or rather in the unsubstantiated claim that the rigour has in fact been achieved, that recent criticism has so often reduced itself to absurdity. Yet the pretensions are so pervasive that not only are there critics who think they can say positively how poems 'should' be written nowadays, but there are even occasional verse writers who take these precepts seriously and try to follow them — thus gaining reputations, not indeed with people who like poetry, but with people who like criticism. . . .

Though it would be false to say that no genuine poetic effort can ever be achieved by the disruption of grammar, sense, and so on yet this is nowadays, as always, so rare that I have thought it scarcely worth achieving a forced catholicity by representing it here [sc. in *New Lines 2*]. On the other hand, the artificial taste for the perverse, which is still to be found in critical and other circles, has a bad effect on poets capable of decent work. It has led, for example, to over-praise for the worst portions of certain poet's work, so that the good in them is often obscured. In some cases, a sadder result still is found – that they are persuaded to adopt forced and frigid mannerisms instead of the genuine poetry they are capable of. And it has been widely noted that there are a number of poets of some talent who have never written a whole poem. There are poets in this volume whose names have been used as banners by advocates of disproportion and distortion. There may be some slight justification for this in their poorer verses. But it will be seen that, on a fairer showing, their work falls neither into empty rant nor into bloodless chinoiserie. As with the other contributors, they follow the central principle of English poetry, and use neither howl nor cypher, but the language of men. . . .

Poetry has no 'tasks' except to be poetry. A poem is moving, in a fashion which has never been adequately defined (though the effect is well described in a general way, by Dr Donald Davie, as being a sort of 'elation' and the poem itself, by Robert Graves, as 'heart-rending sense'). Nor is it possible or desirable for a critic or an anthologist to dictate: all he can do is register. Our own situation has looked worse, superficially, than that which the *Lyrical Ballads* were designed to remedy. But, essentially, the rot never penetrated so deep. Thus we need not speak of restoring the principles of English poetry, but only of registering the fact that, in spite of appearances, these have never really lost their hold. . . .

SOURCE: extracts from: I Introduction to *New Lines 1* (London, 1957), pp. *xi*, *xvi–xvii*, *xvii–xviii*; and II Introduction to *New Lines 2* (London, 1963), pp. *xvii–xxi*, *xxviii–xxix*.

Allen Ginsberg (1959)

. . . Ideally each line of *Howl* is a single breath unit. Tho in this recording it's not pronounced so, I was exhausted at climax of 3 hour Chicago reading with Corso & Orlovsky. My breath is long – that's the Measure, one physical – mental inspiration of thought contained in the elastic of a breath. It probably bugs Williams now, but it's a natural consequence, my own heightened conversation, not cooler average-dailytalk short breath. I got to mouth more madly this way.

So these poems are a series of experiments with the formal organization of the long line. Explanations follow. I realized at the time that Whitman's form had rarely been further explored (improved on even) in the U.S. Whitman always a mountain too vast to be seen. Everybody assumes (with Pound?) (except Jeffers) that his line is a big freakish uncontrollable necessary prosaic goof. No attempt's been made to use it in the light of early xx Century organization of new speech-rhythm prosody to *build up* large organic structures.

I had an apt on Nob Hill, got high on Peyote, & saw an image of the robot skullface of Moloch in the upper stories of a big hotel glaring into my window; got high weeks later again, the Visage was still there in red smokey downtown Metropolis, I wandered down Powell Street muttering, 'Moloch Moloch' all night & wrote *Howl* ii nearly intact in cafeteria at foot of Drake Hotel, deep in the hellish vale. Here the long line is used as a stanza form broken within into exclamatory units punctuated by a base repetition, Moloch.

The rhythmic paradigm for Part iii was conceived & half-written same day as the beginning of *Howl*, I went back later & filled it out. Part i, a lament for the Lamb in America with instances of remarkable lamblike youths; Part ii names the monster of mental consciousness that preys on the Lamb; Part iii a litany of affirmation of the Lamb in its glory: 'O starry spangled shock of Mercy'. The structure of Part iii, pyramidal, with a graduated longer response to the fixed base. . . .

A lot of these forms developed out of an extreme rhapsodic wail I once heard in a madhouse. Later I wondered if short quiet lyrical poems could be written using the long line. *Cottage in Berkeley & Supermarket in California* (written same day) fell in place later that year. Not purposely, I simply followed my Angel in the course of compositions.

What if I just simply wrote, in long units & broken short lines, spontaneously noting prosaic realities mixed with emotional upsurges, solitaries? *Transcription of Organ Music* (sensual data), strange writing which passes from prose to poetry & back, like the mind.

What about poem with rhythmic buildup power equal to *Howl* without use of repeated base to sustain it? *The Sunflower Sutra* (composition time 20 minutes, me at desk scribbling, Kerouac at cottage door waiting for me to finish so we could go off somewhere party) did that, it surprised me, one long Who . . .

Last, the Proem to *Kaddish* (NY 1959 work) – finally, completely free composition, the long line breaking up within itself into short staccato breath units – notations of one spontaneous phrase after another linked within the line by dashes mostly: the long line now perhaps a variable stanzaic unit, measuring groups of related ideas, marking them – a method of notation. Ending with a hymn in rhythm similar to the synagogue death lament. Passing into dactyllic? says Williams? Perhaps not: at least the ears hears itself in Promethian natural measure, not in mechanical count of accent. . . .

A word on Academies; poetry has been attacked by an ignorant & frightened bunch of bores who don't understand how its made, & the trouble with these creeps is they wouldn't know Poetry if it came up and buggered them in broad daylight.

A word on the Politicians: my poetry is Angelical Ravings, & has nothing to do with dull materialistic vagaries about who should shoot who. The secrets of individual imagination – which are trans-conceptual & non-verbal – I mean unconditioned Spirit – are not for sale to this consciousness, are of no use to this world, except perhaps to make it shut its trap & listen to the music of the Spheres. Who denies the music of the spheres denies poetry, denies man, & spits on Blake, Shelley, Christ & Buddha. Meanwhile have a ball. The universe is a new flower. America will be discovered. Who wants a war against roses will have it. Fate tells big lies, & the gay Creator dances on his own body in Eternity.

SOURCE: extracts from 'Notes for *Howl* and Other Poems', in *Fantasy 7006* (1959); reprinted in Donald M. Allen (ed.), *The New American Poetry, 1945–60* (New York, and London, 1960), pp. 416–18.

Frank O'Hara   (1959)

. . . I am mainly preoccupied with the world as I experience it, and at times when I would rather be dead the thought that I could never write another poem has so far stopped me. I think this is an ignoble attitude. I would rather die for love, but I haven't.

I don't think of fame or posterity (as Keats so grandly and genuinely did), nor do I care about clarifying experiences for anyone or bettering (other than accidentally) anyone's state or social relation, nor am I for any particular technical development in the American language simply because I find it necessary. What is happening to me, allowing for lies and exaggerations which I try to avoid, goes into my poems. I don't think my experiences are clarified or made more beautiful for myself or anyone else, they are just there in whatever form I can find them. What is clear to me in my work is probably obscure to others, and vice versa. . . .

SOURCE: extract from article in *Fantasy 7006* (1959); reprinted in Donald M. Allen, op. cit., p. 419.

Gary Snyder   (1959)

. . . I've just recently come to realise that the rhythms of my poems follow the rhythm of the physical work I'm doing and life I'm leading at any given time – which makes the music in my head which creates the line. Conditioned by the poetic tradition of the English language & whatever feeling I have for the sound of poems I dig in other languages. 'Riprap' is really a class of poems I wrote under the influence of the geology of the Sierra Nevada and the daily trail-crew work of picking up and placing granite stones in tight cobble patterns on hard slab. 'What are you doing?' I asked old Roy Marchbanks. – 'Riprapping' he said. His selection of natural rocks was perfect – the result looked like dressed stone fitting to hair-edge cracks. Walking, climbing, placing with the hands. I tried writing poems of tough, simple, short words, with the complexity far beneath the surface texture. In part the lines was influenced by the five- and seven-character line Chinese poems I'd been reading, which work like sharp blows on the mind.

Myths and Texts grew between 1952 and 1956. Its several rhythms are based on long days of quiet in lookout cabins; settling chokers for the Warm Springs Lumber Co. (looping cables on logs & hooking them to D8 Caterpillars – dragging and rumbling through the brush); and the songs and dances of Great Basin Indian tribes I used to hand around. The title comes from the happy collections Sapir, Boas, Swanton, and others made of American Indian folktales early in this century; it also means the two sources of human knowledge – symbols and sense-impressions. I tried to make my life as a hobo and worker, the questions of history & philosophy in my head, and the glimpses of the roots of religion I'd seen through meditation, peyote, and 'secret frantic rituals' into one whole thing. As far as I'm concerned, I succeeded. . . .

SOURCE: extract from *Riprap* (Origin Press, 1959); reprinted in Donald M. Allen (ed.), op. cit., pp. 420–1.

Thom Gunn   (1961)

My Sad Captains

One by one they appear in
the darkness: a few friends, and
a few with historical
names. How late they start to shine!
but before they fade they stand
perfectly embodied, all

the past lapping them like a
cloak of chaos. They were men
who, I thought, lived only to
renew the wasteful force they
spent with each hot convulsion.
They remind me, distant now.

True, they are not at rest yet,
but now that they are indeed
apart, winnowed from failures,
they withdraw to an orbit
and turn with disinterested
hard energy, like the stars.

SOURCE: title-poem from the poetry collection *My Sad Captains and Other Poems* (London, 1961).

Robert Lowell   (1963)

. . . Almost the whole problem of writing poetry is to bring it back to what you really feel, and that takes an awful lot of maneuvering. You may feel the doorknob more strongly than some big personal event, and the doorknob will open into something that you can use as your own. A lot of poetry seems to me very good in the tradition but just doesn't move me very much because it doesn't have personal vibrance to it. I probably exaggerate the value of it, but it's precious to me.

Some little image, some detail you've noticed – you're writing about a little country shop, just describing it, and your poem ends up with an existentialist account of your experience. But it's the shop that started it off. You didn't know why it means a lot to you. Often images and often the sense of the beginning and end of a poem are all you have – some journey to be gone through between those things; you know that, but you don't know the details. And that's marvelous; then you feel the poem will come out. It's a terrible struggle, because what you really feel hasn't got the form, it's not what you can put down in a poem. And the poem you're equipped to write concerns nothing that you care very much about or have much to say on. Then the great moment comes when there's enough resolution of your technical equipment, your way of constructing things, and what you can make a poem out of, to hit something you really want to say. You may not know you have it to say. . . .

SOURCE: extract from Malcolm Cowley (ed.), *Writers at Work: The 'Paris Review' Interviews*, 2nd series (New York, and London, 1963), pp. 268–9.

Philip Larkin   (1964)

Love Songs in Age

> She kept her songs, they took so little space,
>   The covers pleased her:
> One bleached from lying in a sunny place,
> One marked in circles by a vase of water,
> One mended, when a tidy fit had seized her,
>   And coloured, by her daughter –
> So they had waited, till in widowhood
> She found them, looking for something else, and stood
>
> Relearning how each frank submissive chord
>   Had ushered in
> Word after sprawling hyphenated word,
> And the unfailing sense of being young
> Spread out like a spring-woken tree, wherein
>   That hidden freshness sung,
> That certainty of time laid up in store
> As when she played them first. But, even more,

> The glare of that much-mentioned brilliance, love,
>   Broke out, to show
> Its bright incipience sailing above,
> Still promising to solve, and satisfy,
> And set unchangeably in order. So
>   To pile them back, to cry,
> Was hard, without lamely admitting how
> It had not done so then, and could not now.

SOURCE: from *The Whitsun Weddings* (London, 1964), p. 12.

R. S. Thomas (1964, 1975)

. . . One must take the words as one finds them, and make them sing and here arises another question: Are words the poet's servant or master? We are familiar, no doubt, with Mr Eliot's pessimistic conclusions in 'East Coker', although he wins through to some sort of détente in 'Little Gidding'. I think that any practising poet would also agree that there can be no hard and fast rule in this matter. Most poets compose with great difficulty, choosing and rejecting and altering their words, until often the finished draft bears little relation to what they began with. In this way the poet would seem to be the master, forcing the words to do the bidding of the conscious mind. Yet this, also, is a travesty of the position. Words have surprising resilience, and get their own way often by appearing to yield. The idea of the poets' eye 'in a fine frenzy rolling' and of the words flowing ready mixed with the ink off the tip of his pen is, of course, a fiction. Yet here again most poets could tell of periods of inspiration of varying length, when the words and lines did appear to come with agreeable ease. And although we have Yeats's words as a warning against being deceived by an appearance of case, we also have it on Mr Vernon Watkins's authority that he said, too, that a poem is a piece of luck. This is a pregnant statement, but certainly one aspect of it has to do with words themselves – a lucky finding or perception of the right word. . . .

Can one make any useful generalisations? It seems that it has always been easier for poets to evolve theories of language than to stick to them. Wordsworth was a case in point, Yeats another. It was Coleridge who remarked that the lofty and sustained diction which characterised Wordsworth as a poet was a complete contradiction of his theory about the speech of the natural man. And although Yeats had a temporary spasm for deleting from his verse all words which were not understood by Irish washerwomen, fortunately for the state of English poetry the lunacy passed. I would be inclined to doubt whether much poetry of top rank has ever been written in accordance with a theory. Wordsworth at his most puling lends me support. It is far better to observe, not necessarily consciously, what you are able to do with words, and what they can do to you, and on that basis, *post hoc* as it were, to evolve your theory of poetry. Personally I have often agreed that there is something feminine about words, and, of course, the muse herself is female. It is as though, the more one woos words, the more desperately in love with them one grows, the more coquettish and refractory they become, whereas a certain insouciance or aloofness in the writer will often bring them fawning about his feet. . . .

. . . Coomaraswamy said that an artist is not a special kind of man, but that every man is a special kind of artist. This seems to be one of those rather slick half-truths which so often gain currency. Indeed, no one wishes to set up artists as a kind of *herren-volk*. The difference between them and other men is quite possibly a difference in degree and not in kind. But the degree is very great in the best of them. I suppose most men wish to tell others of their experiences. They gratify this wish mainly in talk, that endless noise which goes on in streets and 'buses and pubs. But some few have been born with the urge and the gift to write about their experiences, many in prose, fewer in poetry. I am using experience in a very broad sense to embrace every apprehension of life by the total personality. In other words, as I go through my day at my desk, in my contact with others, or out in the world of nature, I see something, begin to turn it over in my mind, and decide that it has poetic possibilities. The main concern now will be not to kill it; not to make it common, prosaic, uninteresting. If it bores me in the telling, it will surely bore the public in the reading. I must choose words and rhythms which will keep it fresh and have the power to recreate the experience in all its original intensity for each new reader. But in this very process the experience is changed, and will continue to be changed as each new reader apprehends it.

A recurring ideal, I find, is that of simplicity. At times there comes the desire to write with great precision and clarity, words so simple and moving that they bring tears to the eyes, or, if you like, as Wordsworth said, are 'too deep for tears'. I remember also Wordsworth's 'human heart by which we live'. The poet's function and privilege surely is to speak to our condition in the name of our

common humanity in words which do not grow old because the heart
does not grow old.

SOURCE: extracts from *Words and the Poet* (Cardiff, 1964).

The Combat

You have no name.
We have wrestled with you all
day, and now night approaches,
the darkness from which we emerged
seeking; and anonymous
you withdraw, leaving us nursing
our bruises, our dislocations.

For the failure of language
there is no redress. The physicists
tell us your size, the chemists
the ingredients of your
thinking. But who you are
does not appear, nor why
on the innocent marches
of vocabulary you should choose
to engage us, belabouring us
with your silence. We die, we die
with the knowledge that your resistance
is endless at the frontier of the great poem.

SOURCE: from *Laboratories of the Spirit* (London, 1975), p. 43.

John Wain   (1972)

... England, before 1945, was much more of an island than she will
ever be again. And the mood of England, after the long stalemate of
the thirties, had blazed out into something prophetic. Poets of very
different styles and temperaments were agreeing in their passionate
desire to 'kiss the hem of God's robe'. During those years of privation
and danger, their object was to make

> Soul clap its hands and sing, and louder sing
> For every tatter in its mortal dress.

Not all these poets were 'religious' in any formal sense. The prophetic mood runs the entire gamut from Eliot's orthodox Anglo-Catholicism to the home-made constructions of Yeats or Graves, and the almost pantheistic reverence for life, the mere process of life, in Dylan Thomas. Across the Atlantic, Auden, who in his earlier years as an American still seemed to be within the gravitational pull of England, experienced Christian conversion and wrote his two most explicitly Christian works, *New Year Letter* (1941) and *For the Time Being* (1945).

There need be no quarrel here between 'Christians' and 'humanists'. All these poets, by expressing their instinctive belief that life is not a mere biological accident but a sacrament, were pointing to the path that man must follow if he is to avoid being swallowed up by his political systems and enslaved by his technology. The attitude they share, a fundamentally religious approach to the wonder of life, is not merely the best way, but the only way, of giving back dignity and meaning to human existence. . . .

Source: extract from C. B. Cox and A. E. Dyson (eds), *The Twentieth-Century Mind* (London, 1972), p. 370.

SELECT READING LIST

In my Introduction I cite the two texts I think most useful to readers of poetry. One, Bradley's lecture, is reproduced in this selection; the other is Henry James, *The Art of the Novel: Critical Prefaces*, edited by R. P. Blackmur (1934).

For the rest, my advice is for the reader to follow up the critics and poets (particularly the poets) represented here. The selection forms a comprehensive ground for further study. The necessary references are to be found, of course, in the text.

I have not found space, unfortunately, to quote from Kathleen Raine: a fine poet and our most consistent and readable neo-platonist critic. Readers need to sample her work at length if they are to respond fully. I would strongly recommend, as a start, her collection of essays, *The Inner Journey of the Poet* (London, 1982).

It is perhaps needless to remind readers of volumes on individual poets in the Casebook series. These are a natural setting-out point for further study, along with John S. Hill's Casebook on *The Romantic Imagination*. There is also, in preparation for the series, my volume on four 'Post-1950s' poets: Ted Hughes, Thom Gunn, Philip Larkin and R. S. Thomas. Also to be mentioned, among works on individual poets, is C. B. Cox (ed.), *Dylan Thomas: A Collection of Critical Essays* (Englewood Cliffs, N.J., 1966).

Other books are legion. Those mentioned in the Introduction are my first choice – and I would stress again the importance, in general terms, of the work of Freud and, more especially, Jung.

Among the many others dealing with developments of poetic ideas and techniques, the following may be found useful: C. K. Stead, *The New Poetic* (1964), D. E. S. Maxwell, *Poets of the Thirties* (1969), G. S. Fraser, *Vision and Rhetoric* (1959), M. L. Rosenthal, *The New Poets: American and British Poetry since World War II* (1967) and Martin Dodsworth (ed.), *The Survival of Poetry: A Contemporary Survey* (1970).

For 'background' reading to the original Romantic tradition, leading on to the Symbolists, I strongly suggest the two classics by Paul Hazard, for many years now available in English translation, viz. *The European Mind* (1953) and *European Thought in the Eighteenth Century* (1954), together with Basil Willey's equally well-known works: *The Seventeenth Century Background* (1934) and *The Eighteenth Century Background* (1940) and *Nineteenth Century Studies* (1949).

Finally, a note on the 'Geneva School' of criticism (see p. 14 above), and on the excellent work of J. Hillis Miller in explaining its approach to literary texts and its value to artist and student alike.

The Geneva critics all stress that *consciousness*, however conceived, is our supreme experience. Literature is at once a history of human consciousness, at its most intense; and our best personal entré to this heritage.

The critic's task, says Marcel Raymond (b. 1897), is to 'transform states of existence into states of consciousness', recreating the work of art 'within himself, but in conformity to itself'. This process includes access, and renewal. Albert Béguin (b. 1901) hopes that the critic will 'coincide with the spiritual adventure of the poet': if so, then he will experience the life of saints, sinners, men of faith through the ages – indeed (for Béguin was the most orthodoxly religious of the group), of Incarnation and Crucifixion. Georges Poulet (b. 1902) perceives that the 'intimacy' required for criticism 'is not possible unless the thought of the critic *becomes* the thought of the author criticised, unless it succeeds in re-feeling, in re-thinking, in re-imagining the author's thought from the inside': there must be 'absolute transparency with the thought of the other'. Jean Rousset (b. 1910) assures us that 'in art there is no form which is not experienced and worked out from the inside', and sees the critic's rôle as reverse creation, seizing 'the dream by way of the form'. Jean Starobinski (b. 1920) finds the living movement of criticism somewhere between 'a total complicity with the creative subjectivity' and 'a panoramic look from above'. Jean-Pierre Richard (b. 1922) lays stress on 'sensation' and 'depth' in art – experiences into which the critic seeks to enter; and through which he might then encounter some secret void, or fulness, at the heart of reality.

Though these critics were not a formal 'school', they shared supremely important insights. As J. Hillis Miller puts it: 'For the Geneva critics . . . criticism is primordially consciousness of the consciousness of another, the transposition of the mental universe of an author into the interior space of the critic's mind'. Their close links with the Symbolist tradition will be evident; as will their affinity with most of the creative writers represented in this anthology (Parts 2 and 3), and with many of the academic critics (Part 1). For all of them, *creative* reading is initiation into human intensity and diversity, and so, an enormous enlargement of being. As much as original creative writing, it is a quest for meaning – *our* quest, and *our* meaning. Beyond the human richness it opens, lies whatever cosmic revelation we may ourselves discern, or intuit.

Greatly though I regret the absence of J. Hillis Miller's article from this anthology, I trust that readers will turn to it (*Critical Quarterly*, 8, No. 4, pp. 305–21), and then proceed to the original texts. The adoption of the Geneva critics as major 'modern' presences would much enrich our English and American traditions of academic criticism – as it would also, I judge, much that now passes for poetry.

ACKNOWLEDGEMENTS

The editor and publishers wish to thank the following who have given permission for the use of copyright material: Conrad Aiken, extracts from essays on 'The Future of Poetry' and 'Dylan Thomas' in *Collected Criticism of Conrad Aiken*, by permission of Oxford University Press Inc. (1968); Guillaume Apollinaire, extract from 'On Painting', English translation by L. Abel, in *Cubist Painters: Aesthetic Meditations*, by permission of Wittenbron Art Books Inc.; W. H. Auden, extract from 'Squares and Oblongs' in Charles D. Abbott (ed.) *Poets At Work*, by permission of Harcourt Brace Jovanovich Inc. (1948); and from 'Knowing, Making and Judging', 'The Poet and the City' and 'D. H. Lawrence' in *The Dyer's Hand*, by permission of Faber and Faber Ltd (1968); Charles Baudelaire, extract from essay 'Theophile Gauthier' (1861), included in *L'Art romantique* (1868) and in Jacques Crepet (ed.) *Oeuvres Completes de Ch. B* (Paris 1925) Vol III, English translation in Richard Ellmann and Charles Feidelson Jnr, *The Modern Tradition: Backgrounds of Modern Literature*, by permission of Oxford University Press Inc. (1965); Harold Bloom, extract from essay 'Yeats and the Romantics' in *Modern Poetry: Essays in Criticism*, John Hollander (ed.), by permission of Oxford University Press Inc. (1968); Maud Bodkin, extract from *Archetypal Patterns in Poetry: Psychological Studies of Imagination*, by permission of Oxford University Press (1934); Cleanth Brooks, extract 'The Language of Paradox' in *The Well Wrought Urn*, by permission of Dobson Books Ltd; Robert Conquest, extracts from Introduction to *New Lines I* and *New Lines II*, Macmillan (1957, 1963), by permission of Curtis Brown Ltd, on behalf of the author; A. E. Dyson, extract from *Between Two Worlds: Aspects of Literary Form*, Macmillan by permission of the author; T. S. Eliot, extracts from 'Burnt Norton' from *Four Quartets* and 'Choruses' from *The Rock* in *Collected Poems 1909–1962*; and from 'Introduction to Poems of Tennyson' in *The Use of Poetry and the Use of Criticism* (1933); and from 'Tradition and the Individual', 'Dante', 'The Metaphysical Poets', 'Swinburne' and 'Hamlet' in Selected Essays; and from 'Yeats' and 'The Music of Poetry' in *On Poetry and Poets* (1957), by permission of Faber and Faber Ltd; Richard Ellmann, extract from Introduction to his edited volume *The New Oxford Book of American Verse*, by permission of Oxford University Press Inc. (1976); Robert Frost, extracts from 'The Figure a Poem Makes' in Introduction to *Collected Poems of Robert Frost* by permission of Jonathan Cape Ltd and the author's estate; Northrop Frye, extract from *The Anatomy of Criticism: Four Essays*, by permission of Princeton University Press (1957); Helen Gardner, extract *The Art of T. S. Eliot* (1949) by permission of Cresset Press and Hutchinson Publishing Group Ltd; Allen Ginsberg, extract 'Notes for *Howl* and Other Poems' in *Fantasy 7006* (1959) by permission of the author;

Thom Gunn, extract 'My Sad Captains' in *My Sad Captains* (1961), by permission of Faber and Faber Ltd; Donald Hall, extracts from his Introduction to *Contemporary American Poetry*, by permission of Curtis Brown Ltd, on behalf of the author; G. E. Hartman, extract from *Beyond Formalism: Literary Essays 1957–70*, by permission of Yale University Press; T. R. Henn, extract from *The Lonely Tower*, Methuen and Co. Ltd (1950), by permission of Associated Book Publishers Ltd; Herman Hesse, extract from 'Soap Bubbles' in *The Glass Bead Game*, translated by R. & C. Winston, by permission of Jonathan Cape Ltd (1970) and the author's estate; Frank Kermode, extract from *Romantic Image*, by permission of Routledge and Kegan Paul Ltd (1957); and in *The Sense of an Ending: Studies in the Theory of Fiction*, by permission of Oxford University Press Inc. (1967); Philip Larkin, extract 'Love Songs in Age' in *The Whitsun Weddings* (1964), by permission of Faber and Faber Ltd; C. S. Lewis, extract from *An Experiment in Criticism*, by permission of the executors of C. S. Lewis and Cambridge University Press (1961); Robert Lowell, extract from interview in *The Paris Review* (1963), reprinted in Malcolm Cowley (ed.) *Writers at Work: The Paris Review Interviews* (Second Series), by permission of Martin Secker and Warburg Ltd; Ezra Pound, extracts from 'A Few Don'ts by an Imagiste' in *Poetry* (March 1913 issue); and from 'Vorticism' in *Gaudier Brzeska*, by permission of Ezra Pound Literary Property Trust and Faber and Faber Ltd; R. M. Rilke, extract from a Letter of 1920 in *Letters to Merline* (1920), translated by V. M. MacDonald, Methuen & Co. Ltd, (1952), by permission of Associated Book Publishers Ltd; Michael Roberts, extracts from 'Introduction' in *The Faber Book of Modern Verse* (1936), by permission of Faber and Faber Ltd; Gary Snyder, extract from *The New American Poetry 1945–60*, Grove Press (1960), by permission of the author; Wallace Stevens, extracts from 'The Noble Rider and the Sound of Words' in *The Necessary Angel*; and 'The Man with the Blue Guitar' in *The Collected Poems of Wallace Stevens* (1965), by permission of Faber and Faber Ltd; Arthur Symons, extracts from *The Symbolist Movement*, Ballantyne, Hanson (1908), by permission of Mr Herbert Read; Dylan Thomas, extract from Note written in 1951, published in *The Texas Quarterly* (1961), by permission of David Higham Associates Ltd; R. S. Thomas, extracts from *Words and the Poet*, by permission of the University of Wales Press (1964); and 'The Combat' in *Laboratories of the Spirit*, Macmillan (1975); John Wain, extract from essay on 'Poetry' in *The Twentieth-Century Mind*, C. B. Cox and A. E. Dyson (eds) by permission of Oxford University Press (1972); Edmund Wilson, extract from *Axel's Castle: A Study in the Imaginative Literature of 1870–1930*, by permission of Charles Scribner's Sons (1931); W. B. Yeats, extracts from *Mythologies*, Macmillan (1959), *Explorations*, Macmillan (1962), *Essays and Introductions*, Macmillan (1961) *A Vision*, Macmillan (1937), and *Autobiographies*, Macmillan (1956), by permission of A. P. Watt Ltd, on behalf of M. B. Yeats and Anne Yeats. Every effort has been made to trace all the copyright holders but if any have been inadvertently overlooked the publishers will be pleased to make the necessary arrangement at the first opportunity.

INDEX

Themes such as 'Art', 'Beauty', 'Consciousness', 'Creative', 'Exaltation', 'Intention', 'Metre', 'Modern', 'Natural', 'Rhyme', 'Rhythm', 'Supernatural', 'Symbol', 'Truth', 'Value' occur throughout, and are not listed.

This index includes significant references to other important, but less pervasive themes (entries in italics); and to persons mentioned (entries in capitals).

To save space, particular poems and works of art will be found subsumed under the entry for their creators.